MULTICULTURAL
PERSPECTIVES
ON
RACE
ETHNICITY
AND IDENTITY

ELIZABETH PATHY SALETT AND
DIANE R. KOSLOW, EDITORS

NASW PRESS
National Association of Social Workers
Washington, DC

DARRELL P. WHEELER, PhD, MPH, ACSW *President*
ANGELO McCLAIN, PhD, LICSW, *Chief Executive Officer*

Cheryl Y. Bradley, *Publisher*
Stella Donovan, *Acquisitions Editor*
Julie Gutin, *Managing Editor*
Sarah Lowman, *Project Manager*
Julie Palmer-Hoffman, *Copyeditor*
Wayson Jones, *Proofreader*
Bernice Eisen, *Indexer*

Cover by Metadog Design Group
Interior design and composition by Rick Soldin
Printed and bound by Sheridan Books, Inc.

First impression: May 2015

© 2015 by the NASW Press

Chapter 7 has been adapted and updated from one originally published as Miller, R. L., & Rotheram-Borus, M. J. (1994). Growing up biracial in the United States. In E. P. Salett & D. R. Koslow (Eds.), *Race, ethnicity and self: Identity in multicultural perspective* (pp. 143–169). Washington, DC: NMCI Publications. A subsequent revision was published as Miller, R. L., Staggs, S., Watling, J., & Rotheram-Borus, M. J. (2003). Growing up biracial in the United States: A decade later. In E. P. Salett & D. R. Koslow (Eds.), *Race, ethnicity and self: Identity in multicultural perspective* (2nd ed.). Washington, DC: NMCI Publications.

Library of Congress Cataloging-in-Publication Data

Multicultural perspectives on race, ethnicity, and identity / Elizabeth Pathy Salett and Diane R. Koslow, editors.
    pages cm
 Includes bibliographical references and index.
  ISBN 978-0-87101-460-3 (alk. paper) -- ISBN 0-87101-460-2 (alk. paper) 1. Multiculturalism. 2. Race. 3. Ethnicity. 4. Group identity. I. Salett, Elizabeth Pathy, editor. II. Koslow, Diane R., editor.
 HM1271.M8355 2015
 305.8--dc23

2015010437

Printed in the United States of America

To our grandchildren
Amelia, Jessie, Max,
Noah, Siena, Jackson, and Maxie,
who inherit the future

Contents

Preface

The authors take as their premise a shared belief that in the context of a pluralistic society, the values, mores, and status of the group or groups with which we each identify have a profound effect on how we view ourselves and on how we view and interact with others. The book provides an opportunity to delve into the historical contexts and processes that have shaped each of us while navigating the sea of change that will define our future. It urges us to seek the common humanity in those very different from ourselves.

Multicultural Perspectives on Race, Ethnicity, and Identity is a multicultural conversation intended for all those who wish to explore the impact of race, ethnicity, and sense of self on the development of individual and group identity in the increasingly diverse society of the United States in the 21st century. This volume expands on an earlier version, published by the National MultiCultural Institute, titled *Race, Ethnicity, and Self: Identity in Multicultural Perspective,* which was first published in 1994, with a second edition in 2003.

In any book about multiculturalism, there could be dozens of chapters representing different identity groups and many more perspectives addressing any one group. We have chosen to focus here on issues related to race and ethnicity. Multiculturalism is also a broader concept that includes differences such as gender, age, religion, class, sexual orientation, and variations in abilities. It includes different perspectives, worldviews, values, belief systems, and social and economic conditions, often intersecting between and across these differences.

Rapidly changing demographics and transformational social change continue to reshape the racial and ethnic composition of the United States. In some ways, these changes have challenged traditional definitions of race and ethnicity, expanding them to include our ever increasing diversity. In other ways, they have tested the boundaries of our understanding of identity itself.

There is, of course, great diversity within each racial or ethnic group even within the context of the United States; and as the meaning of family and community evolve and expand to reflect the depth and complexity of our interconnectedness, in our homes, in our neighborhoods and cities, and around the world, so too will our definition of ourselves. While acknowledging the multiplicity of this diversity, these chapters underscore the belief that certain experiences or cultural traits are shared by members of particular identity groups and play a role in identity development.

The key terms in this book—race, ethnicity, and identity—are defined differently by different authors. Because these definitions are still evolving and reflect ongoing changes in our society, each chapter establishes its own vocabulary, as well as its own perspective. We believe that the differences presented here will contribute to, rather than detract from, the conversation.

Historically, *race* has been defined as a biological classification of human features and characteristics. In the context of the United States, race has also been recognized as a social construct, a concept of complex and inconstant meaning, influenced by social conflict and political struggle. Race is often also used to differentiate among human beings in social structure and cultural representation and can lead to distortions in self-image and perception of and by others.

Ethnicity generally describes a group's sense of possessing a shared identity informed by a common language, culture, or religion. Racial and ethnic identities often overlap. One person may be Caucasian by race and Anglo-Saxon or Jewish by ethnic group; another may be Latino by ethnic and linguistic group but of African, Caucasian, or Native American racial heritage. As with race, our ethnicity plays a major role in how we are viewed by others, in who we believe we are, and in who we may or may not want to be.

Identity development is a process through which we create a sense of self influenced by history, community, family, and personal characteristics. In the context of the United States, autonomy is one way identity is expressed. In many cultures around the world, however, less emphasis is placed on individual autonomy, and the development process engenders the creation of a "familial" self that reflects an interdependency among family or cultural group members. Whether individual or familial, our perceptions of ourselves are undoubtedly influenced by our interactions with and relationships to one another.

As in many other parts of the world, the United States is undergoing substantial transformation. Increasing immigration, population growth among racial and ethnic minority groups, intermarriage and intermingling across cultures, and technological advances that bring us closer together despite distance and difference all serve to advance the reality of an increasingly multicultural society. These trends continue to challenge and to inevitably shift what have been the dominant social norms and structures, with the creation of new and different ways to understand ourselves and one another. Recognizing our unique identities and the ways in which the world around us forms and shapes these identities remains a fundamental step toward knowing and respecting one another.

Elizabeth Pathy Salett
Diane R. Koslow

Acknowledgments

Multicultural Perspectives on Race, Ethnicity, and Identity is the result of the efforts of many people. First of all, the editors would like to thank the authors for their contributions to this book and for their cooperation and hard work in making it a reality.

We would like to express our great appreciation to Rebecca Joy Norlander, who tirelessly reviewed each of the chapters, provided superb editorial and organizational support, and kept us on track throughout the process. We extend our special acknowledgment and immense gratitude to Elsie Achugbue, who wrote a scholarly and thoughtful introduction to the book and whose wisdom, guidance, and dedication helped us to finalize the manuscript. Thanks to Evelyn P. Boyer for her insightful critiques, to Spencer P. Boyer and Sarah Claire Pierce for their helpful input, and to Stella Donovan for guiding us along the way.

We extend our thanks to Joseph Ponterotto, who from the beginning was an invaluable resource, enthusiastically encouraging us to move forward with the book and writing a strong endorsement.

The authors of chapter 7 remain grateful to Mary Jane Rotheram-Borus for her contributions to the earlier versions of this chapter and to the editors for their very helpful suggestions.

Introduction

Elsie Achugbue

Multicultural Perspectives on Race, Ethnicity, and Identity offers the reader a multicultural and pluralistic perspective on factors that influence our individual and collective identities and perceptions of self and the important role these factors play in defining how we experience our lives and the world around us. The authors introduce and review numerous frameworks and models for understanding racial and ethnic identity development and articulate the unique experiences, past and present, of various racial and ethnic groups in the United States. Each chapter reviews the historical background—the social, economic, and political processes—that has shaped the experience of building and preserving racial and ethnic identities and perceptions of self in U.S. society and identifies the important socioeconomic trajectories that have affected interpersonal and group relations over time. In doing so, the authors, importantly, highlight the very real practical and policy implications that these changes and trends have for our future.

The path to becoming an increasingly multicultural and international society, however, often presents very real challenges to understanding racial and ethnic identity. Every once in a while, a significant or major historical event, such as the 2008 election of Barack Obama as the nation's first black president, spurs a national dialogue in the United States that urges us to examine whether we have become "postracial" and more inclusive and respectful of difference. In recent years, political figures, media pundits, and everyday citizens have pondered this question, and this discourse seems to offer both hope and concern. On the one hand, in the face of collective triumph or shared tragedy, it can seem that we—a nation of many divides—have overcome our most significant barriers to nestle in a place of unity. On the other hand, that the everyday reality for so many Americans, of all different backgrounds, may involve daily indignities or injustices, seemingly based on their race or ethnicity, negates such optimism.

The election of Barack Obama sent ripples of hope throughout the United States and the international community and seeded the notion that the country had transformed itself into a postracial utopia. Meanwhile, race itself, and racism, permeated political and social arenas nationwide as the American public grappled with the question of why and how much the president's, or anyone's, racial and ethnic identity really mattered. This also led to pertinent discussions on the meaning and significance of race and ethnicity in 21st-century U.S. society. Though unified in our thirst for change, America was divided, not necessarily along racial lines but by where we stood on the position of the importance of race and ethnicity as a concept. Some saw racial and ethnic group divides as an important historic institution that formed the basis of a real social hierarchy; others saw these divides as a false notion and a shameful stain on the otherwise polished face of a great nation.

Both the embracing and the backlash surrounding Barack Obama made evident what were still very salient categories in our daily national discourse and experience: color, race, ethnicity, and nationality. Obama's political opponents weren't the only ones who called into question the president's identity; suspicion was evident on both sides of party lines as political figures and the public evaluated their new leader. Could the new president be trusted to represent mainstream America, or would he underhandedly advance black interests? Did he embody real "American" values despite being raised in a nontraditional family by a single mother? What did it mean that the president was also viewed as part of an educated black elite: Was the president black enough? What did it mean that he was rumored to worship amid an Afrocentric congregation: Was he, perhaps, too black? As a child of an interracial marriage, should he be considered black at all? And with ties to relatives in Africa, was he really even an American?

The very public examination of the president's identity, the dissection of his identity into distinct facets of his life experience, illustrates a critical connection between our individual and collective identities and the broader narrative on what it means to be a part of this nation, to be an American. It also made clear that while the shape and form of racial and ethnic identity today is ever changing, it plays as important and central a role in our lives today as it has in the past. It is not only the way many people in the United States define themselves, it is still very much the way in which we define one another.

As we become more aware of our rapidly diversifying society; as so many of our cities are poised on the brink of becoming "majority minority"; as "bi-," "multi-," and "trans-" increasingly preclude our self-identities; and as a growing number of nontraditional families progressively define a "new normal," we, as a nation, embark on an ever more complex examination of the meaning of race and ethnicity today. There is a strong assertion made by social science researchers that our relationship with racism and discrimination is not disintegrating but is simply taking on a different face. Each year, new studies are released that chronicle series of social experiments designed to capture social attitudes in the United States. What we are learning is that where the old racism was overt and obvious, a new racism has taken root that is covert and subtle, yet nonetheless has very real implications for individual, family, and community outcomes. Research has shown that racial and ethnic discrimination and bias remain ever present in everyday interpersonal interactions, in the act of buying or renting a home, applying for a job or bank loan, or purchasing a car, and in our policies and institutions—for example, in education and criminal justice systems. Beyond interpersonal relations, structural racism and systemic bias continue to privilege some and disadvantage others, contributing to real disparities among racial and ethnic groups, in education, employment, health, and household wealth.

Nonetheless, we have developed an ill-fated national culture of deeming it mostly unsuitable, uncomfortable, and inappropriate to talk about race. Although this is often done in an effort to revive that age-old fantasy of a raceless, or postracial, color-blind melting pot, it is in shockingly persistent ignorance of our daily realities. As a result, we unveil race and ethnicity only in reactionary responses to political missteps, sensational media reports, and celebrity blunders or, worse, to police brutality, hate, violence, and, ultimately, tragedy. It is for this very reason that the discussion embarked upon in the following chapters is both critical and timely.

The authors included in this book write about very different populations and subgroups in the United States; however, there are some consistent themes and concepts that transcend cultural boundaries. Each chapter addresses race as a social construct—meaning that at the same time that they acknowledge the very real political, economic, and social significance of race in the United States, they demonstrate a shared understanding of race as a false classification and echo the findings of rigorous scientific research that purports that there is no real biological demarcation that sets one "racial" group apart from another. Perhaps more important than this perspective of race as a social construct is the common insistence that, for many, a deliberate awareness and acceptance of racism and oppression as a reality for some groups—and, accordingly, of privilege and power as a reality for others—is a critical component of healthy identity development. Additionally, the authors place mutual emphasis on establishing and maintaining a sense of belonging as inherent to the psychosocial development process. At the core of the frameworks and models discussed is the need among all individuals, regardless of race or ethnicity, to feel that they are part of a greater community, to connect with others in, and recognize a reflection of themselves within, that community. In this way, despite the persistent notion of identity development as a personal or individual process, it is also almost impossible to separate the individual "self" from family, community, or even the nation as a whole, because each of these environs influences our psychosocial development and perception of our selves. Finally, the authors collectively purport an understanding of identity as transformational, not static throughout one's life, but rather as something that is constantly changing, evolving, redefining, and reshaping itself.

We begin, in chapter 1, with "Identity, Self, and Individualism in a Multicultural Perspective," in which Alan Roland examines the origins of individualism and chronicles the range of pioneering scholarship on identity development. He goes on to differentiate between the individualized and familial conceptions of self that separate the United States, in its Westernized cultural framework rooted in individualism, from many cultures around the world, which instead embrace interdependency and reciprocity. In doing so, Roland draws from his experience working with East and South Asian clients, from Japan and India, respectively, to illustrate Asian societies' emphasis on family, rather than the individual, as the core concept of identity. As an appropriate opener to the subsequent chapters, Roland also stresses the importance of recognizing the role of racism and colonialism in creating identity conflicts and reminds us that new identities are continuously emerging and evolving.

In chapter 2, "African American Identity and Its Social Context," Lee Jenkins builds on Roland's emphasis by defining the various manifestations of racism in U.S. society. Jenkins relates this to recognizing and understanding anger and rage as valid and appropriate responses to the unique position held by African Americans in the United States. He describes this position by borrowing from DuBois's articulation of "twoness," the dual endeavor of affirming a self-identity and maintaining self-respect in the face of a society whose continued exclusion prohibits the same. Jenkins appropriately closely links the African American experience to changes in social trends and economic development policies in the United States that adversely affected social cohesion within African American communities and fortified barriers to integration with the larger society. Jenkins offers a complex view of African American identity in differentiating among the social classes and gender and pays particular attention to the experience of poor urban African American youths.

In chapter 3, "Children of Undocumented Immigrants: Imperiled Developmental Trajectories," Luis H. Zayas and Mollie Bradlee introduce us to the harrowing experience of citizen children living with undocumented parents and siblings in the United States. The chapter focuses on children of mixed-status families of Latin American origin—appropriately so, given that U.S.-born children whose parents were unauthorized immigrants represent an estimated 4.5 million of 9 million people living in mixed-status families in the United States; and that unauthorized immigrants, 58 percent of whom are from Mexico, are primarily of Latin American origin.[1] The authors guide us through the various legal, social–structural, and developmental conditions that contribute to these children's identity development, too often characterized by fear and uncertainty, guilt and shame, detailing the ways in which living in a constant state of "hypervigilance" contributes to emotional insecurity, anger, and depression. At the close of chapter 3, the authors invite us to consider the ways in which immigration policy in the United States "devalues children," especially citizen children, and how this experience will affect not only their psychological well-being, but also their sense of belonging, level of civic duty and engagement, and perspective on their obligation as workers and citizens.

Perceptions of Asian Americans as a social group have undergone substantial transformations over time. In chapter 4, "Racial and Ethnic Identities of Asian Americans: Understanding Unique and Common Experiences," Greg M. Kim-Ju and Phillip D. Akutsu trace the history of Asian Americans, a diverse group composed of over 25 distinct ethnic groups from East and Southeast Asia, in the United States and recount the Asian American experience, from exclusion and marginalization in the 1800s to the stereotypical role of the "model minority" in contemporary times. The authors situate the process of Asian American identity development within the cultural constraints of ethnic traditions, practice, and language and, in reviewing different models of identity development, call out the distinction many Asian Americans make between ethnic and racial identity. The authors then address the various situational influences on ethnic identity, reinforcing our understanding of identity as a variable and continuing process informed by our unique life experiences.

In chapter 5, "Indigenous Identity in the 21st Century: Remembering, Reclaiming, and Regenerating," Sandy Grande, Timothy San Pedro, and Sweeney Windchief encourage practitioners and service providers to do the

---

[1]Pew Research Hispanic Trends Project, "A Nation of Immigrants: A Portrait of the 40 Million, Including 11 Million Unauthorized." Washington, DC: Pew Research Hispanic Trends Project, January 2013.

work of developing a "critical consciousness" in examining their own racial bias as a key component of learning to walk with and be "in a good way" with indigenous peoples. The chapter details the experience of "forced incorporation," endured by indigenous peoples, as unique from other racial and ethnic minority groups. The authors recognize the construction and reconstruction of race in the course of our actions rather than as something we are or possess. Accordingly, they identify the acts of remembering, regenerating, and reclaiming, particularly through the medium of storytelling, as something that indigenous peoples do, not only as a critical component of the process of healing wounds of history, but also in continuing to assert their sovereignty and self-determination, engendering a mode of survival.

Through a historic review of whiteness, Lisa B. Spanierman, in chapter 6, "White Racial Identity Development: Looking Back and Considering What Is Ahead," engages us in an examination of the intricate relationship between race, labor, and economy in the United States. Whereas for many, racial and ethnic identity is defined by an experience of exclusion, contrarily, whiteness in the United States is a story of inclusion, an evolving and expanding definition that transformed over time as was needed to maintain social control by the empowered elite. In this chapter, we learn that whiteness is not removed from the experience of race but is rather inherently defined by it. Spanierman discusses several models of White identity development, each articulating an interdependent relationship between stages of identity development and racist or nonracist attitudes. She chronicles a process in which individuals move first from ignorance to awareness and then to acceptance of racist structures in U.S. society—inevitably paired with White power and privilege—and ultimately culminate in a desired healthy White identity that embodies both a comfortable understanding of and commitment to racial justice. The author importantly reminds us that, as with any other group, whiteness is not a monolithic experience but differs across gender, sexual orientation, and social class divides.

The rapidly rising number of individuals who self-identify as multiracial is pointed to by many as evidence of improved tolerance for mixing among groups. In chapter 7, "Growing up Multiracial in the United States," Robin Lin Miller and NiCole T. Buchanan illustrate how multiracial individuals themselves have often occupied a symbolic position in U.S. society, first as a new and "exotic" category of minority and now emblematic of the realities of an increasingly multicultural society. Nonetheless, these individuals must still navigate the complex hierarchy of social and economic status afforded to different racial groups. Miller and Buchanan depict a compounding process of racial identity development: Akin to the American public's examination of President Obama's identity, they address the question of which label—a self-label, the family's label, or society's label—determines a multiracial child's identity and acknowledge that these labels may, at times, be at odds. The authors stress the importance of ecological and environmental factors in multicultural identity development, offering a critical lesson on the importance of external validation to our internal processes and on how our neighborhoods and communities affect our perceptions of self.

The book aptly ends, in chapter 8, on the question of "What It Means to Be American," through which Jennie Park-Taylor, Joshua Henderson, and Michael Stoyer engage us in an examination of the numerous micro- and macrosystems that influence our understanding of ourselves in relation to our nation. The authors articulate that what it means to be American has changed and continues to change over time, is deeply rooted in our history, and varies depending on the age and generation of the individual. They depict an America in which the experience of being American is not shared, is not uniform, but instead is uniquely crafted on the basis of an individual's position within a fixed social hierarchy that clearly demarcates preferences and privileges based on race, gender, and class. They point out the inconsistencies of an American ideology that values civic participation and freedom but is built on biased and exclusionary rules for belonging and ask us to consider what change is needed to truly become a pluralistic society.

The world of multiculturalism is vast and the diversity of experience seemingly infinite. As such, it is important to acknowledge some of the important areas where additional research and a more in-depth discussion could contribute to and complement this work.

The authors consider the experience of identity development within the context of the United States. Although some of the chapters, particularly regarding Asian American identity and that of citizen children of undocumented parents, incorporate a lens that considers identity development as influenced by foreign policy, immigration law, and individual and familial experiences that transcend borders, the book overall does not deliberately acknowledge the role of internationalism. For example, many immigrants in the United States and their children maintain strong ties with their families and communities in their country of origin. These relationships are evident in both the social–cultural practices of these groups as well as their financial habits, for example, the billions of dollars U.S. immigrants send to their home countries each year. In addition, as discussed by Miller and Buchanan in chapter 7, a growing number of individuals develop blended identities that represent bicultural, multicultural, and international family arrangements. Furthermore, the relative ease and affordability of international travel, compared with what it was just a generation ago, and increased frequency and quality of interaction afforded by technological advancements and social media have served to further strengthen global ties and individuals' connectedness to people and places around the world. Undoubtedly, these factors introduce an additional layer to our understanding of identity that transcends borders and traditional boundaries.

Additionally, although some authors address the differences in experience among men and women, this book does not deeply investigate the complexities of racial and ethnic identity development in the context of gender. Furthermore, for many racial and ethnic groups, the experience of being in that group varies not only between men and women but also among individuals who transcend traditional gender roles: The lesbian, gay, bisexual, transgender, and queer (LGBTQ) experience is another area worthy of further research. The present-day reality for LGBTQ individuals and families is not unlike that of other minority groups in the United States in that they, too, encounter social exclusion and live within the confines of legislative constraints that, at various points in history and up to today, infringe on civil liberties and rights enjoyed by mainstream society. Recognizing this allows us to at least acknowledge the many ways in which the LGBTQ experience warrants the same level of investigation and understanding.

Furthermore, Arab Americans and Muslims in the United States, as increasingly visible minorities in this country, constitute other groups whose voice would benefit from further attention. Although the majority of Arab Americans are Christian, the fastest growing segment of the Arab American population is Muslim. Like other racial and ethnic groups, Arab Americans and Muslims represent great diasporas that span many countries of origin and distinct waves of immigration to the United States. With the United States' continued engagement in the Middle East as well as future involvement in the political and economic arenas of Arab countries—and rising immigration from these countries as a result of this engagement—the experiences of Arab Americans and Muslims will become an increasingly important component of our national narrative and an essential perspective on ethnic and religious diversity in the United States.

Multicultural Perspectives on Race, Ethnicity, and Identity illustrates the multiple ways that racial, ethnic, individual, and group identity and sense of belonging are etched in our collective history, deeply ingrained in the process of our birth and growth as a nation. This has occurred on an internal and individual level, in our understanding of ourselves and one another, as well as an external level, in shaping our national psyche and dominant cultural norms. In doing so, the authors have also chronicled our legislative past, identifying how race and ethnicity have been, and continue to be, so deeply intertwined with the law, governing everything from our interpersonal relationships and neighborhood interactions to our settlement patterns, development, and expansion. The authors present an invaluable examination of how understanding and accepting this history, given its inherent influence in our personal lives, families, and communities, can contribute to much-needed change that will ensure we remain on the path toward becoming a truly multicultural society in which each one of us can participate and thrive. They rightly ask the question of what this means not just for individuals, or various racial and ethnic communities, but for all of us.

Chapter One

Identity, Self, and Individualism in a Multicultural Perspective

Alan Roland

Erik Erikson's (1950, 1968) multifaceted formulations of identity are among the most seminal and fruitful concepts in modern psychoanalysis, especially in interrelating the psychological makeup of individuals with their sociocultural background. A number of mental health professionals and social scientists have taken up his identity theory in their work. There is no question that Erikson's psychosocial concept of identity linking the individual's self with the community's values, norms, and social roles is central to the understanding of ethnic and racial identity in a multicultural perspective. Nevertheless, as is the case with most psychological theories, Erikson's work emerges from within a Western cultural framework and the clinical data of Western people. It is therefore essential to reexamine and reassess Erikson's identity theory for its optimal use in multicultural analyses.

I would like to paint Erikson's identity theory against the backdrop of Western individualism and, more specifically, against the northern European and North American culture of individualism. I shall demonstrate how certain aspects of his multifaceted theory are a strong critique of individualism as it has permeated psychoanalysis and other psychological theories, thereby facilitating the delineation of identity in a multicultural context. Conversely, other aspects of identity theory, particularly Erikson's epigenetic developmental stages that reach their fulfillment in adolescence and young adulthood, simultaneously delineate central psychological processes necessary for functioning in a culture of individualism. As perceptive as this part of Erikson's theory is, it needs to be seriously reexamined if we expect it to shed new light on the ethnic and racial self of different groups in the United States. Otherwise, the "other" may once again emerge as inferior or psychopathological.

Nature and Roots of Individualism

To delve into the relationship of Erikson's concepts of identity and individualism, I shall begin by briefly considering the nature and roots of individualism as the dominant culture of the United States. On a descriptive level, anthropologist Clifford Geertz (1975) has phrased this well:

> The Western conception of the person as a bounded, unique, more or less integrated motivational and cognitive universe, a dynamic center of awareness, emotion, judgment, and action organized into a distinctive whole and against a social and natural background is, however incorrigible it may seem to us, a rather peculiar idea within the context of the other world cultures. (p. 48)

Other descriptions of individualism in current psychoanalytic and psychological theory emphasize the independent, self-contained individual who is highly separate and differentiated from others. These theories describe individuals as self-reliant, autonomous, and self-directed to freely choose their own goals, purposes, beliefs, and values. Individuals are seen as highly reflective of their own unique configuration of internal attributes, traits, and abilities. From these, individuals organize their everyday behavior, which they consider to be essentially their own business.

In Western society, the individual is considered inviolate, the supreme value in and of itself, with each person having his or her own rights and obligations, and each equal to the other. The needs of society are seen as essentially subordinate to the needs of individuals, who are governed by rationality and their own self-interest in mutually consenting contractual relationships. Considerable social privacy is granted to the individual. These cultural valuations of the autonomous individual have come to underlie all of modern European American economic, political, legal, and educational approaches (Allen, 1991; Dumont, 1986), as well as social and psychological theories, including psychoanalysis.

Since the Enlightenment, the rational, thinking person has been seen as the one who is most real and valued and as intrinsically superior to the person who is ruled by emotions. Analytic–deductive, or scientific, modes of thought that explore causal, logical relationships are seen as primary. The world and the cosmos are viewed as essentially secular—that is, knowable through science. All other ways of perceiving reality are discredited as superstition or are demystified, as in the case of religion, magic, and ritual.

What are the roots of this culture of individualism? Very briefly stated, individualism first took primacy in the religious sphere of the Reformation. It then spread to the secular sphere through the philosophers of the social contract, the Jurists, and the philosophers of the Enlightenment—and later to the liberal economic theorists and into the cultural realm of Romanticism.

The Reformation transformed an earlier Christian, otherworldly individualism to a this-worldly one where the onus of salvation is put squarely on the shoulders of individuals who are in a direct, unmediated relationship to a God from whom they are essentially separate and trying to rejoin. In the Calvinist vision, individuals—through independent, active achievement in the world—gauge the degree to which they are among the elect and therefore predestined for redemption. Protestant sects have emphasized values of individualism in taking responsibility for making correct moral decisions and in being self-reliant, self-sufficient, and independent. Rather than being rooted in a hierarchical social collective and cosmic order, as is the case in many other societies, Western individuals are on their own (Dumont, 1986; Kirschner, 1992; Nelson, 1965).

Such 17th- and 18th-century philosophers as Thomas Hobbes, John Locke, and Jean-Jacques Rousseau, each in his own way, then formulated the social contract in which essentially self-contained, atomistic individuals who interact with each other enter into a society with some kind of necessary authority. These philosophers were joined by the Jurists, who reinterpreted natural law as composed of self-sufficient individuals who are made in the image of God and are the repository of reason. This outlook was in turn adopted by various Enlightenment philosophers who laid the cultural groundwork for modern Western individualism in the social and political spheres, with the formation of the modern nation-state as a union of equal individuals with rights and obligations (Dumont, 1986).

Individualism entered the economic realm through Adam Smith and David Ricardo, who assumed a rationally ordered economy of separate, self-contained individuals governed by their rational self-interest rather than that of the community. Philosophical and literary approaches in Romanticism further developed individualism by incorporating the ideal of the highly individuated, self-expressive individual in close relationship with others similarly individuated.

Individualism, Psychoanalysis, and Identity Theory

To understand the context in which Erikson's identity theory relates to individualism, both through counterpoint and continuity, let us first briefly review the position of psychoanalysis in general to this secularized cultural model of self-contained, self-reliant, and self-directed individuals who fulfill their individuality in work and other social relationships. Freud's model in many ways reflects the paradigm of the self-contained individual. In this model, all the motivation and psychological activity arise from within the person. The social surround receives scant attention, except for being the object of a person's sexual and aggressive drives, the source of the content of a person's conscience and of identifications with others, and the reality principle of what a person can or cannot do in the social world (Roland, 1996).

The later development of ego psychology in the United States similarly maintains the stance of the self-contained individual. Ego psychologists further delineate the early childhood developmental processes that enable the child to become a functioning, separate individual in accord with the prevalent cultural and social models of individualism in the United States.

Suzanne Kirschner (1992), a psychoanalytic anthropologist, cogently argued that Margaret Mahler's emphasis on individual autonomy, separation, and individuation (Mahler, Pine, & Bergman, 1975) reflects Protestant Pietistic and Calvinist values of self-reliance and self-directedness. Kirschner also interpreted the strong valuation that ego psychologists place on verbal communication as a reflection of the high Romantic emphasis on individualistic self-expression, as well as of Protestant values of self-reliance and separateness. Nonverbal communication, which is so important in Asian and many other cultures, is then viewed pejoratively as occurring at an earlier developmental level of merger and symbiosis with the mother.

Similarly, Freud and almost all of his followers to this day (with but rare exceptions) have adopted the rational, secular views of the Enlightenment. Religion and spiritual experiences and disciplines are demystified and relegated to the stage of infant–mother symbiotic merger states, or the "oceanic feeling," if not to some form of psychopathology. An even more disparaging attitude prevails with respect to the magic–cosmic world of personal destiny with its connection to astrology, palmistry, the spirit world, and such—all of which are so common to much of the world's population.

These attitudes were further reinforced by social evolutionism, the prevailing colonial theory of the 19th century. It held that the northern European and North American countries were at the top of the social hierarchy with their dedication to rationality, science, and technology. Southern Europeans, Slavs, and Jews were considered inferior, whereas those from Asian, African, and South American countries were deemed primitive, if not savage. It is important to note Freud's reactions to social evolutionism inasmuch as he partly bought into it with regard to religion, spiritual practices, and personal destiny, seeing them as primitive and at times at the level of the savage (Brickman, 2003).

Erik Erikson, as much or more than any other psychoanalyst, introduced the idea that the social, cultural, and historical milieu is essential to a psychoanalytic consideration of the individual self. In his psychosocial concept of self-identity, Erikson saw the individual's identity as an integral part of this milieu rather than being self-contained. Thus, the roles, values, ideals, and norms of the community profoundly shape and are a part of a personal identity. Elaborating on the concept of self-identity in congruence with the insight of Otto Rank (Menaker, 1982) on self-creation, Erikson framed the central psychological dimension of individualism in the United States: the self-creation of one's identity.

Erikson's stages of development stressing autonomy and initiative in the childhood years—in some ways anticipating and paralleling the contributions of Mahler—lay the groundwork for concepts of the adolescent struggle to self-create an identity. Erikson's work perceptively charts the stormy seas that are more often than not encountered in this prolonged act of self-creating: the identity conflicts and diffusion, confusion and crises, the frequent need for a moratorium, the occasional syntheses around negative identities, and eventually (it is hoped) the resolution of a positive identity synthesis.

This self-creation of identity takes place within a social milieu in which contemporary culture in the United States imposes on the individual an enormous degree of autonomy in the adolescent and young adult years. Young people choose who will be their mate or love partner, what type of education and vocational training to pursue, and then what kind of work to do, what social affiliations to make, where to live, and to what kind of ideology or value system to commit. Adolescents and young adults in mainstream U.S. society thus face the enormously difficult intrapsychic task of integrating these adult commitments with the inner identifications with others and self-images developed from expectations within the family. This is the crux of Erikson's elaboration of self-identity. In this sense, self-identity is the psychological process and achievement par excellence of U.S. individualism. Although this psychological description obviously does not apply to all ethnic groups, it is the dominant mode of psychological development in youths in the contemporary United States (Roland, 1988, 1996).

The Individualized and the Familial Self

However perceptive Erikson's description of the development of self-identity in the United States, it does not reflect the experience of youths in most traditional societies. In many African and Asian societies, the experience of childhood, youth, and young adulthood, in either traditional or contemporary urban environments, reflects an emphasis on the family, rather than on the individual, as the core concept of identity. The comments and examples that follow draw on my own experience working with clients from India and Japan.

Manoj, a young Indian psychiatric resident at an excellent residency program in New York City, once related to me that he attended a course on adolescent development given by a highly esteemed psychoanalyst. The analyst at one point proclaimed that unless a person underwent some rebellion as an adolescent, it was impossible to achieve a healthy identity. Manoj went home searching within himself for any signs of rebellion he had felt against either of his parents when he was growing up in India or against any other parental figure as an adolescent. When he could recall no such feelings of rebellion, he concluded that he must be abnormal. This is an example of how the paradigm of identity development—if it is not presented as unique to northern European and North American cultures—can make an immigrant feel inferior or even psychopathological.

Many cultures around the world do not grant individuals the degree of autonomy or the social and cultural options that U.S. culture does. In both traditional and contemporary urban Indian culture, marriages are still arranged, although among many educated urbanites, it is an arranged marriage by introduction by the two families, allowing the young man and woman to make their own decision. Educational and occupational choices are still chosen with predominating parental guidance; social affiliations or friends usually become absorbed by the extended family with no separation of age groups; and a highly integrated Hindu worldview, with certain variations and nuances, is still pervasive and operative. In essence, psychological development and functioning in India do not involve the self-creation of identity as it occurs in mainstream U.S. culture. Rather, they involve processes and organizations of what I call a "familial self" and, among many people, self-transformation toward a more spiritual self (Anandalakshmi, 2014; Roland, 2011).

Developmental stages of childhood throughout much of the world downplay Erikson's emphasis on autonomy and initiative, as well as Mahler's emphasis on separation–individuation. Other cultures typically stress dependency and interdependency, receptivity to others, and reciprocity. Most cultures outside of the northern European and North American culture belt of individualism model some type of familial self, rather than the self-creation of one's personal identity.

In fact, the very idea of a relatively integrated identity, which is so central to dominant North American psychological development, is not particularly relevant to Indians or Japanese or, I believe, to other Asians as well. These cultures experience the personal self as far more relational, varying from one relationship to another. A question may well be asked as to why psychoanalysis and other psychological theories have not until very recently tried to formulate a different and relevant psychology. The answer is again related to Freud's reaction to social evolutionism. To counter the pejorative social–psychological hierarchy of social evolutionism, he framed a new psychology based on universalism, a major Western philosophical concept, that all people are essentially alike, what he termed "the psychic unity of mankind" (Brickman, 2003). Although this was a major advance over social evolutionism, it has made it difficult for psychoanalysis to explore the cultural–psychological differences of those from cultures that are radically different from the West (Roland, 2011).

It may be useful to contrast briefly the suborganizations of the familial self with that of the more individualized self that predominates in the United States and that is so central to Erikson's developmental model of identity. This will serve to highlight many identity issues that ethnic groups who come from outside of the northern European and North American culture belt face in the United States.

The Individualized Self

The individualized self includes an experiential "I-self" as a relatively stable and integrated inner unity, regardless of inner conflicts, with a sharp separation of inner images of self and other. Relatively firm emotional boundaries surround the self, and considerable psychological space exists between self and other in "I and you" social relationships. The individualized self has a conscience that is relatively principled and constant in all situations. Although this is more true for men than for women, who are more contextually and relationally oriented, these inner structures enable both men and women in U.S. culture to function autonomously. Other characteristics of the individualized self include inner directiveness, self-agency, assertiveness, and initiative that call for one's authenticity, individuality, ambitions, and ideals to be implemented in the social world to whatever extent is possible. Cognition in the individualized self is more oriented toward the rational, logical processes of reality testing while thinking in both dualisms and universals. Communication is more verbally expressive, including feelings of anger.

The Familial Self

In contrast to this individualized self, rooted within northern European and North American individualism, is the familial self of much of the rest of the world. The familial self varies considerably from one culture area to another, just as the individualized self varies throughout the countries of northern Europe and North America. I shall delineate the Asian familial self, blurring distinctions among the self of Indians and Japanese (see Roland, 1988, 2011, for a much fuller elaboration of the Indian and Japanese familial self; and Roland, 1996, for descriptions of the Chinese and Korean familial self).

Salient suborganizations of the familial self include an experiential "we-self," with self-experience varying from one relationship to another and much closer emotional connections between inner images of self and other. The familial self also has more permeable, or less delineated, emotional boundaries between self and other, as well as less psychological space between self and other, balanced by a far more private self in emotionally enmeshed "we" relationships. The familial self is also characterized by a dual-self structure that enables an individual to meet the social etiquette of formal hierarchical relationships while maintaining a hidden, private self. In contrast to the individualized self, the familial self has a conscience that is far more contextual or situational to the relationship, situation, and natures of the persons involved. In India, this is related to the prevailing moral theory of *dharma*.

Another aspect of the familial self is that esteem is experienced much more in a "we-self" context and is related to the reputation of the family and the other in various hierarchical relationships. An inner attitude of receptiveness and openness to constant guidance from others is also characteristic, with individuality and authenticity residing much more in a private self rather than being openly manifested in social situations. Cognition is also more contextual than universal (for example, Indian *ragas* are to be played only at certain times of the day or season) and more metonymic on a monistic continuum than dualistic as in the West (for example, an idol of a god or goddess is seen as a partial manifestation rather than as a symbol). Emotion and thinking, and mind and body are on the same continuum. And finally, attributes of interpersonal sensitivity and empathic attunement to nonverbal communication are highly developed in interdependent relationships, to the point that anger is contained within the private self to preserve the harmony of the family and group.

All of these suborganizations of the self allow Asians to function in closely knit familial and group hierarchical relationships. These relationships are characterized by three psychosocial dimensions: (a) the formal hierarchy, with its social etiquette and the expected reciprocities between loyal and deferent subordinates and nurturing and caring superiors; (b) hierarchical relationships of intimacy, with their high degree of dependence and interdependence, considerable nonverbal communication, and reciprocal gratification of one another's needs and wishes without their being voiced; and (c) a hierarchy based on the quality of the person, with deep respect and veneration given to people of superior qualities, whatever their place in the formal hierarchy.

In contrast to the essential psychological process in Western individualism of the self-creation of an identity, the fundamental process in Asians is that of self-transformation oriented to the cultivation of a spiritual self. Such self-transformation may be accomplished through any number of spiritual disciplines, including aesthetic and martial arts (in East Asian cultures), rituals, myths, pilgrimages, or being in the presence of a spiritual person (*darshan*) in South Asia. This is clearly the area of the culture where the greatest psychological individuation takes place and where Asian psychology most particularizes the nature of the person (Anandalakshmi, 2014; Roland, 2005). Moreover, in Asian cultures, the spiritual self and meditative or other disciplines are kept very private, whereas in contemporary American culture, they are openly expressed as an important aspect of one's identity (Roland, 2011).

Identity Theory: A Multicultural Perspective

Having delineated the familial and the individualized self, I will now highlight the relevance of identity theory to a multicultural perspective. Once we recognize that a person's self-identity is profoundly related to his or her community and culture, it becomes apparent that the very makeup of the self can vary significantly.

Thus, central identity issues emerge in intercultural encounters in the United States between immigrants from traditional societies who have a more familial self and those from the mainstream United States who have a more individualized self. To a certain extent, using their radar sensitivity to others and to the norms of different situations, Indians and Japanese, among others, are able to adjust quickly and appropriately to social situations they encounter in the United States.

Veena, for example, recalls her experience at a U.S. college as a 17-year-old fresh from New Delhi. The other students marveled at how quickly she had become "Americanized" in her manner and in her participation in numerous extracurricular activities. In typical Indian fashion, she quickly sensed what it was like to be a student in the United States and acted accordingly. But every few weeks she took a couple of days off and simply stayed in bed all day. She was exhausted from taking on such an unfamiliar lifestyle and adopting a demeanor that stemmed from totally different motivation and inner psychological makeup than her own—namely, the actualization of her abilities and individuality in various activities and relationships.

For some, the contrasts and dissonances between two cultures may prove too strong. Yoshiko, a young Japanese woman happily married to a man from the United States, began working in a corporation in New York City after completing three years of graduate school in the United States. She had chosen to work in a U.S. corporation rather than a Japanese one because she had already become too "Americanized" and too individualized to feel comfortable observing the strict social etiquette and subordination of Japanese hierarchical relationships. But her work experience proved to be intensely upsetting. Her discomfort derived from her having to be verbally assertive and confrontational with clients and from the occasional direct criticism she received for the very rare mistakes she made. Her emotional makeup was much more oriented toward polite, indirect communication, in which it was expected that the other would pick up the innuendos and be cooperative, as was true among the Japanese. Moreover, direct criticism was particularly painful because she was already striving to do everything perfectly, according to her strict Japanese conscience. Thus, major aspects of her familial self around communication, conscience, and esteem were in conflict with the individualized functioning that permeated corporate life in the United States. It was only by my empathizing with the strong contrasts between the psychological functioning typical of the Japanese and American cultures that she could begin to sort out how much to internalize new ways and how much to retain Japanese ways in the formulation of a new kind of identity (for a fuller description, see Roland, 1996).

Many of the dissonances between the familial and individualized self center around issues of intimacy and hierarchy. Asians and Latinos, among others, may expect a greater emotional intimacy and interdependency, especially in insider relationships, than is common in the United States. Particular frustration may result from their expectations of nurturing from bosses, teachers, and school administrators—expectations that are not likely to be met in the contractual, hierarchical relationships typical in the United States (Bhatia, 2007; Purkayastha, 2005; Roland, 1996).

From these intercultural encounters, many Asians, Latinos, and others who are living in the United States begin developing a new identity that encompasses the dominant modes of individualized functioning in a bicultural or expanding self. Often this bicultural self is contextualized in different situations and groups—for example, individualized functioning may be reserved for the work situation, while the familial ways may be retained for family relationships (Roland, 1988). Many immigrants initially experience their two selves as being in stark contrast with each other, coexisting uncomfortably. Gradually, they exist together more comfortably. In the second generation, among children born and raised in the United States, their identity more fully assimilates the individualized self and the culture of individualism in school and work; but the familial self is still very much in evidence in family and other relationships (Roland, 1996). There is at times conflict in this bicultural self, as evidenced by second-generation Indians sometimes referring to themselves as ABCD, American Born Confused Desei (Indian).

Identity Issues Relating to Colonialism/Racism

It is important to recognize that identity conflicts in immigrants may be present well before immigration. Problems with identity issues may be generated within their own families abroad and displaced onto the situation in the United States. Vietnamese Amerasians, for instance, have faced discrimination and marginalization in Vietnam. Immigrants whose home situations have contributed to the lack of a cohesive identity bring the accompanying problems with them to the United States.

Sunil, an immigrant to the United States from India, expressed in group therapy one day that he felt that some members of the group, including me as the therapist, wanted him to become much more independent of his family, or more Americanized. He felt that other group members were supportive of his remaining emotionally enmeshed in his extended family, most of whom had also immigrated to the United States. As his therapist, I was able to see this as an unconscious displacement from an identity conflict within his family in India. His father, an entrepreneur, had deeply identified with British culture, denigrating Indian culture and wanting his sons to become Westernized; his mother remained a traditional Indian woman and mother, representative of Indian culture and family patterns. Thus, a few of the group members had unconsciously come to represent his father in our wanting him to assimilate to the United States, while the other group members represented his mother, who stood for traditional family relationships. This suggests that counselors and therapists need to be alert to identity conflicts that may have been generated even before immigration.

The story of Sunil raises identity issues that emerge from a colonial or racist culture where there is political and economic domination by one group over another. Identity problems in a colonial/racist milieu take on a whole other coloration from those in the intercultural encounters I have delineated above. There is in the description of Veena and Yoshiko, for example, a tacit assumption that they are free to make whatever kind of identity integration they can between their familial selves and their individualized selves.

In a colonial or racist society, there is a profound denigration of the culture and self of those who have been subordinated by the dominant group. On a psychological level, there is an inevitable unconscious projection of the forbidden aspects of the self by the dominant group onto the subordinate "others." Thus, the dominant group views the subordinate group in an intensely negative way. This results not only in a poisonous image being assimilated by those in the subordinate group, but also in a highly rigid, defensive, and superior image being assumed by those in the dominant group (Roland, 2010).

A brilliant analysis of the psychology of British colonialism by Ashis Nandy (1983) demonstrates how British men in India unconsciously projected the rejected feminine aspects of themselves onto the indigenous Indians, resulting in their seeing Indians as effeminate, and therefore ineffectual. This reinforced a British identity of hypermasculinity. Until Gandhi assumed national leadership, most Indians accepted the superior attitude of the British toward them. In his analysis, Nandy depicts the British as well as the Indians as being psychologically adversely affected by colonialism. Although colonialism is by and large over, the attitudes of social evolutionism linger on. Take, for instance, underdeveloped nations compared with developed ones, or Third World countries compared with First World ones. There is clearly still a hierarchy of inferiority and superiority.

In the United States, racism involves an unconscious projection of unacceptable aspects of the self, which are the underside to the predominant ideals of independence, self-reliance, self-directedness, and achievement in work. These repressed aspects of the Protestant ethic and its secularized versions in U.S. individualism are unconsciously projected onto African Americans and others, so that they are seen in negative stereotypes. These stereotypes then serve as justification for exploitation while shoring up the prevailing norms and feelings of superiority in the dominant White group. The whole process engenders rage and self-hate in those onto whom these negativities have been projected, while greatly rigidifying the identity of Whites, again causing them to surrender a part of their own humanity. Neither group emerges with a healthy sense of identity.

Conclusion

With many ethnic groups represented in the United States, new kinds of identities are constantly evolving as persons with very different selves come in contact with each other in ongoing intercultural encounters. When options, opportunities, and choices are relatively available to everyone, these new kinds of identity integrations between different selves can gradually take place. But when racist attitudes predominate, repressed negativities are unconsciously projected onto the other, poisoning the identity of both.

References

Allen, D. (1991, December). *Indian, Marxist, and feminist critiques of the "modern" concepts of the self.* Paper presented at the annual meeting of the American Philosophical Association, New York.

Anandalakshmi, S. (2014). Introspections on culture: Updating the perspective. In N. Chaudhary, S. Anandalakshmi, & J. Volaines (Eds.), *Cultural realities of being: Abstract ideas in everyday life* (pp. 13–22). Sussex, United Kingdom: Routledge.

Bhatia, S. (2007). *American karma: Race, culture and identity in the Indian diaspora.* New York: New York University Press.

Brickman, C. (2003). *Aboriginals of the mind: Race and primitivity in psychoanalysis.* New York: Columbia University Press.

Dumont, L. (1986). *Essays on individualism.* Chicago: University of Chicago Press.

Erikson, E. (1950). *Childhood and society.* New York: W. W. Norton.

Erikson, E. (1968). *Identity: Youth and crisis.* New York: W. W. Norton.

Geertz, C. (1975). On the nature of anthropological understanding. *American Scientist, 63,* 47–53.

Kirschner, S. R. (1992). Anglo-American values in post-Freudian psychoanalysis. In D. H. Spain (Ed.), *Psychoanalytic anthropology after Freud* (pp. 162–197). New York: Psyche Press.

Mahler, M., Pine, F., & Bergman, A. (1975). *Psychological birth of the human infant.* New York: Basic Books.

Menaker, E. (1982). *Otto Rank: A rediscovered legacy.* New York: Columbia University Press.

Nandy, A. (1983). *The intimate enemy.* Delhi, India: Oxford University Press.

Nelson, B. (1965). Self-images and systems of spiritual direction in the history of European civilization. In S. Z. Klausner (Ed.), *The quest for self-control.* New York: Free Press.

Purkayastha, B. (2005). *Negotiating ethnicity: Second-generation South Asian Americans traverse a transnational world.* New Brunswick, NJ: Rutgers University Press.

Roland, A. (1988). *In search of self in India and Japan: Toward a cross-cultural psychology.* Princeton, NJ: Princeton University Press.

Roland, A. (1996). *Cultural pluralism and psychoanalysis: The Asian and North American experience.* New York: Routledge.

Roland, A. (2005). The spiritual self and psychopathology: Theoretical reflections and clinical observations. In A. Vohra, A. Sharma, & M. Mini (Eds.), *Dharma: The categorical imperative* (pp. 192–214). New Delhi, India: Printworld.

Roland, A. (2010). Politics and paranoia: The political exploitation of paranoid anxiety. *Psychoanalytic Review, 97,* 191–356.

Roland, A. (2011). *Journeys to foreign selves: Asians and Asian Americans in a global era.* New Delhi, India: Oxford University Press.

Chapter Two

African American Identity and Its Social Context

Lee Jenkins

In 1903, W. E. B. DuBois established a basis for viewing the identity of African Americans in the United States by referring to a sense of "twoness—an American, a Negro; two souls, two thoughts, two unreconciled strivings; two warring ideals in one dark body" (Dubois, 1903/1961, p. 17). Implicit in this assessment is the difficulty of reconciling two modes of identity that are both viewed as ideals worthy of fulfillment. These two modes are equally incapable of being disowned and are mutually inextricable as a basis of self-identification. DuBois (1903/1961) further spoke of social reality in the United States as yielding the African American "no true self-consciousness, only [letting] him see himself through ... the eyes of others ... measuring [his] soul by the tape of a world that looks on in amused contempt and pity" (p. 17).

This view of twoness—the search for the integrity of self-respecting Black self-representation and the desire to be a full participant in an American society that denied such membership—has been an abiding concern that has been addressed now by the division of African Americans into different social classes. The social critic Eugene Robinson (2011) argued that there are four distinct classes: a mainstream middle-class majority; a large minority or underclass; a small elite with money and power; and two emergent groups—mixed-race individuals and recent Black immigrants. The latter includes people from the Caribbean and Black African immigrants from, for instance, Nigeria and Ghana, who, over the last 10 to 15 years, have been fleeing instability in their native countries. Although many have impoverishment as a primary experience, others come from educated backgrounds of relative comfort in their homelands but were nonetheless stifled by lack of opportunity there.

Their international migration was motivated by the desire for a more complete realization of their personal potential, which they imagined possible in the United States.

The burden of slavery and racial segregation has not had the deleterious effect on Black immigrants in the way that it has on African Americans, resulting in a differing conception of self-identity and expectations of success. It is a situation reminiscent of the way many Black Latinos and people of the Caribbean do not conceive of racial prejudice as an obstacle to their accomplishment. Such attitudes are buttressed by their experiences of an intact ethnic identity and, in many instances, the racial intermingling that has been part of their heritage. Thus, conceptions of autonomy, positive self-regard, visions of opportunities available and socioeconomic success, even visions of what constitutes being Black, vary greatly among the groups, as does the ability to affirm a self-identity that stands apart from the traditionally demeaning attitude of mainstream White society.

That African Americans in the United States have been afforded "no true self-consciousness," in DuBois's terms (1903/1961, p. 17), means that they have been deprived of the means to develop a self-respecting, independently affirmed identity and instead have been conditioned to conform to White superiority–Black inferiority beliefs that apply, without exception, to every aspect of social life.

What are racism and prejudice? Many scholars see the two as still pervasive in the United States and worldwide. *Prejudice* has been defined as "a negative bias toward a particular group of people" (Utsey, Ponterotto, & Porter, 2008, p. 339). *Racism,* conversely, is "based on beliefs and reflected in behaviors that accept race as a biological entity and maintain that racial groups other than one's own are intellectually, psychologically, and/or physically inferior" (Casas, 2005, p. 502). The core of racism essentially includes a "prejudiced sense of superiority in an in-group with a concomitant exercise of power to subjugate an out-group. Thus, whereas prejudice is mainly attitudinal in nature, racism extends the negative attitude into behavior that discriminates against a particular group" (Utsey et al., 2008, p. 339).

We learn early in life to discriminate between in-groups and out-groups and the subtle aspects of discrimination that accompany conceptions of such groups. In one study (Gopnik, 2013), White children ages three to 12 years and adults were shown computer-generated, racially ambiguous faces. Half the faces looked happy, half angry. The adults and the children were more likely to say that the angry faces were black. The Whites also saw the Asian faces as angry, though not as frequently. However, even though Whites are the out-group for Blacks, when the Black children and adults were shown the faces, they showed no bias at all, viewing the White and Black faces in the same way. An explanation for this is that the Black children (and adults) pick up conflicting signals: They know that they belong to the Black group, but they also know that White people have higher status.

Utsey et al. (2008) described the work of the pioneering scholar of racism James Jones, who identified three forms of racism: individual, institutional, and cultural. In institutional racism, social systems and organizations create and implement policies that lead to inequities and disparities among racial groups: Examples include racial profiling, health care disparities, and housing discrimination. In cultural racism, White cultural norms and practices are deemed superior, as this applies to standards of beauty, language usage, and emotional and interpersonal means of self-expression. In individual racism, one can see how, consciously or unconsciously, the attitude of one's own superiority is maintained in relation to another of a different race (Utsey et al., 2008).

The challenge is to make Whites aware of their own unconscious or unintentional racism and unthinking assumption of White privilege. In the increasingly multicultural life we live, Whites could benefit from becoming more aware not only of the common humanity they share with others, but also of the extent to which they seem oblivious to other cultural norms, languages, and customs, without having to suffer economic or social consequences, because of the assumption that being White never requires justification. Speaking about the responsibility to end racism, former NAACP president Benjamin Jealous affirmed that that responsibility falls on the shoulders of Whites, as much as on anyone, just as it is the responsibility of straight people to end homophobia and of men to end sexism and misogyny (Keller, 2013).

Utsey et al. (2008) provided an illuminating discussion of the different ways racism is expressed in society. *Dominative* or old-fashioned racism uses power to enforce its position, a way of doing things that is in decline but still carried out. *Symbolic* or modern racism emerged as a reaction to the end of legal segregation during the civil rights movement and is rooted in cultural values related to the Protestant work ethic and anti-Black fears. It holds that racism no longer exists and Blacks are too demanding of equal rights. *Laissez-faire* racism provides for ongoing racial oppression within the context of changing economic and political realities, rationalizing the economic and political inequities and standing in opposition to affirmative action. *Ambivalent* racism includes coexistence of both positive and negative attitudes. *Aversive* racism (Kovel, 1984) occurs when Whites hold egalitarian principles but still retain views of racial superiority (for example, they may show public advocacy for these principles but privately feel fear and discomfort and avoid personal contact with Blacks). *Color-blind* racism denies or minimizes the ways racism continues to exist and affect people, retains negative stereotypes, blames minorities for their own social challenges, and resists meaningful efforts to remedy social inequality.

The resulting African American psychological profile is one in which accommodating, incompetent, servile behavior is encouraged and internalized. In a complementary fashion, the opposite is held out for Whites: initiative, competence, independence, mastery, risk taking, pride. To be Black, therefore, has been to be the recipient of the coercive and degrading action of Whites, out of which is instituted Whites' conception of themselves relative to Blacks, resulting in the creation of the White dominant self and its social order in opposition to the subservient Black others (Kovel, 1984).

However, at this point, there seems to be confusion about what the U.S. public sees as racism. Old-fashioned expressions of racism are giving way to aversive racism, so that Whites may believe that discrimination is on the wane, racism is no longer a significant factor, and they can personally feel free of bias, believing that equality will soon be achieved (Sue, 2003).

In contrast, Black Americans see racism as a constant and continuing reality and that well-intentioned Whites continue to respond with racial insensitivity, taking their sense of White superiority for granted with the right to govern and control behavior, treating Blacks poorly because of their race. These attitudes are expressed through microaggressions, the new face of racism:

> Racial microaggressions are brief and commonplace daily verbal, behavioral and environmental indignities, whether intentional or unintentional, that communicate hostile, derogatory, or negative racial slights and insults to the target person or group, and are expressed in three forms: micro-assaults, micro-insults, and micro-invalidations. (Sue, 2003, p. 72)

> Micro-assaults are deliberate, conscious, explicit acts; micro-insults are verbal, nonverbal or environmental acts that are rude or insensitive, demeaning a person's racial identity or heritage; and micro-invalidations are actions that exclude, negate or nullify the thoughts, feelings or experiences of persons of color. (Sue, Nadal, Capodilupo, Lin, & Rivera, 2008, pp. 330–331)

Blacks report feelings of rage, frustration, and depression in response to microaggressions. Such aggressions, representing the unconscious worldview of White supremacy, are more harmful than outright expressions of racial hostility because their unintentional nature allows them to exist outside of conscious awareness (Franklin, 2004; Sue et al., 2008).

Six themes have emerged from the content of microaggressions:

1. Assumptions of intellectual inferiority: The Black person is seen as inarticulate, lacking in commonsense; the "complimented" Black individual in question is said to be an exception to the race, because he or she is articulate. Whites are accomplished on résumés, whereas a Black is not supposed to be, and it is a surprise seeing one who is.

2. Second-class citizenship: The Black person is perceived and treated as less than the White individual; he or she may not be waited on properly; clerks may not place change back into the Black individual's hand.

3. Assumption of criminality: Whites avoid Blacks, walking on the other side of the street; Blacks may be viewed as thieves and shoplifters.

4. Assumption of inferior status: A Black person could not be seen as the store manager; Blacks are assumed to be poor or uncultured; they are expected to enter the service entrance or to hold lower-status jobs.

5. Assumed universality of Black experience: An individual may be asked to speak for all members of one's race, as if all Blacks share an identical experience and are interchangeable.

6. Assumed superiority of White cultural values or communication styles: Black communication styles are devalued, as are Blacks' dress, grooming, and hairstyles; Blacks are expected to adapt to mainstream White values and styles (Sue et al., 2008).

Ethnic identification is often equated with racial identity, but race is only a part of ethnic identity; it also involves factors such as family structure; value orientations; differential conceptions of male and female roles; and group ethos with respect to aspirations, accomplishment, and work (Patterson, 1998; Smith, 1991).

Ethnic or racial identity, buttressed by a defining and supporting cultural embeddedness, has much to do with providing a sense of personal and group integrity and worth. The critical issue is not only oppression but status inequality. Oppression is only one result of majority–minority dynamics (Smith, 1991). In addition, as is the case with members of other ethnic groups,

African American culture is diverse with respect to levels of employment or unemployment; education; encounters with the police; economic status; degree of family stability; and degree of identification with, and integration into, the life of White mainstream society (Priest, 1991).

A useful way to examine the importance of a sense of ethnic solidarity and the support provided by shared ideals is to see how such experiences affect the performance of African American secondary school students. The experience of biculturalism is often looked at in terms of the positive effect it may have on African American high school students, beyond the providing of cultural identity and self-esteem (Rust, Jackson, Ponterotto, & Blumberg, 2011). *Biculturalism* is thought of here as one's "sense of belonging to two different cultures without losing a sense of one's original cultural identity; one's ability to differentiate between the rules, norms, and values of both; and one's ability to interact in both cultures without relating them in a hierarchical manner" (Rust et al., 2011, p. 131). Research has found that bicultural individuals have higher self-esteem, better cognitive function, and a stronger sense of well-being when compared with monocultural individuals (LaFromboise, Coleman, & Gerton, 1995; Rust et al., 2011).

The academic achievement gap between Whites and Blacks has lessened over the last 30 years, but African Americans still score lower on tests, achieve lower grades, reach lower levels of educational attainment, and have higher dropout rates than Whites (Kao & Thompson, 2003). Many factors are involved here, including academic tracking and teachers' expectations; stereotyping; limited access to social, political, and economic power and resources; and inferior and underresourced schools (Diamond, 2006; Lawrence, Crocker, & Dweck, 2005).

A much greater effort needs to be made to identify the strengths, protective factors, and sources of competence of African Americans. One attempt to do this in a specialized way is Richard Shin's study (2011) on self-efficacy of African American elementary school children. *Self-efficacy* (Bandura, 1991) refers to an individual's beliefs about his or her ability to generate and maintain the effort needed to achieve a goal. Shin's study found that positive beliefs in one's own competence held significant predictability of higher score outcomes.

There are also cultural differences with regard to the socialization experiences of Black versus White students. As socializing agents, schools reflect, use, and teach the cultural norms of the mainstream. There is an emphasis on individualism and competition in the mainstream culture; in contrast, the Black socialization experience emphasizes collectivism and cooperation (Maryshow, Hurley, Allen, Tyler, & Boykin, 2005). There may therefore be academic disparity between African American and European American students resulting from dissonance between understanding of their own cultural norms and values and those of the mainstream that are instilled in the schools. African American students may disidentify with academic achievement by not incorporating it into their self-concept and not viewing it as an important factor in establishing self-esteem (Rust et al., 2011).

Research has found that the extent to which an individual positively identifies with his or her cultural–ethnic group helps mitigate conflict with intercultural contact (Constantine, Alleyne, Wallace, & Franklin-Jackson, 2006; Rust et al., 2011). However, even though self-esteem is positively related to cultural identity and biculturalism, no significant relationship has been found for African American students between global self-esteem and academic performance.

One explanation for this might be the way subordinate individuals (and others) have been led to think that their performance is equated with their human worth, and one should not have to prove one's human worth by performing well academically. The fear of being found to be academically deficient might be defended against by the feeling that one's human worth precedes academic performance and should not depend on it. Therefore, one might not want to perform well, because to do so would be to accede to the idea that one's worth is dependent on and proved by one's academic performance.

Being forced to accommodate, for any length of time, to an inferior status results in the internalization of such thinking as an appropriate and expected part of oneself (Smith, 1991). This process brings about the fusing of negative images held up to people who are prevented from fulfilling the dominant cultural ideals (Erikson, 1966). The persistent consequence of such a situation, as Pettigrew (1964) suggested, can be devastating—resulting in confusion of self-identity, lowered self-esteem, a perception of the world as a hostile place, and serious sex role conflicts (Berlin, 1969).

Identity thus reflects culture and is a product of the specific culture that creates it, causing people of different cultures to inhabit different worlds. Because of the imposition of prevailing White mainstream cultural and social attitudes, members of minority groups have had to develop bicultural identities and skills. When the African American culture is unable to provide support mechanisms that counteract the negative and contradictory messages from White mainstream society, American Blacks often experience identity conflicts and maladaptive behavior.

The pressures of racial rejection and discrimination in public life and the internal struggle against a negative self-image have imperiled the identity development of many Blacks. They have had to adapt to reduced status and the ambivalent choice between an accommodative or an assertive role, assessing the prospects of meeting the demands of their own group as well as those imposed by mainstream society. Are African Americans to be taught to survive in and adapt to a world of insults or to adopt an attitude that would change such a world? Social scientists are struggling to define what constitutes successful identification and development for African Americans—something that promotes empowerment and cohesive inclusion in their own group membership, because fitting into the group is itself important in defining satisfactory individual development (Billingsley, 1992).

Nevertheless, despite the proven negative effects of racism and discrimination, African Americans have continued to improve their positions in society and succeed in all walks of life. Their coping and resilience in the face of racism have not received the research attention they deserve (Rowles & Duan, 2012). In one study, in terms of the perception of having been victimized by racism, only 30 percent of African Americans reported not having experienced some form of racism within the past year (Sellers & Shelton, 2003). It should also be noted that not all responses to racism are maladaptive. Many African American families have been able to develop the psychological resources to counteract the debilitating effects of subordinate status. It is in the disintegration of the family and the absence of fathers, however, that one sees the effects of discrimination and the undermining of the coping mechanisms to deal with such effects, particularly evidenced in juvenile delinquency, acts of physical aggression, and mental illness. The depressed surroundings of many African American children present so constricted an encounter with the world that their intellectual potential is barely tapped (Pettigrew, 1964).

How have such experiences been dealt with in an attempt to retain psychological well-being? Active coping, in the forms of spirituality, ethnic pride, and racial socialization, is often exercised by African Americans in order to remain resilient (Allen, 1996). Additionally, feeling adequate and competent and having a sense of hope and connectedness help individuals to deal with hardship (Rowles & Duan, 2012). Encouragement also seems to contribute to an individual's resilience and self-worth, regardless of how well or poorly he or she may be treated by others (Evans, Dedrick, & Epstein, 1997).

Racial socialization is one way such encouragement and resilience are instilled: "Orienting children to values, norms, and ways of being within the family, the community and the world, is something taking place in all families to some degree" (Rowles & Duan, 2012, p. 12). For African American families, there would be a specific need to include messages specifically oriented toward race and the meaning of being African American in this society (Fischer & Shaw, 1999; Mosley-Howard & Evans, 2000).

Another way to provide encouragement is through spirituality, not necessarily religious observance, but belief in a higher power as a source of strength (especially for women), persevering in the face of obstacles. This is seen as a key element in family relationships and as "an integral part of self-definition" (Mosley-Howard & Evans, 2000, p. 446). It is important to emphasize the many forms of encouragement that have been used by African Americans in their ongoing response to the effects of racism. I document the vulnerabilities and risks encountered.

Social Trends and Economic Development

The integrationist and civil rights movements of the 1950s and 1960s mobilized the long-suppressed yearning for change into a disciplined assault on the nation's conscience for its failure to fulfill its ideals. The integration movement led by Martin Luther King, Jr., typified the desire of African Americans for full citizenship and the nation's moral obligation to provide it. At the same time, the Black separation movement, symbolized by Malcolm X, articulated Blacks' distrust of Whites as unrelenting antagonists and racist destroyers of Black life and culture and proclaimed the accompanying need for Black self-rehabilitation through separatism (Patterson, 1997; Pinderhughes, 1976).

The Black Pride movement of the 1960s sought to reject White-imposed terms of reference by fully asserting the fact of African American identity as a descriptive category and redefining its interpretive meaning. The movement disavowed the term "Negro" as a legacy from the enslaved past imposed by Whites and affirmed the term "Black" as a basic mode of selfacceptance:

> The overriding fact is that black ... was once a despised term and is now being rehabilitated. The identification with black had been rejected by darker Americans who, tragically, sought to escape the burdens and inconveniences of discrimination by ... adopting white manners and morals and standards of beauty. They coveted the illusion that they could thus be accepted for themselves, without regard to color. (Smythe, 1976, p. xi)

The economic and social gains that were made during the 1960s and 1970s did not bring about the abolition of discrimination but did create greater tolerance. African Americans began to experience a more extensive integration into mainstream society and a greater sense of empowerment, racial pride, and mutual respect. Although a small percentage of Blacks were able to materially improve the quality of their lives and to benefit from civil rights legislation and affirmative action initiatives, a large proportion continue to struggle in impoverishment and powerlessness. Increasingly, militancy and disaffection are some of the consequences, whether on the part of a growing underclass, a marginalized and struggling working class, or among those who see salvation in Black ethnocentrism or in a politicized stance that separates from and denigrates everything considered to be White modes of thinking and behaving.

The 1970s and 1980s brought about the beginnings of a steady erosion of many of the economic advances that had been made by African Americans during the 1960s. Despite a large increase in the number of middle- and upper-income Blacks, the disparity between White and African American incomes has widened during the last two decades. The most enduring and impressive economic gains were made by two-parent, two-income African American households, many of which are composed of urban, upwardly mobile professionals. The increase in their numbers, however, corresponded to an equivalent increase in the number of lower-income African Americans. Today, African Americans comprise a disproportionate share, roughly one-third, of the urban poor (Kneebone & Garr, 2010). An illuminating study of the state of African Americans today was provided by Angela Hattery and Earl Smith (2012) in *African American Families Today: Myths and Realities.*

As much as Barack Obama's presidency is another step in the continuing realization of the promise of full membership of African Americans in American society, the reality is that the lives of too many are stifled and unfilled—and continue to be affected by racial discord:

> Three years after the inauguration of Barack Obama, at the beginning of 2012, African Americans are incarcerated at increasingly high rates, high school dropout rates are higher than ever, fewer African Americans are enrolling in or graduating from college or earning advanced or professional degrees, more African Americans are living in poverty—the wealth gap between whites and African Americans has grown ever wider—and African Americans are more likely to die in their first year of life and they can expect to live shorter lives than white Americans. (Hattery & Smith, 2012, p. 7)

There has been an exodus of stable African American families away from the inner city, leaving behind the least resourceful to succumb to the forces of social disintegration. A culture of poverty, joblessness, and single-parent households has resulted, which may be more significant in determining the fate of impoverished inner-city African Americans than the effects per se of racism. This would simply be another way to speak of what the ultimate consequences of structural racism have become when there has never been an equal opportunity for education, employment, and social advancement. In his controversial book, *The Declining Significance of Race,* the sociologist William Julius Wilson (1978) argued that the racial oppression and antagonism that characterized the economic sector prior to World War II, severely limiting the aspirations of Blacks, have been reduced significantly, especially after the social changes of the 1960s. Wilson saw race as a declining factor and class—in Black and White society alike—as the new source of division. He did not see racism as the sole explanation of Blacks' social ills but pointed to other social trends and factors: poor employment opportunities, inadequate education, a severe shortage of marriageable men, the effects of crime and drugs and welfare dependency, the departure of the African American middle class and the stability it provided, and the impact of this on an increasingly isolated and self-destructive inner-city underclass (Ploski & Williams, 1989; Wilson, 1987).

The African American populace had been seen as divisible into three segments. The first third constitutes the successful middle- and upper-income, college-educated, and professional Blacks, who have a history of stability and achievement and a fully employed, twoworker household. The middle third is composed of a struggling working class, hard working and sacrificing, subject to layoffs and economic and social dislocations. The bottom third is composed of an underclass that is in a state of social chaos and dependency (Ploski & Williams, 1989). It is as much a mistake to equate the Black working poor with the underclass as it is to make no distinction between the Black working class and the Black middle class. Viewing Blacks as a monolithic group is as erroneous as conceiving of Whites as a monolithic racist majority with a vested interest in keeping Blacks in a state of subjugation (Patterson & Winship, 1992).

The African American class structure was updated and further elaborated on by Eugene Robinson (2011) in his provocative book *Disintegration: The Splintering of Black America.* African Americans could not rent, buy, or live in White neighborhoods; they were confronted with "Whites only" educational institutions, stores, hospitals, and restaurants. Places of public accommodation were segregated. Such restrictions led to the development of

African American institutions, businesses, churches, hospitals, higher-education facilities, and a cadre of professionals serving this population. They were confined to their own communities and developed their own social networks. Further, regardless of their social class, they lived in the same neighborhoods, which made them relatively diverse and socially integrated. This meant that "affluent, middle-class and poor African American neighborhoods often bordered each other in ways that created frequent contact among people of differing social class and occupations" (Hattery & Smith, 2012, p. 8). School teachers, plumbers, domestics, and dentists might live with or near one another, promoting a sense of shared purpose and interest as marginalized and discriminated-against Blacks, in comparison, for instance, to poor, middle-class, and affluent Whites, who tended to live in separate neighborhoods and viewed their self-interests differently.

The implementation of integration laws loosened the sense of social cohesion and helped weaken the bond between the Black social classes. Those who could take advantage of new opportunities in the White world increasingly did so, leaving behind the most vulnerable, who had always had the most difficulty managing their lives. Regarding class divisions, I referred earlier to Robinson (2011), who argued that a rift had formed between four social classes or groups: (1) a mainstream middle class invested in full membership in American society; (2) a large, abandoned minority or underclass; (3) a small social elite of wealth and power; and (4) two newly emerging groups—individuals of mixed race and growing communities of Black immigrants, increasingly complicating the idea of what is meant by referring to oneself as "Black" (Hattery & Smith, 2012).

A look at the educational, social, and economic contexts of the lives of Black Americans might help provide an understanding of these class divisions. The acquiring of a good education, from elementary school onward, is of obvious importance for successful accomplishment. The *Brown v. Board of Education* decision mandated the end of legal segregation in schools. In the 60 years since the court's decision, in spite of nationwide efforts made to promote integration, a resegregation of schools has occurred, such that a typical White student today attends a school with a population that is 80 percent White, while a Black student is now more likely to attend a segregated school than his parents, based on geographical rather than legal boundaries. This is a new version of inequitable access, as most Black schools are severely underresourced. The experiences of upper-class Blacks mask the deprived conditions of most Black schools. When Whites see the accomplishment of the fortunate Blacks and see their presence in integrated and White progressive schools, they may think integration has been accomplished.

As of 2010, 61.5 percent of all Blacks graduated from high school, compared with 90 percent of Whites. White females' graduation rate was five points higher than that of White males' (Hattery & Smith, 2012). The Black middle class and the socially elite have rates similar to those of the White community. Yet only 16 percent of African Americans earned a four-year bachelor's degree, even in six years. Complicating this, at the historically Black colleges and universities, which were undermined by integration, the graduation rate in some schools is lower than 25 percent. Legacy admissions, an unacknowledged example of (White) affirmative action, based on status and not qualifications, are also a barrier to Blacks. Another hindrance is the way Blacks do not reap the same advantage from a college degree as Whites do, with respect to the type of degree earned; where it was obtained; and, once one is employed, the kind of work chosen, all of which contribute to the profit-making and socially elevating potential of the career being pursued. Also to be considered are the lure and often false promise of for-profit colleges and institutions, which target minorities, dropouts, and the un- and underemployed (Hattery & Smith, 2012).

African Americans work in all sectors of the economy, but disproportionately few work in professional and leadership roles. The workplace is still segregated in many ways, and Blacks are still less likely to accumulate wealth. This results in less or inferior education, lower-wage jobs, wage discrimination, and discrimination in banking, including high risk of subprime mortgages, all of which prevent wealth accumulation. Housing values in African American neighborhoods remain deflated because Whites often do not buy in Black areas.

According to U.S. Census data for 2012, the median American household income was $49,445, 7 percent below the 1999 figure, with a $52,000 median income for Whites and $32,000 for Blacks. Twice as many African American households (14.4 percent) live on less than $10,000 per year as compared with 7.3 percent of U.S. households combined (Hattery & Smith, 2012, p.103). White Americans are only half as likely as African Americans to be among the poorest households, yet they are nearly four times more likely to be among the wealthiest.

Poverty is rising in severity and frequency, especially after the 2007 Great Recession, which produced an unemployment rate of 9.1 percent but a rate at least twice as high for Blacks, and three times as high for Black men. The welfare rate was 12 percent for Whites versus 40 percent for Blacks. In 2011, the U.S. Census reported that 46.2 million Americans were poor, for an overall poverty rate of 10 percent, which for a family of four was set at $22,113. This means that 9.4 percent of Whites lived in poverty, while 27.4 percent of Blacks did. African Americans continue to be underrepresented in the higher-earning professions, and old-style discrimination still exists, with Blacks with similar credentials as Whites less likely to be hired in any kind of work than Whites. Sometimes, for both Blacks and Whites, there can be a "false sense of individual accomplishment and a fierce blaming of those individuals who fail" (Hattery & Smith, 2012, p. 110). There are African Americans who can interpret their success as resulting from their individual efforts alone, viewing themselves as above the structural inequities that have so undermined others, though this false sense of security was dramatized by the 2007 recession. Nevertheless, a rift has occurred between successful Black and those on the bottom, especially when some of the unsuccessful are friends or members of one's own family.

Complicating this issue is the fact that the efforts and successful adaptation of some African Americans show that African American achievement can occur despite the legacy of the past and continuing resistance in the present. Some Whites, seeing such achievement, may be moved to think that racism no longer exists, within themselves or within the society, and that therefore those left behind have only themselves to blame, and Whites no longer have to be accountable for new, more subtle forms of racism.

Millions of African Americans have escaped the ghetto. In some ways, the ghettoization of the poor may have helped lead to the growth of the African American middle class (Wilson, 1987). These African Americans had always been opposed to the stereotyped and destructive aspects of ghetto culture. Their moving into a middle-class lifestyle, whether in African American or integrated communities, was a natural, expected consequence of their efforts. Their success raises the troubling issue of how to view the underclass: as victims of racism (a liberal attribution) or as perpetuators of a self-destructive lifestyle (the conservation attribution).

Those who left the ghetto tell the story of the successful African American immigrant experience in the United States, not the defeat and failure of the underclass. The desire to realize many of the expectations of middle-class life—achievement, good schools, and safe and prosperous neighborhoods—has always been as much an African American as a White aspiration. African Americans resent the idea that such expectations are often thought of as the exclusive province of Whites and that the desire of Blacks to fulfill their aspirations is seen as an intrusion into the White domain.

The class intermingling of African Americans in the ghetto and the racial integration of Blacks and Whites in society at large have a parallel relationship. Because groups operate as closed, self-sustaining hierarchical systems, only by enlarging the conception of group membership can mutual recognition and mutual assimilation take place. This possibility is negated by segregated practices that inhibit White empathy with the feelings of African Americans, sustain prejudice and inequality, and frustrate social mobility (a direct by-product of residential mobility).

Many African Americans have opted for life in African American communities instead of integrated ones (Dent, 1992). Many have been disillusioned as a result of the difficulties they have experienced as African Americans moving into White communities. They also want to provide African American role models for their children; to protect their children against racist attitudes and images; and to immerse their children in the experience of successful African Americans managing their own economic, political, and social institutions, as had been the case during the period of segregation.

This trend is an example of cultural embeddedness, the desire to live among one's own kind; it may have psychological benefits in strengthening ethnic cohesion and preventing identity conflicts. Greater rates of emotional disorder have been shown to occur among minorities of any group identification living in stressful circumstances among a majority group of a different identification (Smith, 1991).

The stability of the successful African American classes in the segregated community has fostered the determination, discipline, and sense of worth—however tenuous at times and under assault—that are necessary to believe in the eventual assimilation of African Americans and their ability to compete in the White mainstream of the United States, not to mention their ability to survive and prosper within the African American community. Some of those who have become assimilated into White society in the United States have found that this sense of the strength of African American solidarity has become attenuated, and they are searching for it again in an African American communal spirit.

This effort is reflected in the movement toward African American self-help organizations and autonomous actions in addressing a range of social problems. It also is seen in the resurgence of interest in African American literature, culture, and history—in a movement that goes beyond multicultural egalitarianism to, for some, Afrocentric preference. The drift toward separation is particularly strong as African Americans attempt to achieve both self-protection and self-enhancement. African Americans today are focusing less exclusively on desegregation and more on a broader demand for equitable distribution of advantages and benefits comparable to those of Whites. African Americans in the United States at all socioeconomic levels feel in many ways separated and excluded from the life of the mainstream, even as polls continue to show a greater tolerance and acceptance of African Americans and other minorities on the part of Whites. Harvard sociologist Orlando Patterson has written that the United States, though flawed in many ways, "is now the least racist White-majority society in the world" and may become, in the view of others, the "first multiracial democracy in history" (Patterson, as cited in Harrison, 1992, p. C2).

Nevertheless, the need to repair damaged self-esteem on the part of many African Americans—or prevent its occurrence—is often coupled with the perceived need to defend against White perceptions of Black inferiority. The hope is for a generation of young African Americans freed from the effects of a damaged self-image, who are able to help liberate their White counterparts from their own disabling misperceptions.

Gender Socialization and the Relations of Black Men and Women

The socialization of men and women with respect to gender roles is subject to variation according to ethnic, racial, or cultural group identity, but in any patriarchal society the assigned roles tend to be similar (Davenport & Yurich, 1991). Women are generally expected to be the nurturing, dependent caregivers, who foster and find meaning in relatedness to others, while men are expected to be independent, assertive, in control of their fates, sexually adventurous, and autonomous. The attempt to adhere to such stereotyped expectations, however, can be harmful. Perhaps most important, changes in the status of women in the workplace and at home and the increased emphasis on egalitarian sharing of child rearing and domestic duties have all brought about a change in thinking about gender roles.

These gender role conceptions and the issues they raise are linked to the way a person's self-image and sense of worth are defined by his or her status in society. The way status inequality plays out between the races can also apply to gender roles. Those in high-status positions may internalize dominant behavioral traits and a positive self-image, while those in lower-status positions may have a negative view of themselves. Men in lower-status positions often act in unassertive, compliant, and "feminine" ways when they see no opportunity to change their prospects (Davenport & Yurich, 1991).

Slavery and its aftermath had a profound effect on status positions of African American men and women in the performance of gender roles. African American women endured the effects of slavery equally with African American men, achieving a negative equality with men. The conventional image of the woman looking to the man for economic or physical support or protection could not easily be taken as a prevailing description of the relations between Black men and women during slavery and its aftermath of segregation, violence, and denial of opportunity. This was a historical circumstance that brought about its inevitable result, in spite of the ongoing familial collaboration among Black men and women during these difficult times and the heroic, yet commonplace bearing of the burden of hard work and sacrifice on behalf of their families engaged in by the majority of Black men.

Black women were challenged to discover their strength and resourcefulness in a way that women of other racial or ethnic groups have seldom had to do. They were called on to try to survive by functioning in a way that was conventionally considered to fulfill both the male role of provider and the female role of nurturer. Black women were able to secure employment, though at the lowest economic levels, in spheres of work from which Black men might still have been excluded. In this effort, they were, of course, dehumanized and beaten down just as the men were, but their involvement in this conception of what constituted masculine and feminine roles has left its mark.

The development of this phenomenon, over time, as affected by male unemployment and welfare dependency—especially in its elaboration in the social dysfunction of the underclass—has helped contribute to the stereotype of the matriarchal family with a domineering, controlling female and an irresponsible, unavailable male (Davenport & Yurich, 1991; Staples, 1973).

Across socioeconomic lines and levels of education, no set family or gender role pattern can be found for African Americans. However, some investigators (Pettigrew, 1964; Staples, 1988) have concluded that the matriarchal stereotype is more likely to occur among lower-income African Americans. African American women pursue higher education in greater numbers than African American men, jeopardizing their chances of getting a mate, but also reducing their need for one as they can be economically independent.

In contrast to women of other ethnic groups, the roles of African American women have been defined in terms of strength and resourcefulness. One researcher (Danby, 1975) found that being a good provider, the traditional male role, was accepted by 76 percent of African American women as a matter of course, yet both African American men and women view motherhood as a criterion for a woman's fulfillment. African American women are often seen as competent, secure providers who hold a grievance against African American men for not being equally capable partners. The men in turn are subject to anger and low self-esteem, reflecting their perception of their powerlessness and diminished status in society and their inability, except through sports, to gain access to positions of prestige, wealth, or power (Chapman, 1988). African American men, nevertheless, do not appear to be independent, withdrawn beings who disparage closeness and relatedness. Although they give evidence of distrust of Whites and women, they also evince a deep need for supportive, encouraging relationships (Davenport & Yurich, 1991).

Successful African American women sometimes seem privileged in comparison to African American men. Their higher status and educational aspirations often steer them away from the traditional compliant female role. Lacking male partners, they may acquire the connectedness they need through affiliation with their children, their parents, other adults, and the church and other institutions in the community, rather than through a romantic relationship.

Though African American women today sometimes seem to occupy a higher status relative to African American men, the historical reality of their position has always been one of the most status-diminished group, the "mule of the world," in Zora Neale Hurston's phrase (1937/1990), burdened with the work refused by others. In light of the recent focus of attention on the problems of African American men, many activists think that the equally severe problems of African American women have been neglected. However, the problems of African American men—homicide, drug dealing, imprisonment, and irresponsible fathering—take on a sense of urgency because they are viewed as more threatening to society. The problems of African American women are often viewed as the consequence of their own shortcomings and as being threatening only to themselves and their children.

Intimate partner violence (Hattery & Smith, 2012), or domestic violence, is the leading cause of female homicide. Such violence occurs among every race and social class, but the African American family is particularly prone to it. One reason is that African American men are more likely to be unemployed or to have been incarcerated, both of which lead to an increased risk for perpetrating domestic violence. Risk factors for intimate partner violence are marrying young, being poor, and having lots of children. When men are still expected to be breadwinners and are supposed to make more money than their wives, their feeling of being emasculated can lead to violence.

Moreover, incarceration makes men more violent, because in prison they learn violence as a conflict resolution strategy. Great strain is placed on relationships by men newly released from prison who return to their partners with jealous imaginings. Boys who grow up in these situations learn that they are the ones in charge, that women will try to manipulate and control them, and that real men keep their women in line: "boys who grow up in homes where their fathers or stepfathers or mothers' boyfriends beat their mothers are three times more likely to grow up to be batterers themselves" (Hattery & Smith, 2012, p. 60).

African American women have come closer to bridging the gap between their earnings and those of White women but often do so by working longer hours. Moreover, most African American women must support an entire household on one income. Among full-time wage earners, "white men are at the top, then black men, then white women and then the longtime last-place holder, black women" (Britt, 1992, p. F6). In addition, African American women must fight for recognition as career women, resisting both sexism and racism. They are often told by African American men that their success has occurred at the expense of African American males, and they may be subjected to the hostility of African American men who view the concerns of African American women about sexism as an indulgence more suited to White women.

It is a common belief that African American men bear more of the brunt of racism than do Black women. Yet it is the women who raise the children, and their problems need to be addressed. Recent popular movies and fiction have depicted ambitious African American women as materialistic and self-serving, turning them against their men, family, and finally their race (Jones, 1992). They are condemned if they are unmarried, poverty stricken, and childridden and equally condemned if they are highly educated, successful professionals.

All of this can generate anger and resentment, with African American women "seeing themselves as the least powerful, monied and desirable group on the globe" (Britt, 1992, p. F6). This sense of being unappreciated and disrespected is particularly compounded by the recent increase in relationships between African American men and White women. Even though Black–White unions are a tiny minority of all unions (2 percent), compared with those between Asian women and White men (40 percent) and those between Hispanics and Whites (41 percent), African American women are the least likely to marry outside of their race. The majority of people who marry still marry people of the same race. However, there remains a bias against incorporating African American men or women into the matrimonial mainstream: In a recent poll, 46 percent of Republican voters believed interracial marriage should be banned, 80 percent of Americans approved of intermarriage with a White person, and 66 percent supported intermarriage with a Black person (Hattery & Smith, 2012).

African American women have traditionally had the comforts of church or sisterhood and, in the final analysis, their children and their mates to turn to, but they risk losing even the solace of their mates if they voice their grievances too strongly. As a result, they turn their frustration on themselves, their female counterparts, or their children or outward on African American men—who are often viewed in despair as unloving, abandoning, and unredeemable (Britt, 1992). African American mothers are often lauded for being one of the most effective socializing agents of African American males, enabling them to survive in compliance with an accommodating stance imposed by White racism. However, their actions in disciplining young male African Americans may also reflect displaced anger at African American men (Cazenave & Smith, 1991; Pinderhughes, 1976).

Transitions to Adulthood for Poor African American Youths

That African Americans comprise a disproportionate share of the urban poor cannot be overemphasized. Today nearly half of poor African American children live in neighborhoods of concentrated poverty (Austin, 2013). For this reason, the problems facing impoverished African American boys and girls, often as a result of the absence of their fathers and inadequate parenting in general, affect not only the underclass or the lower classes, Black and White, but society in general.

> Fatherlessness consigns children to poverty; children in father-absent households are six times more likely to be poor than children whose homes are headed by a father.... It may lead boys to become hyper-masculine and violence-prone. It deprives inner-city neighborhoods of the quasipolicing function played by good family men.... It leaves the absent fathers without moorings or motivation to pursue lives of hard work and productive citizenship (Taylor, 1992, p. C1).

The symptoms of social disarray also apply to the less visible, predominantly rural, and suburban White underclass, who are greater in absolute numbers and who share with the Black underclass the pathologies of impoverishment—wife beating, incest, alcoholism, the inability to support their families—without the recognition and blame given to Blacks (Patterson & Winship, 1992).

Charles Murray's *Coming Apart: The State of White America* (2012) speaks of this social dysfunction among Whites. We are confronted with what the shift from couples to single households means, a turning away from legal marriage or the forming of partnerships in which people live together and raise children, engaging in long-term cohabitation without being married. The biggest factor with an impact on the likelihood of cohabiting is social class. "Lower-income and poor people are significantly more likely to cohabit than any other social class group. Among women, cohabitation is a transition to marriage for middle class women, but a substitute for poor women" (Hattery & Smith, 2012, p. 20). For poor African Americans, welfare reform had a lot to do with this situation when the requirement was for only the woman and children to receive benefits but not the man to be residing in the home. Thus, low-income women on welfare did not marry the fathers of their children, and over time not marrying became the norm. It might be the case that the best defense against being poor for low-income individuals is not, as we conventionally think, primarily getting an education but also getting married, providing a two-person income.

For poor African American girls, the chances of achieving any one of the markers of adulthood—finishing one's education, getting a full-time job, buying a house, and marrying and having children—are low. So being able to have a child, motherhood itself as something separate from marriage, becomes a significant marker of adulthood and something achievable, providing the mother with a sense of accomplishment and with a child who will always need and love her—and this may be her only way of being able to attach herself to a man (Hattery & Smith, 2012). This dire situation is increasingly the case for both poor White and Black girls.

Poor Black boys are similarly affected with respect to ideas about what constitutes appropriate transitions to adulthood. Many may see going to jail or to the state penitentiary as an expected rite of passage to, or marker of, manhood. In a study of Black boys navigating the experiencing of microaggressions in a traditionally White middle school (Henfield, 2011), one of the participants, speaking for the others, said that being a young man with a degree of high-spiritedness and rebellion is just a phase one goes through, but being Black and not being understood, or being looked down on, lasts forever and never changes. A. A. Ferguson, in *Bad Boys* (2000), puts this into perspective:

A frican American boys are not accorded the masculine dispensation
of being "naturally" naughty [like other boys]. Instead the school
reads their expression and display of masculine naughtiness as a sign
of an inherent viciousness, insubordinate nature that as a threat to
order must be controlled. (p. 86)

Their teachers may not be accustomed to the language or behavioral
differences Black boys present. Some researchers (Henfield, Moore, & Wood,
2008) have concluded that as a reaction to being viewed in such a manner, or
acting out resentment that contributes to their being seen as incorrigible, some
Black boys hide their intelligence during middle school so as not to be seen as
traitors to their race.

When a father is absent, it is hard on both girls and boys. The boys have
no models for manly achievement. They do not learn how to relate to others
with tolerance and respect, conceiving of the world instead as a battleground
for dominance. Unable to acquire self-respect and empowerment through education, loving attachments, and meaningful employment, many turn instead to
gang membership and criminal activities. Girls raised in father-absent households tend to establish similar households themselves, often living with or near
their mothers. Also, in their yearning for the security and reliability of a father,
they may overcompensate by identifying with and giving themselves to the
streetwise, defiant, tough boys who present an image of strong masculinity,
power, and control.

Implications for Treatment

In a discussion of issues involving multicultural counseling, the psychothera-
pist Ronnie Priest (1991) wrote of the necessity for counselors to recognize that

A frican American culture has a deviation that is neither pathological
nor deficient; rather, the culture has strengths and limitations that
simply render it at variance to the majority culture. It is crucial that
clients' cultural distinctions are respected. (p. 214)

What applies in relations between therapist and client similarly applies in
conceptualizing the relations between African Americans and the mainstream
White populace. The relationship between African Americans and Whites is still
"America's most dysfunctional kinship" (Powell, 1998). The most potent way in
which one group can affirm its significance at the expense of another is expressed

in the history of White superiority and Black inferiority. It might not be too much to say that "every white is still responsible [for the continuation of racism] if he or she has done nothing to change the racist traditions he or she inherited, no matter when one was born or came to this country" (Powell, 1998, p. 2).

If the client sees the problem first as environmental, one of societal inequity or racism, the therapist does well to acknowledge this reality and, in recognizing its truth, focus on what its damaging internal consequences have been. It is within this context that issues of self-esteem, character disorders, developmental distortions, and dysfunctional or self-destructive behavior can be identified and later probed at the appropriate depth. Reference to the dynamics of the family constellation may awaken and channel the client's natural rehabilitative and self-enhancement drives. These drives are more likely to be awakened and used in the therapeutic context when acknowledgment is made of the weight that social oppression adds to clinical depression.

Racism's contribution to a client's emotional distress and disease should be addressed by the counselor with sensitivity and flexibility. Counseling for minorities must combine mechanisms for survival and for change (Smith, 1991). Particularly when dealing with lower-income clients, the therapist must recognize that economic insecurity is disastrous to both psychological functioning and physical health, while economic security promotes stability (Ploski & Williams, 1989; Priest, 1991).

The singularity of the African American experience and its damaging consequences cannot be overstated. Neither poor African Americans nor those who are socioeconomically successful are completely untouched by the resulting stigma, depression, paranoia, or damaged self-image. No matter how privileged one is, one can always look backward and see the slavery and shackles of the past. As the psychologist Hussein Bulhan has said, African Americans can trace the route to this country of their African ancestors, who were transplanted to a pro-White, anti-Black environment in which survival was barely possible. "Ahead lay generations of life without space, time, energy, mobility, bonding or identity to call one's own" (French, 1993, p. C4).

Many of the attitudes that African Americans bring to counseling are dynamic reflections of the stresses they experience as a result of their inequitable position in society (Priest, 1991). These attitudes include fear and distrust of the inherent power inequality of the therapist–client relationship; the idea that the need for counseling reflects internal weakness, victimization, or an inability to manage one's life; and the necessity of relinquishing one's independence by having to tell one's business to a (White) stranger and then having to listen to that person's advice, a particular concern for low-income African American men.

The paranoid protectiveness and defensiveness revealed here cannot be addressed until the racist intrusiveness that helped create it and the social vulnerability that helps sustain it are acknowledged. Paranoid defensiveness resulting from intrusive and hurtful experiences in childhood is all too easily fed by the perceived threat of society's readiness to victimize individuals on the basis of their minority-group status. African American clients may believe that, in the final analysis, no one can be trusted and that individuals are motivated only by the exploitative pursuit of their own self-interest.

Such a point of view might be expected because the survival of African Americans has involved a "healthy paranoia," a suspiciousness of the motives of Whites. At the same time, a delicate balancing act is required for African Americans not to lose their grasp on reality. The suspicions of African Americans, however, have often been borne out in the brutal or exploitative treatment they have received at the hands of Whites. This, in turn, has been internalized, to be reenacted in African Americans' treatment of each other.

This dramatizes the automatic power dynamic in the therapist–client relationship: A Black client's fear of being perceived as stereotypically incompetent may be exacerbated when interacting with a White person in a position of power, such as a therapist, whereas a White client's fear of being seen as racially prejudiced may be attenuated when interacting with a Black person who holds some social advantage over him or her, such as a therapist (Jordan, Lovett, & Sweeton, 2012).

A. J. Franklin (1999) introduced the term "invisibility syndrome" to describe how repeated racial slights may result in racially adaptive behaviors, especially for African American men, in their attempts to manage racism when they feel that their "talents, abilities, personality, and worth are not valued or even recognized" (p. 761). These subtle forms of racial indignities tend to occur when African Americans have interracial social contacts, such as in job settings and other social situations (Clark, Anderson, Clark, & Williams, 1999; Franklin, 1999; Franklin & Boyd-Franklin, 2000). Chronic indignation results—with the view that racism is forever embedded in American society—in confusion about the intentions of Whites when the desire to trust some is undermined by the rejection of others (Tovar-Murray & Tovar-Murray, 2012).

Sue and colleagues (2008) have emphasized how psychotherapy and the helping professions have done much to combat overt forms of counselor and institutional bias through production of competency standards and guidelines but have been less successful in addressing forms of racism that affect the worldview of well-intentioned helping professionals and biased policies and practices within the health delivery systems. Getting Whites to become aware of their unintentional racist communications is a major challenge to society and the helping professions.

We know that ethnic and cultural similarity is important. D'Andrea and Heckman (2008) found that "clients from culturally diverse groups were likely to use counseling services more often and drop out of counseling less often when they were matched with counselor/therapists from the same racial/ethnic group as themselves" (p. 358). Instances of therapists and clients being native speakers of the same language were also predictive of better outcomes.

Darrick Tovar-Murray and Maria Tovar-Murray (2012), in discussing African American men susceptible to the invisibility syndrome, indicated that such men would never consider counseling or psychotherapy as a means to ease their distress. These men view going to church and to the barbershop as more appropriate safe havens to talk about racism. They use strategies to guard their integrity and preserve their dignity by not allowing Whites to see that they have the power to injure, by being "cool" and not revealing their vulnerability. These men would not believe that a person who has not experienced racism could help someone who has. However, when asked whether they would consider counseling as a possible option and what counselor characteristics would be looked for, emphasis was placed on warmth and acceptance: The counselor "must be able to emotionally connect with my experiences. He or she needs to acknowledge me for being Black, share my life experiences, and make every attempt to get to know me on a personal level" (Tovar-Murray & Tovar-Murray, 2012, p. 32). Even when the counselor does not fully understand the Black man's experience dealing with oppression, he should still be able to acknowledge that racism exists, not pretend that it no longer exists.

Practitioners must be sensitive to avoid imposing their own cultural biases on their clients, out of a mistaken or unexamined conviction of the universality or objectivity of those values. They must also have a strong conviction as to the therapeutic value of trust between human beings, which cuts across all ethnic and racial lines; this is necessary so that the human vulnerability of the practitioner allows him or her to recognize and accept the circumstances of the client without judgment or condemnation. Yet self-destructive and dysfunctional adaptations and modes of functioning on the client's part must be faced head on and addressed. Only in a situation promoting such trust will the client be able to withstand the scrutiny of self-examination in order to be able to view and address the injury that so often lies beneath the surface of the effects of social and environmental liabilities and handicaps.

Neither should the practitioner succumb to a client's defensive suggestion that the practitioner's privileged position prevents him or her from understanding the special privations of the client's situation. There are no limits to a disciplined and humane imagination. The practitioner's analysis of his or her own life travails can lead to seeing the client's situation as different only in particulars and in degree, not in kind. Intuition and mutual understanding are always a possibility for those who are not afraid to subject themselves to an imaginative experiencing of the life of the other.

A practitioner should understand that when a client speaks of oppression, he or she is often speaking of the workings of power dynamics for both the oppressed and the oppressor. On the part of the oppressed, the result is the internalizing of an alientating, devalued, and fragmented sense of self. On the part of the oppressor, there is a need to maintain power and privileged position over the oppressed because the oppressor sees in those oppressed the inferior and stigmatizing status from which the oppressor is liberated only so long as the difference between the two is maintained.

The psychologist Cheryl Thompson has emphasized how race has presented such a powerful polarity in this country that many psychological issues have become internally defined in terms of the opposition of Black and White, to the extent that the racial factor ought to be viewed as a "unique treatment variable" (Thompson, 1996). The affective components of race, differences between Black and White, and issues of self-definition are usually related to and will unfold around matters of power, privilege, deprivation, rejection, prestige, authority, and self-worth. Race may be equated with an ethnic, cultural, or socioeconomic category with or without value being assigned. To African Americans, there is always the assumption of negative value played out along a range of variables encompassing every aspect of life: self-definition, accomplishment, education, income, skin color, personal appearance, residential area, language, and so forth (Thompson, 1996).

This is another way of viewing the differential consequences of status inequity. The diminished social life and public image of the oppressed individual have their corollary in the self-devaluation and sense of diminishment that can generate a chronic and pervasive state of depression and the rage it masks. This phenomenon is so common as to be taken for granted and therefore not truly appreciated. It is involved in much of the destructive action of young African Americans against themselves and their communities. It is reflected in alcoholism, drug addiction, and misery and the perception of living a meaningless life in a ghetto among others whose lives are failures, in a society of plenty whose bountifulness they will be forever prevented from enjoying (French, 1993).

The adaptation that African Americans have had to make, immense as it is, has its limits. The psychologist Bulhan, a public health specialist who has studied the psychology of oppression worldwide, has spoken of a threshold for what is tolerable. He has described the masks the oppressed learn to wear for different occasions, the sensitivity to the needs and wishes of those in authority, the presenting of acceptable behavior and repressing of what is contradictory and unacceptable, and the refining of strategies for passive–aggressive behavior (French, 1993). Tremendous energy is expended maintaining such postures, often resulting in individuals who are passive–resistant on the job and violently destructive to self and others at home. It is a situation that makes African Americans more vulnerable, according to the Center for Disease Control's National Center for Health Statistics, to alcoholism and drug abuse, cancer, homicide, hypertension, heart disease, and stroke (French, 1993).

Most of my own clients are adults of varying racial, ethnic, and socioeconomic identification. They represent the diversity of the area in which I reside—Manhattan's Upper West Side—and from which many of them come, an area traditionally integrated with respect to class, race, and cultural background. Most are African Americans, Hispanics, Caribbean immigrants, Jews, as well as other Whites and Asian. Many are college graduates with advanced degrees who hold responsible jobs, typically in the academic, health services, artistic, or business worlds. A sizable number of my clients, however, are working-class individuals—for example, a working-class African American man pressed by insoluble domestic or interpersonal problems who sought a sympathetic and understanding African American man to be his counselor. And not infrequently, I may be sought out by a welfare mother who seeks an African American therapist with whom she can attain a more productive rapport than she has found at her Medicaid-sponsored clinic. Even more frequently will I receive a call from a working-class single mother or from middle-class parents who are looking for a Black male therapist to help a son work out academic or behavioral problems.

The problems that a client is experiencing at home will often be mirrored at work. In one instance, an intelligent, forceful, take-charge African American manager of a nationally recognized automobile repair shop experienced conflict when he encountered the slightest questioning of his authority. Either he would be compliant and reasonable, or he would become defensive and overly aggressive. At home, he felt the need to dominate a compliant and dependent wife. In therapy, he began to see the denial of his deep fears of inadequacy, the sense of a lack of masculine potency and worth, and his debilitating ambivalence toward Whites and people in positions of authority. He began to explore the role he had taken on as a child, in which he was the competent fixer and nurturer who would make up for the deficiencies of his alcoholic parents.

Almost all of my African American patients, regardless of class, present in greater or lesser degree maladaptive responses to the injury they sustained as a result of being brought up in an impoverished or dysfunctional family. Many have experienced the traumatic effects on the family resulting from divorce, death, dislocation, or some other event of wrenching consequence. These individuals often feel victimized by fate; by the inequities of class, sex, and race; and by the belittlement they received at the hands of their parents. Damaged self-esteem is revealed in hopelessness, passivity, compliance, and depression. It is defended against in grandiose self-conceptions, in masochistic conceptions of a superior capacity to endure and suffer, or in the power dynamics involved in the provoking of confrontations to display assertiveness and anger; or it may be manifested in a depressed state inseparable from stoic resignation.

Anger and rage must be recognized as appropriate responses to African Americans' experiences of racial subjugation. No African American remains untouched, either in the experience of personal humiliation or in its institutional form. Being oppressed means not exercising authority over one's own existence; being deprived of adequate health, educational, occupational, and residential opportunities; and possessing "little control over the institutions that shape norms, values and practices of society." Innocent acts on the part of Whites may provoke rage, when one is "presumed to be ignorant, hostile, criminal, or inarticulate simply by virtue of one's skin color" (Hardy & Laszloffy, 1995, p. 59).

Whereas anger may be a specific response to a circumstance in which it can be discharged, providing a release of tension, *rage* is a chronic and entrenched experience of suppressed and intense emotion. Rage may be functional and dysfunctional: When functional, it may serve as a protective mechanism to oppose and defend against trauma, providing a measure of relief and self-vindication. When dysfunctional, it can be internalized, expressed as a form of degeneration and erosion of well-being, often revealed as "substance abuse, prolonged periods of sadness or depression, suicidal ideations" (Hardy & Laszloffy, 1995, p. 58).

My being an African American therapist may help initially to persuade an African American client to come to therapy and possibly remain through the beginning phases. I think, however, that the client's encountering of the traumatic data of his or her experience in the transference and the revelation to the therapist of this and similar experiences in life form the restitutive power of the working alliance between therapist and client and become the primary means through which change is effected. Transference occurs without regard for the race of the therapist. Just as my White clients can experience me as a therapeutic object of value, perhaps in ways they had not anticipated or even imagined, a similar situation may obtain between African American clients and non–African American therapists. There is, nevertheless, a need for more African American therapists because there is an increasing number of African American clients, many of whom feel more comfortable working with an African American therapist.

In 2001, the then Surgeon General David Satcher spoke of how therapists and the psychoanalytic profession may have biases or prejudice against the poor, those of low socioeconomic status, and ethnic minorities, often seeing the poor and minorities as indistinguishable groups and attributing negative traits to them. Such negative views are expressed in terms of misdiagnoses, unequal or poor service, disproportionate use of paraprofessionals or support therapy in place of self-exploration, and conceptions of their unsuitability for the disciplined and self-reflective stance required of psychotherapy (Satcher, 2000). Satcher said that people need someone they trust to talk to in order to feel comfortable, someone who understands their culture and how things are expressed in their culture. We must recognize that the analyst's subjectively experienced ethnicity enters into the analyst's interaction as a given in any therapeutic situation, and it assumes particular importance in the situations of socioeconomic, ethnic, and cultural difference between patient and analyst (Moskowitz, 1996; Perez-Foster, 1996).

Psychoanalyst Michael Moskowitz (1996) emphasized that cultural differences must be a necessary part of the matrix that constitutes psychoanalytic work and should be incorporated as part of technique. He noted that

> Freud wrote that psychoanalysis is a cure through love. We are limited in our ability to work psychoanalytically with people only by ... our inability to love and be loved by them. People have loved and been loved across all barriers of culture and class. The question of analyzability then becomes a question of the analyst's capacity to understand

the other, to be able to enter into the person's psychic world. To the extent that a life can be understood, it can be analyzed. (p. 191)

Analysts may feel anxiety in the presence of someone whom they do not understand, whom they are uncomfortable with, and who makes them feel professionally inadequate, with negative or hostile feelings then being projected on the patient (Javier, 1996). I have indicated how the concept of psychological mindedness or suitability is an expression of social biases, with therapists feeling more comfortable working with patients of their own class. Race and ethnicity therefore obscure social class identifications that cast minorities or those of another race as unfamiliar, even though they may be individuals with whom the therapists may share a similar socioeconomic outlook.

These concerns dramatize the need for the relational, interpersonal, or two-person therapeutic model. Not just class differences account for different or divergent ways in which similar life experiences are viewed. It may be that differences from the therapist's socioeconomic class, ethnicity, or political experiences are automatically at risk of being perceived as pathological (Whitson, 1996). The analyst is not offering a tangible service like an internist or surgeon but an intangible, emotive, and intellectual experience, some part of which is a reflection of the quality of interaction with the analyst's own person. Analysts naturally would expect to be in more immediate sympathy with patients with whom they share a similar social outlook and by whom they would expect to be intuitively understood.

Some fascinating research reported by Jordan et al. (2012) suggested that interracial interactions may often initially lead to negative affect, heightening the negative feelings that may have brought the (Black) clients to counseling in the first place. The more one expects to be seen in a prejudiced manner, for both therapist and client, the greater the stress. But people's strategies for avoiding being seen negatively can actually work, making the interaction more mutually agreeable: Prejudiced Whites try harder to be accepting and understanding, with good results, and fearful Blacks self-disclose more, with better results.

Jordan and colleagues (2012) reported that consciously controlling one's thoughts, emotions, and behavior can deplete mental resources and hurt performance on subsequent tasks:

The worse one's prejudice against another racial group, the more cognitively draining interracial reactions can be. This means that professionals may underestimate the cognitive skills of clients temporarily impaired by interracial experiences. Clinicians experiencing cognitive depletion may have trouble focusing attention on their clients.... [It develops that] a client who is coping with preexisting anxiety may be less discouraged by anxiety provoked by the therapeutic encounter when he or she sees it as a typical response to an interracial interaction, rather than as something specific to the self or pathological. (p. 138)

Just mentioning at the intake the research findings on interracial interactions could open up a way to talk about them. Either therapist or client may be nervous rather than prejudiced, thinking about themselves and how they could be seen rather than thinking negative thoughts about the other (Jordan et al., 2012).

Fear of intimacy or closeness is as much an issue for African Americans as for other clients, perhaps more so. A central concern is fear of exposure, of having an inadequate or deformed sense of self revealed, which in the client's view can only provoke in others the rejection and contempt that he or she feels for him- or herself. The client's expectation might be that closeness can only recapitulate the experience of being intruded on, taken for granted, or exploited by others, and the desire may be present to respond in a similar way toward others. For some African American male clients, the associating of closeness with the possibility of homosexual tendencies is an added fear that contends with and distorts the deep need they have for intimacy, understanding, and self-acceptance in a relationship with another male.

The desire of African Americans to seek help and an expectation of its effectiveness can override their fear and reluctance to consult a therapist. But there is often a desire for a quick solution to complex problems. This is a major obstacle because successful therapy requires an ongoing commitment. The need for a quick solution can give way, however, to an appreciation of the therapeutic process and a wonder at self-discovery once the therapy is allowed to unfold and trust develops.

Nevertheless, trust is not an inevitable result of the working alliance, and an attitude of resistance to therapy is not easily defeated. This is especially true when a client has deep-seated cultural or religious ideas about what are acceptable conceptions and sources of help, added to the natural fear of the pain of self-examination. One useful approach is for the practitioner to emphasize that it takes a person of intelligence and depth to recognize that some things cannot be dealt with by mere strength of will or moral rectitude, that some problems require understanding of the kind that one has to work to achieve.

Furthermore, work toward achieving such a goal requires the help of those who understand how the mind works and how its unconscious dimension, impulses, and desires sometimes seem to be in seductive opposition to our best interests.

Final Thoughts for Therapists and Clients

African Americans do not have to endure their mental anguish in silence and shame but need to recognize that mental illness is a disease like any other that requires treatment. Otherwise, its destructive progression will continue, just like that of alcoholism or diabetes or high blood pressure. Although many African Americans may be skeptical of such thinking, it puts the seemingly amorphous therapeutic process into an understandable context. It makes a practical appeal to an individual's desire to recognize a problem and to try to overcome it.

This kind of thinking may also help resolve some of the conflicts that might be felt by the religiously inclined who see the resolution of problems as a matter of faith in God's ability to help. They may accept a suggestion from the therapist that God wants them to see and accept their inner conflicts, to recognize how their life experiences have impaired their functioning. To come into possession of such knowledge may be their responsibility, an idea that might empower otherwise reluctant individuals to act on their own behalf. They might accept the possibility, as one practitioner put it, that "We can't put it all in God's hands. God's busy" (French, 1993, p. C4).

Finally, the practitioner must recognize the client's need to relive and return to the scene of the psychic disturbance or to unknowingly act it out, to free him- or herself from its toxic effects. To do this, the client must rely on the practitioner for help, no matter to what extent his or her behavior seems to refute or negate such an objective. The need for human connectedness exists without regard for differences of race or culture, which sometimes seem to separate human beings from one other.

References

Allen, L. W. (1996). *Strategies that African American female executives and profes-sionals use to manage adversity in the workplace.* Ann Arbor, MI: UMI Company.

Austin, A. (2013, July 22). *African Americans are still concentrated in neighborhoods with high poverty and still lack full access to decent housing.* Retrieved from http://www.epi.org/publication/african-americans-concentrated-neighborhoods/

Bandura, A. (1991). Social cognitive theory of self-regulation. *Organizational Behavior and Human Decision Processes, 50*, 248–287.

Berlin, I. (1969). Two concepts of liberty. In I. Berlin, *Four essays on liberty* (p. 118). Oxford, United Kingdom: Oxford University Press.

Billingsley, A. (1992). *Climbing Jacob's ladder: The enduring legacy of black families.* New York: Simon & Schuster.

Britt, D. (1992, February 2). What about the sisters? *Washington Post,* pp. Fl, F6.

Casas, J. W. (2005). Race and racism: The efforts of counseling psychology to understand and address the issues associated with these terms. *Counseling Psychologist, 33*, 501–512.

Cazenave, N., & Smith, R. (1991). Gender differences in the perception of black male–female relationships and stereotypes. In H. Cheatham & J. Steward (Eds.), *Black families: Interdisciplinary perspectives* (pp. 149–170). New Brunswick, NJ: Transaction Books.

Chapman, A. B. (1988). Male–female relations: How the past affects the present. In A. P. McAdoo (Ed.), *Black families* (2nd ed., pp. 190–200). Newbury Park, CA: Sage Publications.

Clark, R., Anderson, N., Clark, V., & Williams, D. (1999). Racism as a stressor for African Americans: A biopsychosocial model. *American Psychologist, 54*, 805–816.

Constantine, M. G., Alleyne, V. L., Wallace, B. C., & Franklin-Jackson, D. C. (2006). Africentric values: Their relation to positive mental health in African American adolescent girls. *Journal of Black Psychology, 32*, 141–154.

Danby, P. (1975). Perceptions of role and status of black females. *Journal of Social and Behavioral Sciences, 21*, 31–47.

D'Andrea, M., & Heckman, E. F. (2008). A 40-year review of multicultural counseling outcome research: Outlining a future research agenda for the multicultural counseling movement. *Journal of Counseling and Development, 86*, 356–363.

Davenport, D. S., & Yurich, J. M. (1991). Multicultural gender issues. *Journal of Counseling and Development, 70*, 54–63.

Dent, D. (1992, June 14). The new black suburbs. *New York Times,* pp. 18, 25.

Diamond, J. B. (2006). Still separate and unequal: Examining race, opportunity, and school achievement in "integrated" suburbs. *Journal of Negro Education, 75*, 495–505.

DuBois, W.E.B. (1961). *The souls of black folk.* New York: Fawcett. (Original work published 1903)

Erikson, E. H. (1966). The concept of identity in race relations: Notes and queries. *Daedalus, 95*, 145–170.

Evans, T. D., Dedrick, R. F., & Epstein, M. J. (1997). Development and initial validation of the Encouragement Scale (Education Form). *Journal of Humanistic Education and Development, 35*, 163–174.

Ferguson, A. A. (2000). *Bad boys.* Ann Arbor: University of Michigan Press.

Fischer, A. R., & Shaw, C. M. (1999). African Americans' mental health and perceptions of racist discrimination: The moderating effects of racial socialization experiences and self-esteem. *Journal of Counseling Psychology, 46*, 395–407.

Franklin, A. J. (1999). Invisibility syndrome and racial identity development in psychotherapy and counseling African American men. *Counseling Psychologist, 27*, 761–793.

Franklin, A. J. (2004). *From brotherhood to manhood: How black men rescue their relationships and dreams from the invisibility syndrome.* Hoboken, NJ: John Wiley & Sons.

Franklin, A. J., & Boyd-Franklin, N. (2000). Invisibility syndrome: A clinical model of the effects of racism on African-American males. *American Journal of Orthopsychiatry, 70*, 33–41.

French, A. (1993, June 20). In black despair: John Wilson and the plague of African-American depression. *Washington Post*, pp. C1, C4.

Gopnik, A. (2013, May 18–19). How early do we learn racial "us and them?" *Wall Street Journal*, p. C2.

Hardy, K. V., & Laszloffy, T. A. (1995). The cultural genogram: Key to training culturally competent family therapists. *Journal of Marital and Family Therapy, 21*, 227–237.

Harrison, L. E. (1992, June 21). The ultimate ghetto trap: Why does America ignore the black success story? *Washington Post,* pp. C1, C2.

Hattery, A. J., & Smith, E. (2012). *African American families today: Myths and realities.* New York: Rowman & Littlefield.

Henfield, M. S. (2011). Black male adolescents navigating microaggressions in a traditionally white middle school: A qualitative study. *Journal of Multicultural Counseling and Development, 39*, 141–155.

Henfield, M. S., Moore, J. L., III, & Wood, C. (2008). Inside and outside gifted education programming: Hidden challenges for African American students. *Exceptional Children, 74*, 433–450.

Hurston, Z. N. (1990). *Their eyes were watching God.* New York: Harper & Row. (Original work published 1937)

Javier, A. R. (1996). Psychodynamic treatment with the urban poor. In R. Perez-Foster, M. Moskowitz, & R. A. Javier (Eds.), *Reaching across boundaries of culture and class: Widening the scope of psychotherapy* (pp. 93–113). Northvale, NJ: Jason Aronson.

Jones, L. (1992, May 19). Bring the heroines. *Village Voice*, p. 43.

Jordan, A. H., Lovett, B. J., & Sweeton, J. L. (2012). The social psychology of black–white interracial interactions: Implications for culturally competent clinical practice. *Journal of Multicultural Counseling and Development, 40*, 132–143.

Kao, G., & Thompson, J. S. (2003). The racial and ethnic stratification in educational achievement and attainment. *Annual Review of Sociology, 29*, 417–442.

Keller, B. (2013, July 29). Profiling Obama. *New York Times,* p. A17.

Kneebone, E., & Garr, E. (2010). Income and poverty. In *State of metropolitan America: On the front lines of demographic transformation* (p. 140). Washington, DC: Brookings Institution Metropolitan Policy Program.

Kovel, J. (1984). *White racism.* New York: Columbia University.

LaFromboise, T., Coleman, H.L.K., & Gerton, J. (1995). Psychological impact of biculturalism: Evidence and theory. In N. R. Goldberger & J. B. Veroff (Eds.), *The cultural and psychological reader* (pp. 489–535). New York: New York University Press.

Lawrence, J. S., Crocker, J., & Dweck, C. S. (2005). Stereotypes negatively influence the meaning students give to academic settings. In G. Downey, J. S. Eccles, & C. M. Chatman (Eds.), *Navigating the future: Social identity, coping, and life tasks* (pp. 23–44). New York: Russell Sage Foundation.

Maryshow, D., Hurley, E. A., Allen, B. A., Tyler, K. M., & Boykin, A. W. (2005). The impact of learning orientation on African American children's attitudes toward high achieving peers. *American Journey of Psychology, 118*, 603–618.

Moskowitz, M. (1996). The end of analyzability. In R. Perez-Foster, M. Moskowitz, & R. A. Javier (Eds.), *Reaching across boundaries of culture and class: Widening the scope of psychotherapy* (pp. 179–193). Northvale, NJ: Jason Aronson.

Mosley-Howard, G. S., & Evans, C. B. (2000). Relationships and contemporary experiences of the African American family: An ethnographic case study. *Journal of Black Studies, 30*, 428–452.

Murray, C. (2012). *Coming apart: The state of white America.* New York: Crown Forum Press.

Patterson, O. (1997). *The ordeal of integration.* Washington, DC: Civitas/Counterpoint.

Patterson, O. (1998). *Rituals of blood.* New York: Basic Books.

Patterson, O., & Winship, C. (1992, May 3). White poor, black poor. *New York Times,* p. 17.

Perez-Foster, R. (1996). What is a multicultural perspective for psychoanalysis? In R. Perez-Foster, M. Moskowitz, & A. R. Javier (Eds.), *Reaching across boundaries of culture and class: Widening the scope of psychotherapy* (pp. 3–20). Northvale, NJ: Jason Aronson.

Pettigrew, T. F. (1964). *A profile of the Negro American.* Princeton, NJ: Van Nostrand.

Pinderhughes, C. A. (1976). Black personality in American society. In M. Smythe (Ed.), *The black American reference book* (pp. 128–158). Englewood Cliffs, NJ: PrenticeHall.

Ploski, H. A., & Williams, J. (1989). *The Negro almanac: A reference work on the African American* (5th ed.). New York: Gale Research.

Powell, K. (1998, November 22). Myths that I'd like to see unmade. *Washington Post,* p. C3.

Priest, R. (1991). Racism and prejudice as negative impacts on African American clients in therapy. *Journal of Counseling and Development, 70*, 213–215.

Robinson, E. (2011). *Disintegration: The splintering of black America.* New York: Doubleday.

Rowles, J., & Duan, C. (2012). Perceived racism and encouragement among African American adults. *Journal of Multicultural Counseling and Development, 40*, 11–23.

Rust, J. P., Jackson, M. A., Ponterotto, J. G., & Blumberg, F. C. (2011). Biculturalism and academic achievement of African American high school students. *Journal of Multicultural Counseling and Development, 39*, 130–140.

Satcher, D. (2000, February). A report of the surgeon general—Executive summary. *Professional Psychology: Research and Practice, 31*(1), 5–13.

Sellers, R. M., & Shelton, J. N. (2003). The role of racial identity in perceived racial discrimination. *Journal of Personality and Social Psychology, 84*, 1079–1092.

Shin, R. Q. (2011). The influence of Africentric values and neighborhood satisfaction on the academic self-efficiency of African American elementary school children. *Journal of Multicultural Counseling and Development, 39*, 218–228.

Smith, E. J. (1991). Ethnic identity development: Toward the development of a theory within the context of majority/minority status. *Journal of Counseling and Development, 70*, 181–188.

Smythe, M. (1976). A note on terminology. In M. Smythe (Ed.), *The black American reference book* (pp. xi–xiv). Englewood Cliffs, NJ: Prentice Hall.

Staples, R. (1973). *The black woman in America: Sex, marriage, and the family.* Chicago: Nelson-Hall.

Staples, R. (1988). An overview of race and marital status. In H. P. McAdoo (Ed.), *Black families* (2nd ed., pp. 187–189). Newbury Park, CA: Sage Publications.

Sue, D. W. (2003). *Overcoming our racism: The journey to liberation.* New York: John Wiley & Sons.

Sue, D. W., Nadal, K. L., Capodilupo, A. I., Lin, G. C., & Rivera, D. P. (2008). Racial microaggressions against black Americans: Implications for counseling. *Journal of Counseling and Development, 86*, 330–338.

Taylor, P. (1992, June 7). Life without father: Why more and more dads are drifting away, leaving the kids in poverty and violence. *Washington Post,* pp. C1, C4.

Thompson, C. (1996). The African-American patient in psychodynamic treatment. In R. Perez-Foster, M. Moskowitz, & A. R. Javier (Eds.), *Reaching across boundaries of culture and class: Widening the scope of psychotherapy* (pp. 115–142), Northvale, NJ: Jason Aronson.

Tovar-Murray, D., & Tovar-Murray, M. (2012). A phenomenological analysis of the invisibility syndrome. *Journal of Multicultural Counseling and Development, 40*, 24–36.

Utsey, S., Ponterotto, J., & Porter, J. (2008). Prejudice and racism, year 2008—Still going strong: Research on reducing prejudice with recommended methodological advances. *Journal of Counseling and Development, 86*, 339–347.

Whitson, G. (1996). Working-class issues. In R. Perez-Foster, M. Moskowitz, & A. R. Javier (Eds.), *Reaching across boundaries of culture and class: Widening the scope of psychotherapy* (pp. 143–157). Northvale, NJ: Jason Aronson.

Wilson, W. J. (1978). *The declining significance of race: Blacks and changing American society.* Chicago: University of Chicago Press.

Wilson, W. J. (1987). *The truly disadvantaged: The inner city, the underclass, and public policy.* Chicago: University of Chicago Press.

Chapter Three

Children of Undocumented Immigrants: Imperiled Developmental Trajectories

Luis H. Zayas and Mollie Bradlee

Found among the categories of vulnerable children in the United States are those born to undocumented immigrants, individuals who either entered the country illegally or stayed in the country after their temporary visas or permits expired. Their children are part of the millions who live in mixed-status families, or families composed of at least one undocumented parent and U.S.-born citizen children. In reality, though, many mixed-status families include undocumented children, offspring who were brought to the United States during infancy, middle childhood, or adolescence by their undocumented parents.

This chapter is about the developmental potentialities of children in mixed-status families. These complex families and their children warrant our research and service attention, for they are not an inconsequential part of our population: Presently, about 10 million individuals in the United States live in mixed-status families. Of the approximately 11.7 million undocumented immigrants in the United States, about 5.7 million (49 percent) are parents of 1 million undocumented children and 4.5 million U.S.-born children under the age of 18 (Taylor, Lopez, Passel, & Motel, 2011). Because of the circumstances of their birth, citizen children of undocumented immigrants have rights that neither their undocumented parents nor their undocumented siblings enjoy, a fact that puts them in positions that are distinct from those of their family members. Living under the cloud of their parents' and siblings' deportability and actual deportations can have devastating effects on children's social, emotional, and identity development. Therefore, we focus this chapter on how the developmental pathways of citizen children and their undocumented siblings are imperiled. (We do not include in this chapter another highly vulnerable group of immigrant children—undocumented, unaccompanied minors—who enter without parents or legal documents. They represent an exceptional group of child refugees.)

To further contextualize our discussion, we note that this chapter highlights children of mixed-status families of Latin American origin. The vast majority—81 percent—of undocumented immigrants in the United States have come from Latin America, mostly from Mexico (Hoefer, Rytina, & Baker, 2009), and more is written about them than about any other undocumented immigrant group. Inasmuch as it is immigrant Hispanics with whom we are most familiar, our illustrations will be of children from this group. A more important caveat is that there is a dearth of developmental research on the children of the undocumented, and the literature that exists is mostly descriptive and clinical. Therefore, we do not purport to provide an empirically based examination of the development trajectories of these young lives. Rather, by synthesizing the extant literature with our clinical research, practice experience, and personal knowledge of children in mixed-status families, we offer a snapshot of what these children face everyday and how their healthy development is compromised.

It is worth beginning our discussion with an understanding of the different legal, social–structural, and developmental positions that create precarious circumstances for children in mixed-status families. The parents, of course, are foreign-born undocumented immigrants; their legal status sets the grounds for the situations facing the entire family. Their U.S.-born children are American citizens at birth, but the undocumented siblings of these children are not eligible for citizenship. Added to this is the fact that some of the undocumented children in mixed-status families, mostly those in their teenage and early adulthood years, are what are commonly known as "DREAMers," a moniker applied to them for the legal eligibility they would have received through the unsuccessful DREAM (Development, Relief, and Education for Alien Minors) Act of 2001. The DREAM Act, which was passed by the House of Representatives but failed in the Senate, provided a path to citizenship to undocumented immigrant children meeting several criteria contained in the bill. These undocumented youth may now be eligible under President Barak Obama's executive order titled "Deferred Action for Childhood Arrivals," issued in June 2012 by the U.S. Department of Homeland Security, which stated that people who entered the United States illegally as children may qualify for consideration of deferred action from immigration enforcement for a period of two years, subject to renewal, and would be eligible for work authorization. But this grant of deferred removal action does not confer lawful immigration status, nor does it alter an individual's existing immigration status or provide a path to citizenship. The memorandum directs U.S. Customs and Border Protection, U.S. Citizenship and Immigration Services, and U.S. Immigration and Customs Enforcement (ICE) to exercise prosecutorial discretion. Others, however, may be ineligible for any relief as undocumented persons.

Living Every Day in Mixed-Status Families

Children who grow up with undocumented parents—under the legal and structural conditions just enumerated—face a myriad of stressors ranging from economic insecurity to fear of family dissolution. For children who do not experience a parent's deportation, living in a world in which they are easily identified as the children of parents who many Americans think "don't belong" in our country and "should go back where they came from" can cause serious psychological harm. Vicious public rhetoric about their parents coupled with the very aggressive government deportation policies undertaken in the first and second decades of the 21st century undoubtedly leave lasting marks on the developmental paths of these young lives, sometimes permanently. Moreover, it can affect their self-concepts, their cultural and ethnic identities, and their sense of belonging to a national or collective identity.

The lives of the typical children of undocumented immigrants consist of moments of blithe inattention to their parents' legal status interspersed by sudden and frightening reminders of their parents' vulnerability to arrest, detention, and deportation. These are not distinct experiences, for they coexist and are indistinguishable in the children's daily lives. Children live with a gnawing consciousness even in the most carefree moments at the playground or at school that things could turn very badly for their families at any minute. Within the privacy and fragile security of their homes, mixed-status families are wary as they are never too far away from their beleaguered existence. They can be quickly brought out of their homes' quiet reveries by an unexpected knock at the door. There is no respite from the wariness.

Children often learn at a very early age that their parents are *sin papeles* (without papers). At first, their understanding of what not having papers really means is limited; young children cannot yet integrate the concepts and facts cognitively or emotionally. In spite of this, they understand early on that something dire can happen if their parents' legal status is revealed. Children as young as five may learn that their parents are undocumented or "illegal," either through a purposeful explanation by the parents or through an inadvertent disclosure in everyday conversation (Zayas, 2015). By about the age of seven they gain a better understanding of what "undocumented" really signifies. They understand that being without papers means that they, their parents, or siblings were born in another country, that they entered the United States without permission, and that they do not possess the requisite documents to be in the country. With this conception, a seven-year-old might simply ask, "so where do you get the papers?" By the age of 10, they put together an appreciation of their parents' birthplace, unauthorized entry, why parents cannot easily get the necessary papers, and what the consequences can be for the entire family.

With this fuller comprehension, children begin to worry about their parents and themselves. Although young children may understand illegality as committing a crime, like stealing or robbing or killing someone, they may not understand the complexities of illegality when it refers to being in a country without authorization. They might consider their parents' legal status as a private family matter, not as a generalizable principle. At an age when cognition is concrete and egocentric, it is viewed as a problem for only their parents. Only with cognitive maturation is legal status understood as something shared by many others and that it operates in a broad governmental and political environment. The older youth comes to understand that legal status is a public issue that includes structural determinants that affect not just their parents but others, too (Dreby, 2012; Gonzales, 2011). All told, children's comprehension of their families' dilemmas increases with age, but their worry does not cease.

Mixed-status families dread every encounter with law enforcement or governmental organizations that might ask about their status. Being undocumented and living in a state of deportability is aggravated by the persistent threats from immigration enforcement, insults by those with anti-immigrant sentiments, the stress of staying in the shadows, and instability of employment and housing. Deportability, according to Dreby (2012), brings about "fears of separation among children regardless of their own legal status or family members' actual involvement with immigration officials" (p. 830). Hypervigilance inevitably becomes part of the life of the children of the undocumented. They live with fear—not an imagined fear but a real one that is harmful through its chronicity. In a state of constant alertness, even hyperalertness—at school, the playground, the mall—the child's confidence and mental calm are eroded.

The frequent economic hardship of undocumented immigrants often compounds this day-to-day stress and worry. Children of the undocumented are more likely than other children to live in poverty, which often means they are uninsured, underuse medical services, change homes and schools frequently, and experience privations that affect their behavioral and academic performance. In addition to having fewer visits for medical care than other poor but legal families (Ortega et al., 2007), undocumented parents are less likely to have a consistent medical provider or medical home. (The *medical home,* a model and philosophy of primary care that is patient centered, comprehensive, team based, coordinated, accessible, and focused on quality and safety. The medical home enables strong trusting relationships among patients, providers, and staff. Overall, it is a model to achieve the highest possible care in a manner that best suits a patient's needs.) What's more, parents may not seek benefits and services for their U.S.-born children (who are entitled to many benefits) because they fear being identified as undocumented. Food and housing insecurity can be common among mixed-status families struggling economically. It is exacerbated when a parent is deported. In a study of undocumented families caught up in the immigration raids conducted by ICE, displaced families underwent housing instability that lasted from weeks to months, sometimes longer. About one in four families had to move in with relatives, and nearly half of families lost their homes when banks foreclosed on their mortgages for failure to pay (Chaudry et al., 2010).

As parents experience transitory or chronic poverty and homelessness, their stress is evident to their children. Economic hardship—unemployment and earnings loss—raises every family member's stress but especially the undocumented primary breadwinner, whose lowered self-worth and irritability may cause tense interactions with spouse and children. The effects of these circumstances on young children are both serious and pervasive. Children experiencing the stress of poverty may display emotional and conduct problems, somatic problems, poorer school performance, and lowered aspirations. In time, children's measured intelligence, academic achievement, social competence, and emotional functioning may decline (Blair & Raver, 2012; Yoshikawa, Aber, & Beardslee, 2012). Altogether, these deficits in the lives of citizen children and their undocumented siblings place them at developmental risk.

Worry, Responsibility, and Development

The constant possibility of parental deportation often leaves children in a state of anxiety and vigilance (for example, De Genova, 2010; Dreby, 2012; Talavera, Núñez-Mchiri, & Heyman, 2010). Worry and fear are important human emotions that alert us to impending danger and prepare us to flee or fight. These emotions may be natural and helpful, but in excess, fear and worry are detrimental to human functioning. Our brains naturally activate the fight-or-flight response immediately upon feeling threatened, and heart rate and blood pressure rise (Sapolsky, 1994). After the danger abates, the body returns to its natural state. But for people facing chronic adversity—including children in poverty and children in families vulnerable to deportation—the stress system is constantly active, and the brain and body do not have time to recover from the stress. Research in the neurosciences shows that constant vigilance and stress damage children's biological and regulatory systems as well, with long-term effects seen in above-average susceptibility to chronic diseases in adulthood (Evans & Kim, 2013). Under such conditions, perception and problem-solving abilities are negatively affected, and memory becomes distorted. At a period in life when the brain is growing, persistent fear, worry, and stress affect social, emotional, and cognitive functioning. Among children of the undocumented, we spot the corrosive effect of prolonged worry or fear in anxiety, sleeping and eating problems, changes in conduct, and the appearance of somatic complaints. Finally, chronic stress can affect social interaction and the child's sense of self. Children must be on guard for any threat to their parents' legal status, and with chronic stress, damage is done to children's mental health, often resulting in increased risk for posttraumatic stress and depression.

Compounding the physiological effects are emotional ones. Citizen children and their undocumented siblings often grow to feel that they bear responsibility for protecting their families, an inescapable reality. Misbehavior at school or in another public space that attracts the attention of others can have devastating effects. For undocumented parents, imposing many rules on the behaviors of their children is an adaptive part of child rearing. They tell their children not to yell, argue, or conduct themselves in public in any way that brings the attention of others, especially law enforcement. Children of undocumented immigrants describe how insistent their parents are that they behave well in public and keep quiet about family matters, especially their parents' legal status. We have heard these children say, "My parents could get in trouble if I talk to people about it"; "My mom tells me not to tell anyone she doesn't have papers because I can get her into trouble"; and "Because I don't want to get my mom in trouble ... she always tells me that I have to tell people that she does have papers" (Zayas, 2015). Violating this important lesson can have effects on families unlike those that the average family encounters. When the average child misbehaves in public, parents may get glares from other people and perhaps feel embarrassed. In a very serious situation, a child's misbehavior could lead to a visit from police. For children of undocumented parents, however, misbehaving or simply misjudging what they say or do can bring their parents to the attention of immigration authorities. Family trips to the mall or to visit relatives are punctuated by the tension that parents produce as they watch for police speed traps or other checkpoints. When border patrol or police vehicles pull alongside them at traffic lights, tension abruptly takes over as the family tries to become invisible. For children, this entails being quiet and sitting still, behaviors imparted to them along with a sense of responsibility for the family's protection. Abdicating this enormous responsibility can have shattering results on the parents and the family as a whole.

But what can happen when a child worries that he might disclose his parents' legal status? What can happen when a child errs in not observing the rules that parents impose or when she drops her guard? What if the child fails to exercise good judgment? In these cases, the child may experience guilt—that human emotion that comes from feeling that we have failed to do something that was expected of us or that we have committed a wrongful act. Commonly defined, guilt is an internal awareness that one's conduct or actions have hurt someone. It feels uncomfortable because we recognize the pain of those we have hurt. We feel regret, worry, remorse, fear, anxiety, and tension (Roos, Hodges, & Salmivalli, 2014; Tangney & Gearing, 2002). As you can see, guilt has some prosocial value in that the sense of culpability we experience is a sign of obligation, if not empathy for the other. Thus, it helps regulate our behaviors. Among the children of the undocumented, guilt is related to the potential negative results their behavior might bring on their parents, siblings, and themselves. Children of undocumented immigrants often express worry that they might cause their parents to be apprehended by immigration authorities, including when the children have done nothing wrong (Zayas, 2015). Alternatively, they may feel that by abandoning their responsibility or lowering their vigilance, they may have committed a wrong. This is a colossal responsibility to carry, and it shapes how children perceive themselves.

The other powerful emotion that children can carry with them if they perceive that they have caused a parent to be detained and deported is shame, an emotion related to but different from guilt. Unrelenting guilt can lead to shame. Shame, much more than guilt, is pathogenic; it condemns an action or failure to take action, condemns the person, threatens the self, and is devoid of any health or social benefit (Niedenthal, Tangney, & Gavansky, 1994; Roos et al., 2014). Guilt may say, "I did something awful"; shame says, "I am awful." And the sense of shame (or guilt) does not have to come from an actual deed. It can come from a perceived deed. For instance, if a child violates the rules about talking about her parents' legal status or misbehaves in public, and as a result, the parents are detained and deported, then the guilt and the shame that she feels are easier to understand. There is a direct cause and effect. But let us take the example of a child who violates the same rules and only by happenstance are her parents detained and deported: She may still feel guilt and shame, that it was her misbehavior that caused her parents' troubles. Despite the fact that her behavior had nothing to do with the encounter with law enforcement, she may still feel the shame of her actions. The dejection of shame is then accompanied by helplessness, inefficacy, disgrace, worthlessness, and a sense of the self as bad. Persistent shame is often at the core of depression, other internalizing disorders, and suicide (Ferguson, Stegge, Miller, & Olsen, 1999).

Take the case of young Maricela and the burnt toast. Maricela is the older of two daughters of an undocumented immigrant couple from Mexico in a small rural town in the Midwest. One day, the parents went to the store "for two minutes" and left the girls alone. While their parents were out, Maricela tried to toast bread for her hungry sister, but it became stuck in the toaster and began to burn. At the time of this incident, the family lived next to a fire station. Within minutes, a woman dressed in a uniform, possibly a firefighter or emergency medical technician, came to their door and asked whether everything was all right. Frightened, Maricela showed the woman the smoke in the kitchen. The woman easily took care of it. When their parents returned, their home was surrounded by police, rescue, and fire vehicles. The parents were handcuffed and placed in police cars, with both girls witnessing the arrests. The parents were taken away, and the girls were transported to the police station, where they were interviewed by child protective services and ultimately released to the custody of an uncle and aunt. For four long days, the girls did not hear from their parents. On the fourth day, their father was released, but their mother was not; she was detained for a month, with very little communication and no certainty as to how long she would be detained. The girls clung to their father and cried daily during their mother's detention. They insisted on sleeping with their father and worried that he would not come home from work every evening.

Worse, it became clear that the children began to shoulder blame for their family's circumstances. When her mother was finally released, Maricela promised, "I'll be a good girl and that won't happen to you again," displaying the guilt of the family trouble that her attempt to toast the bread had brought. Maricela and her sister often tell their parents to "put on your seatbelts so the police don't stop us" and are frightened when they see police cars on the road. When they drive past the house in which the traumatic events occurred, both girls cry. Maricela often says, "You don't have money to buy things, so I won't ask." She is afraid of causing her parents additional stress, costs, or discomfort and is guarded against making her feelings or needs known. She fears that "someone will come here and take someone from my family away" or "that someone will die." It is evident that her guilt has edged into shame and is affecting her emotional health. Maricela says she feels like crying every day and she shows signs of depression, posttraumatic stress, low self-worth, and low self-efficacy. Although she was reunited with her parents, and they were granted legal permanent residency by immigration courts, these symptoms are persistent and threaten her healthy development. The psychological trauma that Maricela bears cannot be undone by a change in legal status.

Deportation Exiles and Orphans

Both citizen and noncitizen children of undocumented parents in the United States grow up identifying as Americans; they attend school, pledge allegiance to the flag, speak English, and generally enjoy all the advantages of living in the United States. Yet despite this identity, even U.S. citizen children cannot fully enjoy the rights and privileges to which they are entitled. Parents in deportation must make the painful decision to take their children with them, leading them into exile, or to leave them behind. To take the children is to uproot them from everything they have ever known, but they are assured that the family is together, in the poverty they are likely to face in the country they go to. To leave them is to dissolve the family, a decision that keeps the child rooted to schools, communities, friends, and places they call "home." The children will continue to enjoy the fruits of a prosperous society—but without their parents. Their parents' legal status leaves them susceptible to becoming de facto exiles or de facto orphans.

Children can become exiles when parents are deported and make the decision to leave together and remain as a family in another country (one that the children have perhaps never known). The term *exile* refers not just to a person banished from his or her country but also to a state of mind with deep psychological effects. The Chilean writer Roberto Bolaño (2003/2011) described the psychological impact in this way: "To be exiled is not to disappear but to shrink, to slowly or quickly get smaller and smaller" (p. 49). Exiles must essentially leave all that they know. Citizen children and often their undocumented siblings may have never left the United States, especially those who came at a very young age. They may remember only their lives in the United States. The disruption of leaving home is painful and places children in situations for which they are not prepared. Children may suddenly be faced with new lives in countries they have never known; a language they don't speak well; cultural nuances with which they are not acquainted; school systems that may not have the learning and remedial resources they need; and a loss of familiar friends, places, and activities. Under conditions of coercion, the adjustment is far more complicated than when families move volutarily, such as when parents relocate for employment reasons or to be closer to relatives.

Coerced exile is enough to cause children to question their identities. Listen to how several children exiled to Mexico experience the state of exile and the psychological dislocation they feel.[1]

A nine-year-old girl who moved with her mother and siblings to Oaxaca, Mexico, never really wanted to be there but she couldn't do anything about it. Her father had stayed behind in the United States because he was not under deportation proceedings. She misses living in California and is often homesick. She had been a good student in the United States and is now having difficulty adjusting to school in Mexico, especially in classes on Mexican history and geography. Her Spanish is below grade level. The girl feels helpless to do anything about the legal circumstances her parents are in. She has no power to convince her parents to send her back to live with friends of the family. She says she hopes her father will not come to Mexico because "if my dad comes here, we will not go back [to the United States] again." She is certain that if her father returns to Mexico, she will be permanently confined to her circumstances. It is hard for her to imagine a time when she will be able to make the decision to return to California. She wishes that she can gain some power in the future. "I always thought that when I grew up," she said, "I would fix it so they could go back."

A 14-year-old girl held similar feelings. Now living in Sinaloa, she is anxious and worries about crime, kidnappings, and her future. As an

[1]Cases presented in this chapter were taken from a study on the impact of deportation on the mental health of citizen children by Luis H. Zayas that was funded by the National Institute of Child Health and Human Development (R21 HD068874) and from his clinical practice.

adolescent, she hopes that in just a few years life will change, [and] she can return to the United States and go to college. She imagines that with a college education and a good job she will be able to advocate for her deported mother and grandmother. Moreover, one day "my mom could go to visit me in the United States and maybe in the future I can buy a house in Mexico and come for vacations."

A 10-year-old boy who had been in Oaxaca for just four months speaks with longing for the television shows he watched in Washington state, his good grades, and his membership on the football and baseball teams. Things have not gone well in Mexico: His parents are unemployed and the family is rapidly going through their savings, teetering close to poverty. His mother admires the free education in the United States, access to free lunches and school supplies. She misses opening the refrigerator that was always stocked with food. The family lived in trepidation of deportation when they were in the United States. Now their son worries for his father who is planning to reenter the United States to work. He envisions a day when he will call for his family to join him somewhere in Washington. But the boy now has another worry. "If my father tried to return to where we lived, he would have to walk but *el desierto está muy duro para cruzar* [the desert is too hard to cross]. I thought that if he tries to pass there, he might stay in the desert," he said, perhaps using unknowingly a euphemism for death. Taken together, to stay in the desert is to die in the desert.

In contrast to exiles who stay with parents in perhaps less than ideal circumstances, the de facto orphan is deprived of a parent's or parents' presence, care, affection, and attention. We use an inclusive definition of orphan in this instance, because the parents do not have to be dead. Deportation orphans may be taken in by the surviving parent, other kin, or close family friends, or they can enter the child welfare system if they are not yet at the age of majority. These other surrogates may provide care, maybe loving, devoted care, but they are no substitute for the biological or psychological parents. Many citizen children and noncitizen children of undocumented immigrant parents worry about becoming orphans, including those whose parents have never been arrested or detained. A girl in Chico, California, feels that she would be taken in by extended family if her parents are deported. She tries not to think too much about her parents' unauthorized status and the possible deportation that could happen at any moment, but inevitably she considers the various options and scenarios she might face. She says,

You know, I think about it and then stop because I don't like to think about it. I feel scared because I think that maybe one day they can just take them away, like that, in a second [snapping her fingers]. Then me and my little brother would have to go to foster homes and I really don't want that. Maybe we would have to go with foster parents but that means that we can't live the life that we used to live. Because I wouldn't have my regular parents and I might have different parents and you never know how they might treat me.

Deportation orphans tell very painful stories. Though citizen children can travel to see their parents and return easily to the United States using their passports, they are generally unable to exercise this option, as minor children left in poverty can neither afford to travel nor travel alone without special arrangements. The following are just some of the experiences of children who suffered the fracture of their families.

A boy we met in Texas had seen his father deported three times. Each time, his father was determined to come back to his wife and children. The boy was showing signs of loss, the feelings of an orphan. Adding to those losses was the uncertainty of what would happen if immigration officers discovered his father again. This boy was often apprehensive of the future. Would his father be arrested and detained again? Would it be his mother this time? Or could it be both of his parents at once? What would become of him? Not surprisingly, he appeared sad and frequently tearful when he spoke about this topic. Since his father's detention, his relationships with friends had changed. He was getting into fights at school, a new occurrence according to his mother. "I became, like, meaner," he said. "I felt like something bothering me. I always went to my dad to talk about stuff. But when he went, I couldn't do anything. But when my dad came back I was back to like normal." About the depression that beset him after his father's detention and deportation, he described that "to me, [every-thing] looked like gray or something. Like bad feelings were around. Like sadness or pain, anger."

A 14-year-old, insulin-dependent diabetic girl had seen her father deported to Mexico three months before. It had been a long road to the deportation, as her parents had challenged removal in immigration court but lost their case. The daughter attempted suicide just days before the judge's ruling. She said that the attorneys and judge "wanted me to go to court but I could not 'cause I had school, and back then I was really focusing on not missing school. My dad was still in jail, I think, when they wanted me to go to the immigration things. Mainly, I just didn't want to see my dad because they were going to show him on the screen, or something like that, and I was like, 'I'm not going to see my dad, not even talk to him, so what's the point of having him right there and seeing him, and not being able to be with him?' I thought it was pointless to even go. It would hurt me even more to see him there." She concluded her conversation by saying, "It hits a nerve now when kids complain about how their dads are this way and that way. And I'm like, 'You just shut up. At least you have him; at least he is there with you. He might not support you and stuff, but at least he is there for you.' My dad is all the way in Mexico. I can't see him every day. I can't tell him I love him every day. It's like, 'You don't know how it is to lose a parent, knowing that they are in another country.'"

Pervasive Effects of Loss

The traumatic loss of parents and the rupture of children's attachments to primary caregivers (and to the places they call home) can leave children susceptible to mental disorders, especially when the loss is not resolved naturally or through therapy (Bendall, Jackson, Hulbert, & McGorry, 2008; Grubaugh, Zinzow, Paul, Egede, & Frueh, 2011; Nickerson, Bryant, Aderka, Hinton, & Hofmann, 2013). The effects of the loss of primary caregivers can have crippling consequences, such as emotional dysregulation; problematic personality development; and relational problems of trust, intimacy, dependency, and insecurity. In the short term, losing an important attachment figure produces traumatic loss and symptoms of acute grief; losing the sense of belonging to a place disrupts the sense of continuity and of self. With support and stability in their lives, children undergo a process of adaptation over time and incorporate the loss as part of their lives. However, when left without stability or a period of therapeutic intervention, some children who experience the sudden, inexplicable loss of parents' presence and of place may enter a process of a drawn-out, pathological, and complicated grief.

A loss due to deportation is often shrouded in ambiguity. Although most loss contains elements of ambiguity—whether sudden or over a period of time—in the case of deportation orphans, the experience is similar but unique. Because of the sudden and confusing nature of detention and deportation, children are frequently unable to locate their parents, find out how they are doing, or determine when or if they are coming home. For this reason, we classify this kind of loss within the concept of "ambiguous loss" (Boss, 1999, 2002), that is, loss characterized by a lack of clarity and absence of closure or finality. Children do not know where their parents are or if and when they will be reunited; orphans of deportation do not know if the separation from their parents is temporary or permanent. In the case of the boy whose father was deported three times before recrossing the border again, the uncertainty of when his father would be arrested and deported again and whether he would make it back to the family safely is altogether psychologically and physically exhausting. When children are separated from their parents because of an immigration arrest, it is difficult for the children to cope as the split-ups are not only sudden but in some cases permanent (Baum, Rosha, & Barry, 2010). Exiles are moved to other countries, and orphans are moved to new homes with people who are not their parents. These children wonder whether they will ever return to the place they once called home and be with the people they knew.

In immigration and refugee resettlements, researchers have found that there are high rates of parent–child separation (Luster, Qin, Bates, Johnson, & Rana, 2009). Such separations cause a multitude of negative effects, such as damaged emotional attachment of parents and children; communication problems in parent–child relations; and different psychological problems, including depression, in both children and parents. Chaudry et al. (2010) recognized several reactive attachment problems among the children of undocumented immigrants ensnared by the workplace raids undertaken by ICE in 2006 and 2007. Children showed withdrawal and despair; the parents' arrests and detention destabilized many of the important sources of structure in their family lives (for example, routines like family dinners, getting ready for bed, and walks in the neighborhood). Over one-third of the children in the study were angry, clingy, and anxious, behaviors that continued more than six months after the parent's initial arrest, as well as in cases where the parent returned. Nearly half of the children were withdrawn, and parents reported the emergence of behaviors in their children that either had been overcome in the past as part of the children's natural development (for example, separation anxiety in the first 24 months of life, compliance with parents' requests) or were entirely new (for example, rebellion, dependency, and anxiety). Common symptoms included excessive crying, problems sleeping, loss of appetite or otherwise irregular eating patterns, and disruptions to other daily habits and practices. Families in which a parent was detained for more than a month reported much more frequent symptoms of childhood loss, especially in cases where the child had to adjust to a new primary caregiver. Even nine months after the arrest, children between the ages of 6 and 11 exhibited difficulty returning to their daily habits and practices. Both the duration and severity of these symptoms demonstrate the intense emotional effects that parents' arrests and detention can have on young children.

Identity, Territorial Belonging, and Citizenship

We posit that three aspects of identity development in the children of undocumented immigrants must be considered if we are to advance our research and our clinical practice with them. The first is that of personal or individual identity, the development of a self-concept, an amalgam of personal characteristics and social interactions, of how we view ourselves and how we are treated and viewed by others. Across life, but particularly during childhood and adolescence, identity emerges and is elaborated; it defines the individual to herself or himself as well as to others. A sense of continuity and uniqueness in the formation of one's identity is accompanied by a sense of affiliation to others.

What are the possible effects of living as a citizen but marginalized by parents' legal status as undocumented immigrants on the identity development and sense of self of the citizen child and his undocumented sister? Growing up in a mixed-status home with the specter of deportation hovering nearby and living in a social and political environment that serves up a mix of derision from some quarters and support from others is confusing. If self-concept is the sum of knowledge about and understanding of one's self, including our physical being, psychological makeup, and social attributes, then for marginalized children the process of identity development is a complicated one. How can a child develop a strong self-concept, a personal identity, while living in the shadows?

The second element of children's self-concept that we must consider is their cultural or ethnic identity. U.S.-born and undocumented siblings of immigrants of Latin American origin may identify as Americans while simultaneously identifying as Latinos or Hispanics, a shared sense of membership in a group derived from a common regional origin, genealogy, or ancestry. But faced with all the negative depictions of immigrants and the public contempt of undocumented parents, identity formation can become confused and difficult to achieve. It is undermined by negative rhetoric and anti-immigrant sentiment. In a study of Latino children's perceptions of American attitudes, children were asked to finish the phrase "Most Americans think we are" with an adjective or clause (Suárez-Orozco & Suárez-Orozco, 2001). The most prevalent answers included the words "useless," "garbage," "thieves," "lazy," and "gangsters"; other notable responses were "drug-addicts that only come to take their jobs away," "bad like all Latinos," and "we don't exist." Mexican children in particular gave the most adverse responses, with three-quarters of the children responding with negative adjectives or phrases. Most groups of children of immigrants had a fair proportion of negative responses, but the results were significantly lower for other groups, with less than half of Chinese children of immigrants responding negatively. These prejudices and stereotypes are internalized by children and adolescents, who may begin to see themselves as the world does. Although some may actively resist and seek to change stereotypes, for others it can become a self-fulfilling prophecy as they begin to engage in self-defeating behaviors. Children may submit to others' perceptions, subscribing to the mentality of "You think I'm bad? Let me show you how bad I can be" (Suárez-Orozco & Suárez-Orozco, 2001, p. 100).

The third identity of relevance to our discussion consists of ethical and philosophical principles around which nation-states form and are linked inextricably with living in a land or territory. It is a *collective* or *national identity*. Social psychologists see this identity as a combination of a person's cognitive, moral, and emotional connections with a national community, its practices, and its institutions (Mead, 1934; Polletta & Jasper, 2001). This self-concept comes through a perceived identification with a nation on the basis of its landmarks and iconography, facts and lore, documents and symbols, and the values that the nation represents. Ties to a land can have powerful implications—physically, psychologically, socially, economically, and politically. It is more than an identity to a local community or a cultural or ethnic group, and it supersedes a sense of personal identity. Overall, the consolidation of a personal identity and cultural–ethnic identity is complemented by the sense of belonging to a nation. To be a citizen or possess a national identity associated with a country includes a sense of "territorial belonging" (Bhabha, 2009, p. 93), a bond between a person and country with overwhelmingly significant implications for the individual's identity and well-being. Bhabha (2009) elaborated how citizenship and territorial belonging affect development and social and psychological functioning:

It affects children's life expectancy, their physical and psychological development, their material prospects, their general standard of living. The fact of belonging to a particular country determines the type, quality, and extent of education the child receives, as well as the expectations regarding familial obligations, employment opportunities, gender roles, and consumption patterns. It determines linguistic competence, social mores, vulnerability to discrimination, persecution, and war. It affects exposure to disease, to potentially oppressive social and cultural practices, to life-enhancing kinship, social, and occupational networks. (p. 95)

Citizen children, in theory, enjoy many protections that come with U.S. birth. Their undocumented siblings may not be protected by citizenship, but they have protection through their status as minors. Immigration law, however, undoes many of the citizenship rights applicable to the U.S.-born children of undocumented immigrants. Children cannot fully exercise their rights as citizens or their protected status as minors, effectively rendering them unequal to other citizens. They are left to ask, "Who am I?" and "What am I?" and "What's my place?" Immigration law devalues children, especially citizen children, and works against their welfare by separating children not just from their parents in the case of deportation, but also from the protection of the state (Thronson, 2011). When parents are citizens, their rights extend to protect their offspring. But children cannot use their citizenship to extend benefits or protections to their parents. What we have then is a situation in which the general structure of American law that is intended to protect family unity is undermined by the effects of immigration laws. That is, American family law and immigration laws are at odds when it comes to citizen children and their undocumented parents and siblings. In the case of divorcing parents, family courts typically consider that the child's "home" is the place where the child will reside most of the time. Regardless of which parent is given custody, or even if it is shared custody, home is where the children live primarily. Legal scholar Jacqueline Bhabha (2009) noted, however, that

if families face separation because of immigration law, the presumption is that the anchoring role of the child must give way, their primacy evaporating. If children have no right to use their citizenship as a basis for exercising family reunion or shoring up family unity, then—if their parents face deportation—the children too risk constructive deportation, despite being citizens. (p. 71)

Deported parents are forced into a decision of leaving their children behind to continue benefiting from all of the advantages of an affluent nation or taking their children with them to avoid fragmenting or dissolving their families. With no power to exert their rights or advocate for themselves, their parents, or their siblings, children effectively have no say. Citizen children forfeit the fundamental citizenship right to residency in the United States to maintain their right to the companionship of their parents. Thus, the right to live in their country of birth (without losing the ties to their parents) is annulled. And to have this define one's place in society impairs identity development and pride in a larger national identity.

Adversity, Strength, and Implications for Development

In this chapter, we have detailed the many adversities converging on the lives of undocumented immigrants' children that affect normal development. But we want to make clear that we are not implying that mixed-status families and their children are defenseless and weak. Parents and children have many strengths that they show every day. Adversities that children confront certainly pose challenges to them, but they bring assets to the hardships, capacities like resiliency, ego strengths, coping abilities, willfulness, self-confidence, courage, judgment, reasoning, wiliness, persistence, and other psychological and social skills. The fortitude that their parents exhibit in taking the risks to immigrate and the approach they take to working, protecting their families, and following the law are transmitted to children and instill capacities for behavioral and emotional self-regulation. Parents' aspirations for their children's future and devotion to the family unit model strengths. Families recognize their vulnerability to deportation and persevere in spite of it. For children, abilities such as bilingual skills that enhance cognitive functioning and biculturalism help them negotiate the cultures and environments in which they live, enhancing their adaptability in challenging situations. With awareness of the challenges they face as a unit, family members grow closer and more interdependent, elements that ultimately strengthen their bonds and their capacities.

Our perspectives on both the assets and deficits of citizen and noncitizen children of undocumented immigrants stem from experiences working with them in various community activities and advocacy practice. Research is sorely needed to explore further the development of citizen- and noncitizen children in mixed-status families. Research must include much more than we have been able to discuss in this chapter, such as more information on family dynamics and tensions; child-rearing patterns in mixed-status families; how differences in legal status affect sibling relations; the developmental course of citizen and undocumented children who are exiles or orphans and those who have never experienced the deportation of a parent; the adaptation and identity consolidation of U.S. citizen children growing up in other countries with their deported parents as well as the development of their undocumented siblings who identified once as Americans; and many, many other issues. Developmental research on children of undocumented immigrants affords us the opportunity to examine the intersection of public policy and human development as well as the disparities that our policies may intentionally or unintentionally create.

Detention and deportation undermine the development of our nation as a whole, not just the development of our young and vulnerable children. How does a nation mature and grow strong and healthy when its policies effectively cause children, who represent the future, to be exiled and orphaned? Quite obviously, it cannot mature without a well-trained, engaged labor force. But a large workforce and strong economic environment alone do not predict the nation's developmental health (Keating & Hertzman, 1999). A nation's health is made up of much more. It consists of the general social environment—its laws, institutions, and natural and man-made physical environment (for example, buildings, parks, roads)—and the physical, social, mental, cultural, moral, and spiritual well-being of its people. It is the quality of the person–environment interaction that determines our national well-being. As civic engagement enhances competencies for the greater good, children must feel engaged as efficacious members of their local and national communities. However, laws and social policies that create measurable inequities between groups of people are one of the greatest dangers to our national developmental health. Weakening people's collective sense of efficacy also weakens the relationship among people and their connection to social institutions. When the immigrants of our times and their children are made to feel like outsiders, subject to angry public words and policy pronouncement, insensitive laws and aggressive deportation, we all are weakened. Individual development is damaged, but so is a nation's development.

We cannot continue to ignore the children of the undocumented. The undocumented are "viewed in current policy debates as lawbreakers, laborers, or victims—seldom as parents raising citizen children" (Yoshikawa, 2011, p. 2). Social and legal policies that impede the chance for personal development will cost our country economically, socially, politically, and morally in the long run. Knowing that the early success of the very youngest predicts the future productivity and the success of our nation, if we do not invest today in our children and in reforming our immigration laws and immigration enforcement, we will see in the future the untoward effects on the developmental health of our country. Only strong social environments can ensure the competence and capacity of the population to keep the country growing and prospering, an endeavor fundamentally undermined by inequality and disparity. When children grow up in communities with low collective efficacy, they frequently experience a host of environment conditions that affect their physical, social, and behavioral outcomes. Housing insecurity, inadequate schooling, unemployment, and violence can in turn lead to dysfunctional home lives, educational setbacks, physical and mental health problems, and children's increased use of violence. All of these outcomes affect a child's future capacity to become an effective, well-educated, contributing member of society. What will the long-term psychological effects be on the citizen children and their parents and siblings living under the threat of deportation? What will the long-term effects be for those who are exiled or orphaned? How will the experiences of citizen children affect their sense of belonging and civic engagement once they are old enough to work, vote, and serve on juries? How might citizen children of deported parents conceptualize civic duty if and when they choose to return to the United States as children or adults? What will be their capacity and tolerance for understanding and participating in U.S. civic processes? What skills will they bring to fully realize their potentials and contribute to U.S. society? What tolerance will they have for social inequities? For those we call orphans, what will be their reactions and long-term attitudes? To what extent will their government's disbanding of their families affect their obligations as citizens and workers? There is no doubt that today's action or inaction in answering these questions will have long-lasting effects.

References

Baum, J., Rosha J., & Barry, C. (2010). *In the child's best interests? The consequences of losing a lawful immigrant parent to deportation.* Retrieved from http://www.law.berkeley.edu/files/IHRLC/In_the_Childs_Best_Interest.pdf

Bendall, S., Jackson, H. J., Hulbert, C. A., & McGorry, P. D. (2008). Childhood trauma and psychotic disorders: A systematic, critical review of the evidence. *Schizophrenia Bulletin 34*, 568–579.

Bhabha, J. (2009). The "mere fortuity" of birth? Children, mothers, borders, and the meaning of citizenship. In S. Benhabib & J. Resnick (Eds.), *Migration and mobilities: Citizenship, borders, and gender* (pp. 187–227). New York: New York University Press.

Blair, C., & Raver, C. C. (2012). Child development in the context of adversity: Experiential canalization of brain and behavior. *American Psychologist, 67*, 309–318.

Bolaño, R. (2011). Exiles. In *Between parentheses: Essays, articles and speeches (1998–2003)* (N. Wimmer, Trans.; pp. 49–60). New York: New Directions. (Original work published 2003)

Boss, P. (1999). *Ambiguous loss: Learning to live with unresolved grief.* Cambridge, MA: Harvard University Press.

Boss, P. (2002). Ambiguous loss in families of the missing. *Lancet, 360*, 39–40.

Chaudry, A., Capps, R., Pedroza, J., Castañeda, R. M., Santos, R., & Scott, M. (2010). *Facing our future: Children in the aftermath of immigration enforcement.* Washington, DC: Urban Institute.

De Genova, N. (2010). The deportation regime: Sovereignty, space and the freedom of movement. In N. De Genova & N. Peutz (Eds.), *The deportation regime* (pp. 33–65). Durham, NC: Duke University Press.

Dreby, J. (2012). The burden of deportation on children in Mexican immigrant families. *Journal of Marriage and the Family, 74*, 829–845.

Evans, G. W., & Kim, P. (2013). Childhood poverty, chronic stress, self-regulation, and coping. *Child Development Perspectives, 7*, 43–48.

Ferguson, T. J., Stegge, H., Miller, E. R., & Olsen, M. E. (1999). Guilt, shame, and symptoms in children. *Developmental Psychology, 35,* 347–357.

Gonzales, R. (2011). Learning to be legal: Undocumented youth and shifting legal contexts in the transition to adulthood. *American Sociological Review, 76*, 602–619.

Grubaugh, A. L., Zinzow, H. M., Paul, L., Egede, L. E., & Frueh, B. C. (2011). Trauma exposure and posttraumatic stress disorder in adults with severe mental illness: A critical review. *Clinical Psychology Review, 31*, 883–899.

Hoefer, M., Rytina, N., & Baker, B. C. (2009). *Estimates of the unauthorized immigrant population residing in the United States: January 2008.* Washington, DC: Office of Immigration Statistics, U.S. Department of Homeland Security.

Keating D. P., & Hertzman, C. (Eds.). (1999). *Developmental health and the wealth of nations: Social, biological, and educational dynamics.* New York: Guilford Press.

Luster, T., Qin, D. B., Bates, L., Johnson, D. J., & Rana, M. (2009). The lost boys of Sudan: Ambiguous loss, search for family, and reestablishing relationships with family members. *Family Relations, 57,* 444–456.

Mead, G. H. (1934). *Mind, self, and society.* Chicago: University of Chicago Press.

Nickerson, A., Bryant, R. A., Aderka, I. M., Hinton, D. E., & Hofmann, S. G. (2013). The impacts of parental loss and adverse parenting on mental health: Findings from the National Comorbidity Survey. *Psychological Trauma: Theory, Research, Practice, and Policy, 5*, 119–127.

Niedenthal, P. M., Tangney, J. P., & Gavansky, I. (1994). "If only I weren't" versus "if only I hadn't": Distinguishing shame and guilt in counterfactual thinking. *Journal of Personality and Social Psychology, 67*, 585–595.

Ortega, A. N., Fang, H., Perez, V. H., Rizzo, J. A., Carter-Pokras, O., Wallace, S. P., & Gelberg, L. (2007). Health care access, use of services, and experiences among undocumented Mexicans and other Latinos. *Archives of Internal Medicine, 26*, 2354–2360.

Polletta, F., & Jasper, J. M. (2001). Collective identity and social movements. *Annual Review of Sociology, 27*, 283–305.

Roos, S., Hodges, E.V.E., & Salmivalli, C. (2014). Do guilt- and shame-proneness differentially predict prosocial, aggressive, and withdrawn behaviors during early adolescence? *Developmental Psychology, 50*, 941–946.

Sapolsky, R. M. (1994). *Why zebras don't get ulcers: A guide to stress, stress-related diseases, and coping.* Boston: W. H. Freeman.

Suárez-Orozco, C., & Suárez-Orozco, M. (2001). *Children of immigration.* Cambridge, MA: Harvard University Press.

Talavera, V., Núñez-Mchiri, G. G., & Heyman, J. (2010). Deportation in the U.S.–Mexico borderlands: Anticipation, experience and memory. In N. De Genova & N. Peutz (Eds.), *The deportation regime* (pp. 166–195). Durham, NC: Duke University Press.

Tangney, J. P., & Gearing, R. L. (2002). *Shame and guilt.* New York: Guilford Press.

Taylor, P., Lopez, M. H., Passel, J. S., & Motel, S. (2011). *Unauthorized immigrants: Length of residency, patterns of parenthood.* Washington, DC: Pew Hispanic Center.

Thronson, D. B. (2011). Clashing values and cross purposes: Immigration law's marginalization of children and families. In J. Bhabha (Ed.), *Children without a state: A global human rights challenge* (pp. 237–254). Cambridge, MA: MIT Press.

Yoshikawa, H. (2011). *Immigrants raising citizens: Undocumented parents and their young children.* New York: Russell Sage Foundation.

Yoshikawa, H., Aber, J. L., & Beardslee, W. R. (2012). The effects of poverty on the mental, emotional, and behavioral health of children and youth: Implications for prevention. *American Psychologist, 67*, 272–284.

Zayas, L. H. (2015). *Forgotten citizens: Deportation, children, and the making of American exiles and orphans.* New York: Oxford University Press.

Chapter Four

Racial and Ethnic Identities of Asian Americans: Understanding Unique and Common Experiences

Greg M. Kim-Ju and Phillip D. Akutsu

What does it mean to call oneself an "Asian American," "Chinese American," or "Chinese" in the United States, and what does this self-designation mean for someone who is a member of an Asian ethnic group? Who determines how a person of Asian ethnic descent should be identified, and how does this ethnic or racial label present certain beliefs about this individual? Are Asian Americans a racial group, ethnic group, or both? These types of questions may play prominent roles in the process of self-examination for individuals of Asian ethnic heritage or descent and often perplex those who work with Asian American clients.

The development of an Asian American identity can be a complex process for members of Asian ethnic groups and is influenced by their immigration history and generational status in the United States, postcolonial and nationhood experiences, citizenship status, and persistent designation as a model minority. Any discussion about Asian American identity formation is further complicated by the basic acknowledgment and understanding that there is not a single homogenous racial group of Asian Americans (Chang & Kwan, 2009).

Asian Americans today represent over 25 distinct ethnic groups with different languages, traditions, customs, and histories in the United States. The term "Asian American" includes East Asians (for example, Chinese, Japanese, and Koreans) and Filipinos, who voluntarily immigrated to the United States in the late 1800s and early 1900s; Asian Indians, the majority of whom are relatively recent immigrants who arrived in the late 1990s and 2000s; and Southeast Asians (for example, Vietnamese, Cambodians, Laotian, Hmong, and Mien), who involuntary arrived in large numbers as refugees in the 1970s and 1980s.[1] Asian Americans currently represent 4.9 percent (single race) of the U.S. population, and their numbers increased 43.3 percent between 2000 and 2010, making them the fastest growing racial group in the country (Hoeffel, Rastogi, Kim, & Shahid, 2012). It is interesting to note that 60 percent (or 9 million) of the Asian American population is foreign-born, with nearly one in three having come to the United States between 2000 and 2009. Given these changing demographics as well as emerging identity politics in the United States, social scientists and scholars examine the larger economic, social, political, and cultural conditions associated with ethnic group relations to better understand the ways in which ethnic and racial identities play out at the individual and interpersonal levels.

Thirty-year-old Jennifer is a second-generation Thai American who has struggled to understand her place and identity in the United States but has, with age, come to increasingly accept and identify with her Asian background. Below she describes the process of developing a racial identity within a society that often has preconceived notions about what an Asian American is:

> Back then, I just wanted to fit in, so I kind of did it more by identifying as White because that would help me fit in. As I grew older, I started appreciating my Asian background more, wanted to learn more about it to express it more. I didn't start identifying as Asian until I got to college, when I started to have more confidence in myself, more self-esteem. Once I felt better about myself, I felt better about who I was and not trying to be White.

In contrast, Steve, a second-generation Korean American at an Ivy League university, continues to struggle with Asian ethnic identity issues, especially his sense of marginalization, as someone who sees himself as neither Korean nor Korean American:

> I don't like associating with Korean Americans, being Korean American. I would rather be just considered Korean or [a] Korean who happened to have grown up in America, whereas my personality comes

---

[1]The term "refugee" refers to those individuals who had to leave their country because of persecution (for example, religious or political) and have resettled in the United States (Chung & Bemak, 2007). This definition conforms to 101(a)(42) of the Immigration and Nationality Act as part of the 1980 Refugee Act and is consistent with the Status of Refugees in the 1951 Convention. Although the circumstances of their resettlements may vary, some Asian American ethnic groups that would be considered refugees include the Vietnamese and Cambodians.

from American culture. It's kind of a reaction against that kind of an approach or that kind of an identity. I mean the more and more I study Koreans in Korea, I realize I'm not that. I'm trying to deal with that right now, I'm trying to figure out—because I'm not really comfortable being Korean American, either. I know I can never be Korean, but I'm not comfortable with being Korean American. I want to wholly identify with Koreans in Korea, but I can't because I grew up in America.

In light of these types of experiences, it is not surprising that scholars have long assumed that members of ethnic minority groups in the United States may suffer from a sense of "double consciousness," "twoness," or "identity confusion" (DuBois, 1903; Erikson, 1968), descriptions of a psychological conflict believed to be the core experience of racial and ethnic minority-group members. This psychological conflict is based on the notion that racial and ethnic minority individuals inevitably internalize conflicts that arise from living in two cultures—the dominant culture and their culture of ethnic or racial origin—in their sense of a "social self." However, to characterize the experiences of racial and ethnic minority-group members in such a way oversimplifies and overgeneralizes the dynamic and complex nature of the development and maintenance of ethnic and racial identities.

In this chapter, we examine theory and research related to (1) the conceptualization of ethnicity and race as important components of social identity, (2) ethnic and racial identity indicators, and (3) the stability of ethnic and racial identity over time and across contexts. In addition to reviewing the literature to add clarity to a diverse body of work, we critically examine underlying assumptions of major theoretical approaches to ethnic and racial identity and its development, to pay particular attention to defining ethnic and racial identity for Asian Americans. In doing so, we acknowledge the unique differences among Asian American subgroups while addressing more common issues and themes of ethnic and racial identities and related factors, such as acculturation, citizenship, and nationalism among Asian Americans.

Race and Ethnicity

Developing a better understanding of racial and ethnic identity is critical to examining how Asian Americans develop a sense of self as they navigate and negotiate within their own Asian ethnic subcultures and American culture.

Racial identity refers to a person's sense of social identity with a designated racial group in U.S. society that involves an increased understanding of what this racial status means in society, including racial oppression and ethnic minority status (Alvarez, Juang, & Liang, 2006). With regard to Asian Americans as a racial minority group, their status in U.S. society began to change dramatically in the 1950s and 1960s. In contrast to African Americans and Latinos, who were viewed in negative terms, specific Asian American groups began to be touted as a model minority who overcame racism to achieve the American dream and achieved noted accomplishments in the face of discrimination and oppression. This seemingly positive characterization of Asian Americans as a successful minority group became the larger narrative in which politicians and educators defined Asian Americans, using it to motivate other racial groups to succeed economically and academically, and served to alienate Asian Americans from other racial minority groups. Moreover, this single homogenous designation failed to reflect the immense heterogeneity of Asian subgroups and the diversity in their social, cultural, educational, and economic opportunities and experiences in the United States.

At the same time, members of different Asian groups started to work collectively to create a pan-ethnic Asian American identity to align with the civil rights movement of African Americans. As such, individuals from different Asian ethnic groups who began to describe themselves as Asian Americans saw this as a conscious act of sociopolitical revolution and rebellion against the corrupt forces that worked against any racial minority group that sought to make significant advances in U.S. society. However, in the years since the civil rights movement, much of the political rhetoric relating to the term "Asian American" has dissipated, and the current designation of identifying as an Asian American is less political.

In contrast, the term "ethnic identity" has had more to do with an individual's feeling of personal belongingness and connection to an ancestral national or ethnic heritage group (Berry, Poortinga, Segall, & Dasen, 1992). That is, members of an Asian ethnic group often share common values and national origins, and specific cultural characteristics are used to distinguish between in-group and out-group status (for example, language, values, practices). In this way, for many individuals of Asian ethnic descent, ethnic group membership or ethnic identity may be a more salient and significant designation than the larger racial group designation of being Asian American.

Similar to Latinos, who also represent a large group of nationalities and ethnic groups, Asian Americans represent a diverse host of Asian ethnic group cultures (for example, Chinese, Korean, Asian Indian, Vietnamese, Bhutanese, and Japanese), which help to delineate important cultural and ethnic group differences. Although there are shared beliefs and customs that are valued by many Asian ethnic groups, many have very different cultural values, worldviews, practices, traditions, and histories that make them unique and distinct from other Asian groups. In this sense, ethnic identity provides a sense of personal connection or belongingness to a person's ancestral national or ethnic culture. For many Asian Americans, the concepts of ethnic identity and racial identity are viewed as distinct and separate entities. Whereas the former speaks to a personal connection to their native ancestors as well as their beliefs, customs, and traditions, the latter speaks more to understanding the sociocultural and historical implications of race and its impact on social, economic, and political forces in the United States. Whether it is ethnic identity or racial identity under consideration, an integral part of these identities is that identification with a group is considered to play a crucial role in defining who the individual is and who the individual is not and, in turn, influences that person's psychological well-being (Yoo & Lee, 2005).

Social Identity Framework

A large body of work on ethnic and racial identity has been influenced by the social identity perspective (Liu & László, 2007; Tajfel, 1981). From this perspective, social identity is strongly linked to group belongingness, defined by the specific characteristics of social groups with which one identifies psychologically. Specifically, social identity is defined as "that part of the individual's self concept which derives from his knowledge of his membership of a social group together with the value and emotional significance attached to that membership" (Tajfel, 1981, p. 255). Typically, the identification process for Asian Americans involves social comparisons in which there is a claim of membership to their Asian ethnic group and a contrast of that group with another ethnic group. This involves a categorization process that distinguishes perceived similarities from perceived differences with members of another ethnic group, including other Asian groups. An Asian American individual is said to internalize this social categorization process to the extent that it becomes a part of his or her self-concept, and negative value-loaded comparisons with other ethnic groups are often made to enhance that person's self-concept about his or her race or ethnicity.

The social identity approach is unique from previous approaches to ethnic identity in that it attempts to link the individual and society in its analysis (that is, social categories). In doing so, this approach affords an analytic tool that allows for a deeper examination of social groups, such as Asian Americans, and how their relative power and status define the social structure and hierarchy of American society. Furthermore, in its formulation of ethnic identity, there is a strong emphasis on intrapersonal processes, presumably because of the theory's reliance on cognitive processes of categorization. For an Asian American to integrate into mainstream society, that person must negotiate conflicting attitudes, values, and behaviors between his or her Asian ethnic group and the dominant American culture. The underlying issue here is whether Asian ethnic group members need to choose between two identities or whether they can establish a bicultural identity. This issue has been addressed more directly by the acculturation literature.

Acculturation Framework

In ethnically heterogeneous societies, where there is contact between two or more ethnic groups, ethnic identity becomes significant and meaningful to the individual. To Asian ethnic group members, acculturation is a process of psychosocial adaptation that requires the learning of new American symbolic meaning and value systems and the discarding of prior Asian customs, beliefs, and behaviors (Burnam, Telles, Karno, Hough, & Escobar, 1987). Broadly speaking, acculturation involves how ethnic groups deal with cultural attitudes, values, and behaviors that result from contact between two cultures—the traditional Asian ethnic culture and dominant American culture (Berry, 1995). This acculturative process is relevant mainly to the experience of first-generation newcomers, though it has relevance, in principle, to later generations as well. That is, many Asian American groups continue to pass on certain traditional Asian values, customs, and practices to the next generation to facilitate a connection to what it means to be, for example, Asian Indian or Korean, at the same time that an Asian ethnic individual is trying to navigate the process of learning what it means to be American.

The acculturation model determines people's orientation of ethnic identity on the basis of two issues: the value of maintaining identification with the culture of Asian ethnic origin and the value of developing relationships with the dominant American group. On the basis of people's orientation to their own Asian ethnic group and the majority group, there are four possible resolutions to ethnic identity: assimilation, separation, biculturality, and marginality.

Assimilation occurs when an individual identifies exclusively with the dominant culture and chooses to forgo or neglect his or her culture of origin. For example, an Asian person may view himself or herself as American and reject any attempt by others to identify him or her as being Asian in any shape or form. *Separation* occurs when the individual does not identify with the dominant culture but instead chooses to identify strictly with his or her culture of origin. From this perspective, an Asian person may speak primarily an Asian language and live in an ethnic enclave (for example, Chinatown, Little Saigon) and only sparingly interact with others in the dominant culture. *Biculturality* or integration occurs when an individual identifies with both the culture of origin and the dominant culture. This type of Asian American will often have mixed ethnic friendships and feel comfortable in the company of Asian Americans and other ethnic groups. *Marginality* involves the absence of self-identification with either the culture of origin or the dominant culture. Such Asian individuals will often feel ostracized by both members of their own Asian ethnic group and the American or White culture.

The acculturation framework focuses on how Asian individuals experience their culture of Asian ethnic origin and the dominant American culture, the factors that influence this adaptation, and the implications of acculturation for interpersonal and intergroup contact and psychological adjustment. The types of settings (for example, school, family) and groups (for example, friends, community) may shape their ethnic identity, self-esteem, and psychological well-being, with assimilationist and integrationist modes potentially offering more positive outcomes than the other modes.

There are two important issues raised by the acculturation framework for Asian Americans. The first concerns the extent to which Asian ethnic groups maintain their ethnic identity when in direct contact with other ethnic groups, particularly the White American dominant group. The second issue concerns the impact of acculturation on the psychological adjustment of Asian ethnic minority-group members. A primary focus of psychological adjustment for Asian Americans concerns *acculturative stress,* which refers to a set of stress behaviors that one experiences during the acculturation process (for example, feelings of marginality and alienation, identity confusion, anxiety; Berry, 1995). The underlying theme in both of these issues is the culture conflict that may arise from negotiating the more traditional Asian ethnic culture and the dominant American culture, its challenges and possible resolution, and the related psychological consequences that may occur in this acculturative process.

Asian American Ethnic Identity Models

Models of ethnic identity have inherently focused on certain aspects of people's ethnic affiliation. For Asian ethnic groups, ethnic identity or ethnic group membership is often associated with a certain measure of ethnic authenticity, which may be assessed by knowledge of specific Asian customs or practices. Family members, social peers, and others in a specific Asian ethnic group may have certain expectations about what members of their specific ethnic group may know and practice on a regular basis, including language proficiency and food preferences. Despite self-identified ethnic group membership and knowledge of familial and social expectations, individuals may choose to adopt certain traditional values and practices but reject others in forming an evolving sense of what it means to be a member of that particular Asian ethnic group.

For example, many Asian ethnic groups may frown on Asian individuals marrying outside of their specific Asian ethnic group. However, with greater exposure to non-Asian members in public schools, churches, and other settings, the occurrence of out-marriage, especially for Asian women, has steadily increased. Faced with such a conflict with traditional views versus modern changing standards, Asian ethnic identity formation may require a certain level of compromise, conformity, or rejection, which can lead to confusion and conflict for the Asian ethnic group member. Cultural standards have evolved for Asian ethnic cultures with greater exposure to American culture and changing times, which demand changes in specific areas. However, even with such cultural changes, there continue to be certain members in Asian ethnic groups who have the power and status to serve as the standard bearers (for example, community leaders, shamans) in determining who is authentically a part of an Asian ethnic group.

Phinney (1989) proposed a three-stage ethnic identity development model based on the theoretical contributions of Erikson (1968) and Marcia (1966, 1980) that is applicable across ethnic groups, including Asian Americans. Compared with an earlier ethnic identity model by Cross (1971), which focused on racial oppression experienced by African Americans and subsequent attitudes toward the African American group and the dominant White group, Phinney's model focuses on the exploration of ethnicity in light of experiences of one's ethnic group, which may or may not include racial oppression or racist treatment by the dominant group in the larger society. That is, although Asian Americans may experience discrimination or racism, these experiences do not necessarily lead to a rethinking of issues related to their ethnicity or ethnic identity.

In Phinney's model, the first stage, *unexamined ethnic identity,* is characterized by a lack of active exploration of one's own ethnicity. In this stage, an Asian ethnic individual is said to internalize societal or parental views of his or her own Asian ethnicity, which does not necessarily imply preference for the dominant White or American culture. The key feature of this stage is that the Asian individual has not critically explored or examined his or her own Asian ethnicity. The second stage, *ethnic identity search,* is characterized by an exploration into one's culture of origin. Usually, the Asian individual is motivated to explore his or her Asian ethnicity because of a growing awareness that not all values of the dominant American group are beneficial to ethnic minority group members. The growing awareness is said to be cumulative and becomes the basis for initiating a search or exploration of Asian ethnicity or culture, in which the person questions and develops a personal sense of ethnic identification. The final stage, *ethnic identity achievement,* is characterized by an appreciation for one's ethnicity and resolution of conflicts with the dominant group. As the Asian ethnic individual actively learns more about his or her own Asian ethnicity and culture, that person comes to a deeper understanding and appreciation of ethnicity through a resolution of two issues: cultural differences between one's own Asian ethnic group and the dominant White group and the status of that Asian ethnic group in American society (Phinney, 1990).

More important, this model does not necessarily assume that there are negative psychological consequences or outcomes for being an Asian ethnic minority group member. It is a conceptual model that is committed to a vision of psychological maturity that reflects the ability to think for one's ethnic self, to be autonomous in interpreting the world and one's ethnic experiences, and to be able to take action in view of one's personal meanings. Phinney has since refined her original discussion of ethnic identity formation to focus more on two major concepts: a sense of belonging to one's ethnic group and an active search and examination of the cultural traditions, history, and heritage of one's ethnic group (Phinney & Ong, 2007).

Asian American Racial Identity Models

The conceptual and theoretical work on racial identity offers different points of emphasis and carries different assumptions concerning human behavior and processes that are influential in racial identity development. Using these frameworks, scholars and practitioners have developed different models to understand and examine Asian Americans and their identities. The *racial/cultural identity development* model (R/CID) (Sue & Sue, 1990), largely derived from counseling settings, was developed to examine the nuances of Asian American experiences. Similar to developmental stage models, the R/CID is a stage model that includes five stages: *conformity, dissonance, resistance and immersion, introspection,* and *integrative awareness.*

In the first stage, conformity the Asian ethnic individual has a preference for the dominant White culture. The second stage, dissonance includes a cultural conflict that challenges an Asian ethnic individual's existing worldview with respect to race and identity. In the third stage, *resistance and immersion,* the Asian ethnic individual rejects the dominant White culture and immerses himself or herself to better understand his or her Asian ethnic culture of origin and minority-group status. *Introspection,* the fourth stage, is characterized by the Asian ethnic individual reflecting more deeply about self and identity; and the fifth stage, *integrative awareness,* includes developing an understanding and balance between his or her culture of Asian ethnic origin, appreciating its unique aspects, and the dominant White culture.

Collectively, these models of Asian American racial and ethnic identity have been useful in examining and understanding Asian Americans and their social identities, though there are questions about which specific dimensions, for example, subjective feelings or behavioral aspects, relate to ethnic and racial identity that they may be assessing. To examine these questions of racial and ethnic identity, it is important to understand how these terms are operationalized and measured and how they may manifest themselves at the individual level. We next examine indicators of ethnic and racial identity in the psychological domains of cognition, behavior, and emotion or affect, in relation to the experiences of Asian Americans.

Indicators of Ethnic Identity: Being Asian American

By and large, there are several core components, or indicators, of ethnic and racial identities that have received the most attention in research. These are (1) ethnic or racial self-identification with one's own ethnic group; (2) cultural familiarity reflected in language use, behavior patterns, cultural practices, and religious involvement; and (3) positive or negative attitudes toward one's own ethnic or racial group that includes a sense of belongingness. Many researchers use *ethnic* or *racial self-identification* as a starting point to assess ethnic identity or racial identity. This indicator refers to a person's choice of ethnic or racial label or category. Researchers have assumed that the ethnic or racial label or category that one applies to oneself such as "I am an Asian American" or "I am a Japanese American" accurately reflects the recognition that one's ethnicity or race is a shared characteristic with a group of people with a common ethnic heritage or racial label. It is important to keep in mind that the choice of ethnic or racial labels, which may be reflective of personal choice (Kiang & Luu, 2013), can also be shaped by the ways in which others ascribe specific ethnic or racial identities to individuals. For instance, Cambodian American adolescents may struggle with their Cambodian identities versus their Asian American identities because of perceived stigma and shame that may be associated with the former label (Chhuon & Hudley, 2010).

The degree to which one identifies as Asian or American may further depend on one's birth location and level of generation in the United States, with U.S.-born individuals and those from a second or later generation referring more to their American lifestyle as a distinct aspect of their identity compared with foreign-born or immigrant Asian Americans (Tuason, Taylor, Rollings, Harris, & Martin, 2007). For example, although Asian Indians are often seen as a single homogenous Asian ethnic subgroup, specific community or geographic, premigration, and subnational factors can highlight more meaningful ethnic identifiers for some Asian Indian individuals, including the designations of being Punjabi versus Sikh or Bengali versus Hindu (Niyogi, 2010).

Researchers have also focused on *cultural familiarity* with one's ethnic group traditions and practices as a symbol or indicator of ethnic group membership; the stronger one's cultural familiarity with ethnic group traditions and values, the stronger one's ethnic identity is considered to be. Specific indicators of cultural involvement in one's ethnic group often include knowledge of ethnic group history and traditions, choice of social relationships (for example, family and friends), membership in ethnic group organizations, and religious practices. Among these indicators, Asian language use and fluency are considered to be the most important markers for many Asian ethnic groups. Language as a behavioral component refers to the preference for and use of one's native Asian ethnic language and the contexts in which this native language is used. It has been shown to be an important dimension of ethnic identity for both Asian American children (Rogers et al., 2012) and young adults (Miller, 2007). As an example, Chinese Americans considered Chinese language proficiency to be an important aspect of their ethnic identity, and it has been found to be strongly related to their self-esteem (Tsai, Ying, & Lee, 2001).

The importance of heritage language for Asian Americans as a component of ethnic identity, however, can vary by generation, with it being more important for children of immigrants (Rogers et al., 2012) than it is for later generations (Kim & Chao, 2009). Still, even when their dominant language is English and their language ability within their "native community" may be limited, Asian

American children can claim and forge an ethnic identity through specific language practices called "self-styling." As an example, Sri Lankan youths may intentionally adopt verbal and nonverbal language reflective of their ethnic group and culture that highlights their in-group solidarity (Canagarajah, 2012). The relationship between ethnic identity and cultural familiarity or use of a native Asian language has been raised as an important factor by many Asian American scholars. Whether specific behavioral components of ethnic identity formation are measured by Asian language use, cultural practices, or religious affiliations, we should keep in mind the significant influence of gender and its uneven effects on the acculturation process for Asian American ethnic groups (Suinn, 2010).

Another indicator of ethnic or racial identity has been attitudes toward one's ethnic or racial group. Developmental models of ethnic identity maintain that positive attitudes reflect strong identification with one's ethnic group, whereas negative attitudes reflect weak identification (Phinney & Alipuria, 1990). Affective ties to one's ethnic group are clearly an important part of what is meant by close attachment to or identification with one's Asian ethnic group. The affective dimension of ethnic group identification has special importance for understanding the ethnic identity of Asian Americans from the social identity framework. Affective elements such as feelings of bonding, feelings of shared fate and interdependence, and feelings of attachment with one's Asian American ethnic group may be important aspects of people's bonds with their cultural group. For instance, social connectedness with one's cultural heritage is considered to be an important dimension of Asian American identity (Oyserman & Sakamoto, 1997). It appears that social connectedness and support afford opportunities for ethnic identity exploration, which, in turn, leads to ethnic identity affirmation and belonging (Whitehead, Ainsworth, Wittig, & Gadino, 2009). Similarly, collective self-esteem, a group-based affect, may reflect how closely evaluation of one's cultural group corresponds with how one perceives others to evaluate one's cultural group (Crocker, Luhtanen, Blaine, & Broadnax, 1994). That is, high collective self-esteem may reflect a close emotional attachment with one's own ethnic group.

These indicators, ethnic or racial self-identification, cultural familiarity, and attitudes toward one's ethnic group, represent a broad and diverse range of measures that researchers have used to assess ethnic group affiliation. Comparatively, Asian Americans differ from White and Black Americans in the extent of their evaluation of their ethnic group. Studies point to the importance of affective connection with one's ethnic group operating through self-esteem and religious participation as well as friendships and social networks as indicators of ethnic group identification. These indicators may tap into a collective cultural dimension of Asian Americans. Specifically, researchers have demonstrated that Asian Americans place more emphasis on harmony in relationships, interdependence with groups, and familial or communal obligations (Markus & Kitayama, 1991). Asian Americans' emphasis on these characteristics may explain why dimensions such as religious participation, affective attachment with one's ethnic group, and friendships are important signs of ethnic group identification for Asian Americans.

An important question related to ethnic identity development concerns the degree of stability or continuity of ethnic identity across social settings and over time. For Asian Americans, social situations present unique challenges as cultural practices dictate that one should act in a manner that is socially responsive to the needs of the collective or group situation. As such, the concept of a stable ethnic identity may not be as culturally relevant for Asian Americans who are meeting cultural standards of reciprocity, group harmony, and collectivism. A discussion of short-term variations and long-term changes in ethnic identity is addressed in the next section.

Changes in Ethnic Identity

I know that when I sit with a mixed group of Asian Americans it feels differently from when I am the sole Asian American in a group of whites. I know that when I sit with Japanese Americans it feels differently than if I'm with a mixed group of Asian Americans. And I know that when I'm with a group of people of color it feels differently from being with any of these other groups. And as an artist, I know that when I read my work to an Asian American audience the response is different than from a white audience. (Mura, 1994, p. 202)

Researchers using developmental models focus more on stable aspects of ethnic identity, whereas those using a social identity perspective focus more on situational influences of ethnic identity. Although acculturation and developmental approaches to ethnic identity implicitly adopt the view that identity achievement, once it occurs, is largely stable, there are also situational aspects of one's ethnic identity that have yet to be addressed accordingly. As the excerpt above by Asian American writer David Mura (1994) illustrates, ethnic identity for Asian Americans may be reactive to social situations. First, the degree to which salience of one's ethnicity in social relations between ethnic groups varies and how one understands one's ethnic identity may not necessarily be consistent across situations (Sodowsky, Kwan, & Pannu, 1995; Yip, 2009). Second, there are situational determinants of ethnic identity whereby a person may feel differently according to the context (that is, a person may feel more ethnically identified in one context versus another; Kim-Ju & Liem, 2003). Finally, how one understands and explores one's ethnicity at different points in the developmental life cycle may also bring about changes in ethnic identity over an extended period of time (Parham, 1989). We begin first with a discussion about salience of ethnic identity as a function of context and short-term changes of ethnic identity.

Short-Term Changes in Ethnic and Racial Identity

The point at which ethnic and racial identities become an important aspect of one's life, for Asian Americans, may depend on a number of factors, including social situation, peer relationships, and life span. One useful way to examine how ethnic and racial identities are situationally influenced is to first explore the most variable aspect of these identities, that is, the extent to which they are salient, conscious aspects of one's sense of self at any given moment in time. Whereas ethnic identity, per se, focuses on the extent to which an Asian American identifies with his or her culture of origin, self-awareness of ethnicity focuses more on how this more stable identification and specific characteristics of different situations interact to determine how salient ethnicity becomes at any particular moment for an Asian American (Kim-Ju & Liem, 2003). That is, an Asian American may be aware of his or her ethnicity in some situations, while completely oblivious to it in others even though his or her basic ethnic identity orientation (that is, ethnic identity development stage, ethnic group label) is relatively constant. Although an Asian American's identification with his or her ethnic group membership may be relatively constant, how much this particular aspect of social identity comes into play or is a conscious feature of one's self-awareness can vary substantially according to immediate social circumstances. It is important to note that these identities may be related to the attitudes and emotions that Asian Americans experience and express in different situations.

Although there is some variability in ethnic and racial identity, the major assumption in psychological approaches is that these identities, in adulthood, have substantial continuity. As the discussion above suggests, however, salience of one's ethnicity or race can have a large impact on the way one perceives and understands one's ethnic or racial identity. Salience depends on the ethnic or racial composition and intergroup influences in social settings as well as other situational factors. For example, in social situations with many Asian Americans of the same ethnic or racial group, the importance of ethnic or racial identity for an Asian individual may be very salient, and the social pressures to engage in behaviors that are culturally appropriate would be required to retain cultural respectability. In such instances, the concept of face plays a critical role for many Asian Americans as it is very important for Asian individuals to act accordingly to the cultural dictates of ethnic protocols and social graces based on ethnic traditions and practices.

Long-Term Changes in Ethnic and Racial Identity

In contrast to short-term variations in ethnic and racial identities, long-term changes may occur as an Asian American explores and evaluates the meaning and implication of his or her ethnicity and race throughout the life course. According to developmental models of ethnic and racial identity (Cross, 1995; Phinney, 1992), these identities can be conceptualized as a process in which one progresses through stages: from an early stage, where there is little exploration of one's ethnicity or race; to a period of active exploration; and on to an ethnic or racial identity that is characterized by understanding one's ethnicity or race and how it relates to one's status and experiences in the larger dominant society. It appears that Asian American adolescents, compared with other ethnic minority groups, tend to be more consistent with their ethnic identities over time (Nishina, Bellmore, Witkow, & Nylund-Gibson, 2010), though their "American" identity has been shown to increase over the same period (Kiang, Witkow, & Champagne, 2012). By and large, most of these developmental models of ethnic and racial identity for Asian Americans tend to be limited to adolescence and young adulthood.

A significant contribution to ethnic identity developmental models has been the application of a life-span perspective by Parham (1989). However, like Phinney, Parham (1989) proposed that adolescence and early adulthood are the earliest periods in which the individual is capable of experiencing a sense of ethnicity or ethnic identity. Prior to this period, one's views regarding ethnicity are believed to be reflective of parental or societal views, which have been uncritically internalized by young ethnic minority-group members. Because of the nature of developmental tasks through the life course, Parham (1989) suggested that experiences related to ethnicity are qualitatively different for each life-span phase (for example, adolescence versus middle or late adulthood). The challenges unique to each life-span phase may induce "recycling" through some of the stages. In other words, at a later time, having already gone through the different stages, an individual may have new identity issues that need to be addressed later in life, and as a result, that person may experience some of the ethnic identity stages again. For example, a young Filipino immigrant might explore his or her own ethnicity for the first time as a single college student who recently came to the United States. During this time, this individual may successfully address identity questions important to early adult functioning, such as socially fitting into an ethnically diverse environment. Later, marriage or parenthood may stimulate new questions about ethnicity for this individual, such as how to ethnically or racially socialize his or her children.

These new questions necessitate a reexamination of what it means to be Asian American, not only for the individual, but also for his or her children. The individual searches for new answers and meanings of ethnicity in his or her life in relation to age-appropriate developmental or life-cycle concerns (Cross, 1995; Parham, 1989). As such, Asian Americans may undergo multiple levels of ethnic identity development and examination because this is a critical issue not only for the individual, but also for other family members who play a vital role in the person's life. Specific difficulties have arisen in many Asian American families and multigenerational households where there are intergenerational differences in ethnic identity and the cultural traditions embraced and followed by different family members (Chun & Akutsu, 2009). Thus, members of Asian American families may undergo various cultural changes and adoptions throughout life because of how the acculturation process can influence individual members at different life stages.

Conclusion

The development of ethnic and racial identities for Asian Americans can be a very complex process. For some, their ethnic and racial identities are the cultural lens through which they engage with others in culturally meaningful ways that show respect to their ethnic culture and provide a sense of cultural wholeness or self. For others, ethnic and racial identities may play a minimal role in their daily life, and there may be little attempt to self-reflect on the meaning of their ethnic or racial identity in social interactions or day-to-day experiences. Invariably, each individual of Asian descent will undergo his or her own personal process of self-reflection about ethnic and racial identities and what they mean for self-identifying as Chinese, Korean, Asian, or Asian American in the United States.

Ethnic and racial identities may have a profound effect on Asian individuals and may serve as a powerful influence on the relationships that Asian Americans have with family members or other Asian Americans in the community. Furthermore, the role one's racial or ethnic identity plays depends on the social situation and cultural expectations of the individual and others. We acknowledge the possible impact ethnic and racial identities may have on an individual's self-growth, psychological health, and social well-being, or how the ethnic or racial identity development process may alter the social and cultural dynamics of an Asian ethnic family or community. However, to presume that such social identities are prominent in the daily roles and experiences of an Asian individual could foster a false impression of how important or salient ethnic and racial identity may be for an Asian individual. One must be cautious in determining how and when ethnic and racial identities play a critical role in the social realities of Asian Americans and recognize that cultural exchanges or situations may be fraught with pitfalls and challenges for losing cultural respectability or face. The theoretical framework and models of ethnic and racial identities as well as the indicators and issues associated with being Asian American may serve as a starting point for increasing in-depth discussions and analysis and fostering a better understanding of Asian American identity.

References

Alvarez, A. N., Juang, L., & Liang, C.T.H. (2006). Asian Americans and racism: When bad things happen to "model minorities." *Cultural Diversity and Ethnic Minority Psychology, 12*, 477–492.

Berry, J. W. (1995). Psychology of acculturation. In N. R. Goldberger & J. B. Veroff (Eds.), *The culture and psychology reader* (pp. 457–488). New York: New York University Press.

Berry, J. W., Poortinga, Y. H., Segall, M. H., & Dasen, P. R. (1992). *Cross-racial psychology: Research and applications.* New York: Cambridge University Press.

Burnam, M. A., Telles, C. A., Karno, M., Hough, R. L., & Escobar, J. I. (1987). Measurement of acculturation in a community population of Mexican Americans. *Hispanic Journal of Behavioral Sciences, 9*, 105–130.

Canagarajah, S. (2012). Styling one's own in the Sri Lankan Tamil diaspora: Implications for language and ethnicity. *Journal of Language, Identity, and Education, 11*, 124–135.

Chang, T., & Kwan, K.-L. K. (2009). Asian American racial and ethnic identity. In N. Tewari & A. N. Alvarez (Eds.), *Asian American psychology: Current perspectives* (pp. 113–133). New York: Taylor & Francis.

Chhuon, V., & Hudley, C. (2010). Asian American ethnic options. *Anthropology & Education Quarterly, 41*, 341–359.

Chun, K. M., & Akutsu, P. D. (2009). Assessing Asian American family acculturation in clinical settings: Guidelines and recommendations for mental health professionals. In N.-H. Trinh, Y. C. Rho, F. G. Lu, & K. M. Sanders (Eds.), *Handbook of mental health and acculturation in Asian American families* (pp. 99–122). Totowa, NJ: Humana Press.

Chung, R.C.-Y., & Bemak, F. (2007). Immigrant and refugee populations. In M. G. Constantine (Ed.), *Clinical practice with people of color: A guide to becoming culturally competent* (pp. 125–142). New York: Teachers College Press.

Crocker, J., Luhtanen, R., Blaine, B., & Broadnax, S. (1994). Collective self-esteem and psychological well-being among white, black, and Asian college students. *Personality and Social Psychology Bulletin, 20*, 503–513.

Cross, W. E. (1971). The Negro-to-black conversion experience: Toward a psychology of black liberation. *Black World, 20*, 13–27.

Cross, W. E., Jr. (1995). The psychology of nigrescence: Revisiting the Cross model. In J. G. Ponterotto, J. M. Casas, L. A. Suzuki, & C. M. Alexander (Eds.), *Handbook of multicultural counseling* (pp. 93–122). Thousand Oaks, CA: Sage Publications.

DuBois, W.E.B. (1903). *The souls of black folk.* Chicago: A. C. McClurg.

Erikson, E. (1968). *Identity: Youth and crisis.* New York: W. W. Norton.

Hoeffel, E. M., Rastogi, S., Kim, M. O., & Shahid, H. (2012). *The Asian population: 2010* (Census 2010 Briefs No. C2010BR-11). Retrieved from www.census.gov/prod/cen2010/briefs/c2010br-11.pdf

Kiang, L., & Luu, J. (2013). Concordance in self and ascribed ethnic labels among Asian American adolescents. *Asian American Journal of Psychology, 4*, 93–99.

Kiang, L., Witkow, M. R., & Champagne, M. C. (2012). Normative changes in ethnic and American identities and links with adjustment among Asian American adolescents. *Developmental Psychology, 49*, 1713–1722.

Kim, S. Y., & Chao, R. K. (2009). Heritage language fluency, ethnic identity, and school effort of immigrant Chinese and Mexico adolescents. *Cultural Diversity and Ethnic Minority Psychology, 15*, 27–37.

Kim-Ju, G. M., & Liem, R. (2003). Ethnic self-awareness as a function of ethnic group status, group composition, and ethnic identity orientation. *Cultural Diversity and Ethnic Minority Psychology, 9*, 289–302.

Liu, J. H., & László, J. (2007). A narrative theory of history and identity: Social identity, social representations, society and the individual. In G. Moloney & I. Walker (Eds.), *Social representations and history* (pp. 85–107). London: Palgrave-Macmillan.

Marcia, J. (1966). Development and validation of ego-identity status. *Journal of Personality and Social Psychology, 3*, 551–558.

Marcia, J. (1980). Identity in adolescence. In J. Adelson (Ed.), *Handbook of adolescent psychology* (pp. 159–187). New York: John Wiley & Sons.

Markus, H., & Kitayama, S. (1991). Culture and the self: Implication for cognition, emotion, and motivation. *Psychological Reviews, 98*, 224–253.

Miller, M. J. (2007). A bilinear multidimensional measurement model of Asian American acculturation and enculturation: Implications for counseling interventions. *Journal of Counseling Psychology, 54*, 118–131.

Mura, D. (1994). A shift in power, a sea change in the arts. In K. Aguilar-San Juan (Ed.), *The state of Asian America: Activism and revolution in the 1990's* (pp. 180–204). Boston: South End Press.

Nishina, A., Bellmore, A., Witkow, M. R., & Nylund-Gibson, K. (2010). Longitudinal consistency of adolescent ethnic identification across varying school ethnic contexts. *Development Psychology, 46*, 1389–1401. doi:10.1037/a0020728

Niyogi, S. (2010). *Crafting identities: Ethnic incorporation of two sub-groups among Asian Indians in the San Francisco Bay area* (Order No. 3404928). Available from ProQuest Dissertations & Theses full text: The Humanities and Social Sciences Collection (518818208). Retrieved from http://search.proquest.com/docview/518818208?accountid-10358.

Oyserman, D., & Sakamoto, I. (1997). Being Asian American: Identity, cultural constructs, and stereotype perception. *Journal of Applied Behavioral Science, 33*, 435–453.

Parham, T. (1989). Cycles of psychological nigrescence. *Counseling Psychologist, 17*, 187–226.

Phinney, J. S. (1989). Stages of ethnic identity in minority group adolescents. *Journal of Early Adolescence, 9*, 34–49.

Phinney, J. S. (1990). Ethnic identity in adolescents and adults: Review of research. *Psychological Bulletin, 108*, 499–514.

Phinney, J. S. (1992). The multigroup ethnic identity measure: A new scale for use with adolescents and youth adults from diverse groups. *Journal of Adolescent Research, 7*, 156–176.

Phinney, J. S., & Alipuria, L. L. (1990). Ethnic identity in college students from four ethnic groups. *Journal of Adolescence, 13*, 171–183.

Phinney, J. S., & Ong, A. D. (2007). Conceptualization and measurement of ethnic identity: Current status and future directions. *Journal of Counseling Psychology, 54*, 271–281.

Rogers, L. O., Zosuls, K. M., Halim, M. L., Ruble, D., Hughes, D., & Fuligni, A. (2012). Meaning making in middle childhood: An exploration of the meaning of ethnic identity. *Cultural Diversity and Ethnic Minority Psychology, 18*, 99–108. doi:10.1037/a0027691

Sodowsky, G. R., Kwan, K. K., & Pannu, R. (1995). Ethnic identity of Asians in the United States: Conceptualization and illustrations. In J. Ponterotto, M. Casas, L. Suzuki, & C. Alexander (Eds.), *Handbook of multicultural counseling* (pp. 123–154). Newbury Park, CA: Sage Publications.

Sue, D. W., & Sue, D. (1990). Issues and concepts in cross-cultural counseling: Racial/cultural identity development. In D. W. Sue & D. Sue (Eds.), *Counseling the culturally different: Theory and practice* (pp. 93–112). New York: John Wiley & Sons.

Suinn, R. M. (2010). Reviewing acculturation and Asian Americans: How acculturation affects health, adjustment, school achievement, and counseling. *Journal of Asian American Psychology, 1*, 5–17.

Tajfel, H. (1981). *Human groups and social categories: Studies in social psychology.* Cambridge, United Kingdom: Cambridge University Press.

Tsai, J. L., Ying, Y. W., & Lee, P. A. (2001). Cultural predictors of self-esteem: A study of Chinese American female and male young adults. *Cultural Diversity and Ethnic Minority Psychology, 7*, 284–297.

Tuason, M. T., Taylor, A., Rollings, L., Harris, T., & Martin, C. (2007). On both sides of the hyphen: Exploring the Filipino-American identity. *Journal of Counseling Psychology, 54*, 362–372.

Whitehead, K. A., Ainsworth, A. T., Wittig, M. A., & Gadino, B. (2009). Implications of ethnic identity exploration and ethnic identity affirmation and belonging for intergroup attitudes among adolescents. *Journal of Research on Adolescence, 19*, 123–135.

Yip, T. (2009). Simultaneously salient Chinese and American identities: An experience sampling study of self-complexity, context, and positive mood among Chinese young adults. *Cultural Diversity and Ethnic Minority Psychology, 15*, 285–294. doi:10.1037/a0013937

Yoo, H. C., & Lee, R. M. (2005). Ethnic identity and approach-type coping as moderators of the racial discrimination/well-being relation in Asian Americans. *Journal of Counseling Psychology, 52*, 497–506.

Chapter Five

Indigenous Peoples and Identity in the 21st Century: Remembering, Reclaiming, and Regenerating

Sandy Grande, Timothy San Pedro, and Sweeney Windchief

The broad aim of this chapter is to build deeper understanding about what it means to be Indigenous in both historic and contemporary contexts. For reasons of brevity, we focus on Indigenous peoples of Native North America and particularly the United States. Within this context, we map the production of Indigenous identity in a manner that accounts for the material effects of "forced incorporation"[1]—namely, the current system of federal recognition and tribal citizenship—and for spaces of Indigenous resistance and resilience, both of which have significant implications for identity development.

For the purposes of this chapter, "Indigenous peoples" refers to those societies that "exercised powers of self-governance prior to colonization by and, incorporation into, the modern nation state" (Grande & Nichols, in press). Such peoples are distinct from other racialized, ethnic, or minoritized[2] groups in that the primary issue framing Indigenous–settler state relations is "not racist exclusion ... but forced incorporation into the state" (Rifkin, 2011, p. 342). Whereas histories of "exclusion" shared by African Americans, Latinos, Asian Americans, and women, among others, have given rise to political projects organized around demands for inclusion, enfranchisement, and the extension

---

[1] As noted by Rifkin (2011), Indigenous peoples and their sovereign nations were absorbed or "incorporated" into the settler state by force.

[2] Burman and Chantler (2005) used the term "minoritized" (as opposed to minority) to highlight that marginalized peoples and communities are not designated as such because of some inhabited trait but rather occupy this social location through sociohistorical processes enacted by the "majority."

of civil rights, Indigenous histories of "forced incorporation" render a very different political project, one defined by sovereignty and self-determination.

Indigenous sovereignty or the right for tribes to make their own laws and be governed by them predates the formation of the United States and is recognized through various treaties negotiated with tribes on a "government to government" basis. The unique status of "federally recognized tribes"[3] as "sovereign" but "domestic dependent nations" obligates the U.S. government through general trust responsibilities to not only protect Indigenous rights to self-government, tribal lands, and resources but also to provide necessary services, including the provision of health care. Beyond this basic understanding, however, sovereignty remains a highly contested and complex set of relations that, more than anything, reflects the long history of colonial domination between the United States and Native nations.

Specifically, federal policies and practices of genocide, removal, and forced assimilation and incorporation have created an inconsistent if not arbitrary system by which tribes and their citizens are recognized as "Indian." Consequently, the question of "Who is Indian?" has preoccupied both academic and community forums. Vigorous debate circulates among those who adhere to positivist measures like blood quantum and tribal rolls and others who argue on the basis of language and culture. "Lost in these disputes," noted Lyons (2010),

> is the recognition that Indian identities are constructed; that they do not come from biology, soil, or the whims of a Great Spirit, but from discourse, action, and history; and finally that this thing is not so much a thing at all, but rather a social process. Indian identity is something people do, not what they are. (p. 40)

Thus, he suggests that the central question of Indian identity should not be who is or is not Native American but rather, "What *kinds* of Indian identities are in production during a given historical moment and what is at stake in their making?" (Lyons, 2010, p. 60).

---

[3]Laws surrounding "federal recognition" require American Indians and Alaska Natives to prove that they have continued to exist over time as stable, prima facie peoples and "tribes." Acknowledgment of tribal existence by the Department of the Interior is highly valued as it theoretically guarantees federal protections, services, and benefits. Specifically, "federal recognition exempts a tribe from state and local jurisdiction and laws including laws relating to taxation and gambling, and it sustains the trust relationship between the federal government and the tribes which allows lands to be held in trust for tribes by the U.S. In addition, the tribes qualify for funding and services from the Bureau of Indian Affairs, funding which can be channeled into programs for the benefit of tribal members" (Riley, n.d., p. 4).

Moving discussions of identity beyond a set of inherited or quantifiable traits (something one possesses) and into the realm of mediated experience emphasizes the relational, a constantly negotiated and constructed space defined by and through sociohistorical and political processes (Bird, Lee, & Lopez, 2013; Lyons, 2010; Quijada Cerecer, 2013). This critical shift opens up spaces of resistance, agency, and possibility, extending the question of "Who is Indian?" to include the more politicized query of "Who is asking and for what purpose?" The power to name, reveal, and define one's people (the right to self-determination) is arguably the truest expression of sovereignty.

The purpose of this chapter is, therefore, not to define who is and is not Indian but rather to map the production of Indigenous subjectivity in a manner that accounts for both the fluidity of social processes and the more fixed markers of the "given historical moment" (Lyons, 2010, p. 60). Specifically, we maintain that there are compelling reasons to understand issues of Indigenous identity as defined through the processes of federal recognition as well as the ways in which communities disregard such processes, constructing identity through community-based and relational practices.

We begin by providing a historical context for the emergence of the settler state and its impact on Indigenous peoples. Although countless laws, policies, and treaties serve to govern Indigenous–state relations, we focus on two of the most significant federal policies affecting Indigenous identity: the General Allotment Act (1887) and the Indian Citizenship Act (ICA) of 1924. After discussion of the legacy of "federal recognition" and Indigenous identity, we examine identity as a social construction, embedded in social processes. Finally, we address the myriad ways in which Indigenous communities have sustained identities through "indigenizing projects," such as remembrance, reclamation, and regeneration.

Indigenous Identity and the Settler State

Prior to European invasion, there were no "Indians," only distinctive peoples (for example, Diné, Pequot, Cherokee, and Choctaw) who were later collectivized under the invented construct (Bruyneel, 2007). Thus, as noted by Gone and Trimble (2012), it was the colonial encounter that "ultimately brought the 'American Indian' into existence" (p. 133). Settler colonial policies such as "land appropriation, resources extraction, population control, and coercive assimilation served to forge commonalities in experience, expectation, and outlook among formerly disparate indigenous peoples" (Gone & Trimble,

2012, p. 133). Therein lies the central organizing principle of settler colonialism: "elimination of the natives" (Wolfe, 2006).

Unlike other forms of colonialism, which eventuate a period of decolonization followed by postcolonial forms of imperial control, settler colonialism is marked by historical continuity with no anticipation of decolonization (Strakosch & Macoun, 2012). Because "settlers come to stay—the primary motive for elimination is not race (or religion, ethnicity, grade of civilization etc.), but access to territory" (Wolfe, 2006, p. 388). To achieve this dubious end, the state uses a variety of eliminating strategies: genocide, warfare, forced removal, imposed citizenship, racialization, religious conversion, child abduction, and resocialization, among other assimilative forces (Wolfe, 2006).

To bring into sharper relief how the "logic of elimination" differs from schemas of racial domination, consider Wolfe's (2006) analysis of the ways in which Native and Black peoples have been "racialized in opposing ways that reflect their antithetical roles in the formation of U.S. society" (p. 387). That is, Blacks-as-enslaved peoples augmented settler wealth, they were subject to an expansive taxonomy—the "one-drop rule," whereby any amount of African ancestry made a person "Black" (thus, the more enslaved peoples, the more wealth). Yet, the opposite is true of Indigenous peoples, who inhibited settler wealth by obstructing access to land. As such, a calculus of elimination was devised whereby the more non-Indian blood or ancestry, the less one was identified as Indian. In other words, "one drop" did not an "Indian" make.

Such strategies of elimination were codified through federal policies organized around the perceived humanitarian principle of "kill the Indian, save the man" (Pratt, 1973, p. 261). Arguably among the most pernicious were the Federal Allotment Act (or the Dawes Act) (1887) and the (ICA) (1924).

By the mid-nineteenth century, ownership of private property was (ICA) viewed as the primary agent of "civilization," turning the Indians "from a savage, primitive, tribal way of life to a settled, agrarian, and civilized one" (Royster, 1995). After the Civil War, settler anxieties about racial classification and segregation peaked along with increased desire for land and westward expansion. Indian lands, "though seemingly protected by treaties negotiated in the 1840s and 1850s[,] were increasingly subject to invasion" (Washburn, 1976, pp. 17–18). The Federal Allotment Act (1887) was proposed as the solution to the "Indian problem," permitting the federal government to break up communally held reservation land into individual parcels or allotments. In accordance with the act, individual tribal members (specifically male heads of household determined by the government as eligible) would each receive a parcel of land to farm, with "surplus" lands opened for sale to White settlers. Though primarily viewed as the central mechanism for land dispossession, the Dawes Act also more broadly affected tribal organization, family and kinship structures, gender relations, spiritual practices, and the legal status of individual Indians.

Specifically, although private property was perceived as the gateway for fostering individualism and economic self-interest, reformers also viewed it as a means of disrupting or eliminating tribal kinship and matrilineal systems perceived to undermine the social order (Stremlau, 2005). As noted by Chang (2011), prior to the Dawes Act, tribal membership "allowed for the entry of new members into the community through ways not figured by genetic descent," often absorbing not only new individuals but also new bands and villages (p. 113). Although kinship systems varied among tribes, it was typical for Native families to live in multiracial, intertribal, multigenerational, multifamily (and often matrilineal) households. One of the express aims of the Dawes Act was to "fracture these extended indigenous families into male-dominated, nuclear families, modeled after middle-class Anglo-American households" (Stremlau, 2005, p. 265). Moreover, although Dawes did not use blood quantum as the exclusive criterion for tribal membership, it did inhere use of 19th-century racial classification systems, creating segregated rolls that identified (1) Indians by blood,[4] (2) intermarried Whites, and (3) freedmen.[5]

In the final accounting, the impact of Dawes was profound. Specifically, it (1) reduced the aggregate Indian land base from approximately 138 million to 48 million acres; (2) legally preempted the sovereign right of Indians to define themselves; (3) introduced the specious notion of blood quantum as a legitimate criterion for defining Indians; (4) institutionalized divisions between full-bloods and mixed-blood, Black and White Indians; and (5) disrupted gender and kinship structures of tribal organization.

Nevertheless, Dawes did not prove to be the "final solution" to the Indian problem as anticipated. So in 1924, the federal government passed the ICA as a cleanup measure, extending citizenship to all Indians not previously designated and born within the territorial United States. Theoretically, the ICA represents a dual citizenship wherein Native peoples do not lose civil rights because of their status as tribal members, and individual tribal members are not denied tribal rights because of their American citizenship (Deloria &

---

[4] Individuals were also forced to choose only one tribal affiliation, even in instances where one had direct lineage to more than one tribe.

[5] The creation of racially segregated tribal rolls and denial of allotments to black freedmen situates allotment "at the center of present-day political and legal struggles over the question of the citizenship of people of African descent in American Indian nations" (Chang, 2011, p. 110).

Lytle, 1984). However, because Indigenous peoples did not generally desire citizenship (further incorporation into the state), the ICA was viewed more as a violation of sovereignty than as an emancipatory act, creating a class of "ambivalent Americans" who existed neither fully inside nor fully outside the political, legal, and cultural boundaries of the United States (Bruyneel, 2004).

As a result of and despite the struggles, Indigenous peoples remain. According to the last census, 4 million self-identified as Native American, comprising 1.4 percent of the population.[6] There are 566 tribal entities currently recognized and eligible for funding and services by the Bureau of Indian Affairs. Compared with the non-Hispanic White population, Native peoples are younger (median age of 31.9 years as compared with 40.1 years), more economically distressed (median income of $31,600, about $17,000 less), and less educated (about 75 percent are high school graduates versus 90 percent) (Gone, 2004; U.S. Census Bureau, 2007). Moreover, according to recent reports from the U.S. Department of Health and Human Services, there are significant health disparities between American Indian/Alaska Natives (AIAN) and other racial–ethnic groups. Specifically, diabetes, suicide, drug and alcohol abuse, heart disease, tuberculosis, and posttraumatic stress, among other health disorders, all occur at higher rates within the AIAN population compared with other groups, contributing to overall poorer health and lower life expectancy (Barnes, Powell-Griner, & Adams, 2005).

But what do these statistics really tell us? Erased by and within these numbers is their historical production, which is to say the ways in which they serve as containers for dominant understandings of Indigenous peoples as defined by settler colonialism. As noted by Gone and Trimble (2012), it is "historical fact" that the onset of community epidemics emerged after the relegation of Indigenous peoples to "reservation captivity" and lives of "forced sedentarization" (p. 151). This, then, begs the question, who or what is served by these statistics? And how are Native communities adversely affected when definitions of health and well-being are tied to settler narratives?

---

[6]The U.S. Census relies on a process of self-identification and does not require proof of tribal citizenship. Therefore, there is often a discrepancy between Census data and that generated by the Bureau of Indian Affairs. Consider, for example, that although 4 million people self-identified as American Indians/Alaska Native (AIAN) in the last U.S. Census (U.S. Census Bureau, 2007), only 1.9 million AIAN peoples met federal eligibility requirements to receive services through the Bureau of Indian affairs. The discrepancy can be explained, in part, by the continued existence of nonfederally recognized peoples, including "over 200 state-recognized tribes; Black-Indian descendants of mixed-blood freedmen who were historically disenfranchised by their own (formerly slave-holding) tribal communities; and, the multitribal offspring of tribal citizens who would not qualify for enrollment in any single tribe due to blood quantum requirements" (Gone, 2004, p. 11). The rest can likely be attributed to the problematics of self-identification and prevalence of ethnic fraud.

In the following sections, we shift the discussion away from what material or essentialist traits define Indianness and toward how Indigeneity is enacted. As G. Smith (2003) notes, Indigenous identities must be "won on at least two broad fronts; a confrontation with the colonizer and a confrontation with 'ourselves'" (p. 2). Whereas the first section of the chapter accounted for some of the major confrontations with the colonizer, the following section undertakes confrontation with self.

Indigenous Identity: The Importance of Relationship and the Co-Construction of Consciousness

As previously discussed, land is central to Indigenous identity, and the (sovereign) struggle to retain land is deeply tied to the struggle to retain identity; for Indigenous peoples, "where they are, *is* who they are" (Wolfe, 2006, p. 388). The centrality of place, however, does not mean that Indigenous identity is geographically determined, fixed in time and space. Lumbee scholar Bryan Brayboy's (2005a) metaphor of an anchor helps our understanding of the relationship between peoples and land, identity and culture: Identity is

> simultaneously fluid and dynamic, and at times—fixed and stable. Like an anchor in the ocean it is rooted to some place.... The anchor shifts and sways, like culture, with the changing tides, ebbs, and flows of the ocean or the life, contexts and situations of Indigenous peoples. (p. 943)

In other words, the anchor illustrates the "rootedness" of Indigenous identity in place (land) at the same time that it recognizes the fluidity of, and interactions with, its changing environs. What remains essential is relationship: to land, to community, and to being and becoming.

In moving beyond analyses of identity as something one possesses or is assigned, we move to discuss identity as a negotiated, social, and co-constructed process (Bird et al., 2013; Lyons, 2010; Quijada Cerecer, 2013), particularly as undertaken in clinical and educational settings. Keeping the anchor in mind, this does not suggest a wholesale embracing of the excesses of postmodern—where everyone is everything—but rather recognizing the changing tides, ebbs, and flows, the dialogics of identity formation. By necessity, the dialogical process of Indigenous identity formation must be built on a foundation of understanding, of the ongoing impact of settler colonialism, the continued disruption of tribal community life, and the ways that Indigenous peoples have been resilient in preserving cultures, knowledge, language, and systems of governance.

This foundation (the confrontation with the colonizer) is distinct but contingent on confrontations with self. How I see myself, the internal negotiation of identity (San Pedro, 2014), is deeply informed by the external world: How do others see me? In Indigenous contexts, inter- and intrasubject dialogue is the primary means by which relations to self, other, tribe, clan, history, and place are developed, shaping the following questions: How do I see myself in relation to you? How do you see yourself in relation to me? Yet in the typical (Western) clinical and educational settings, conversations tend to be one-sided, with one person asking questions while the other is answering. In such one-sided interactions, only one demand is stated: Tell me who you are in the absence of me. The inherent asymmetries of power raise yet another question: What is at stake (and whose interests are served) in a power dynamic where only one person is asked to reveal him- or herself?

As such, practitioners working with and in Indigenous communities must learn to confront their own values, conceptual frameworks, techniques, and attitudes in a way that aligns with the community they are serving. Without this level of self-confrontation, "therapeutic" practices may actually prove harmful to Indigenous peoples (Gone, 2004). On this issue, Gone (2004) writes, quite pointedly:

> It remains exceedingly difficult for us to concede ... that our most prevalent therapeutic technologies and techniques may actually harbor risk in the form of cultural displacement and assimilation.... And yet, given the cultural origins of most conventional clinical practices—grounded in and emerging from the "Western" traditions of individualism, dualism, and secular modernity—is it really so difficult to imagine that ... clinicians are, in several quite crucial respects, subtly and inadvertently prescribing Western selves (or, more accurately, subjectivities) through their therapeutic ministrations to their distressed Indian "clients"? (p. 14)

Given what is at stake, it is critical that practitioners work beyond self-awareness, to confrontation; examining and challenging their own assumptions about the relationship between culture and (mental) health, assessing beyond traditional models of well-being to include the views of the community with which they are working. Such a model requires practitioners to (1) learn from and with whom they are working, (2) connect the trajectory of past occurrences to current situations, and (3) incorporate local knowledge and cultures as important frames of reference. Together, such practices help to engage, build, and sustain relationships, which are "at the heart of what it means to be Indigenous" (S. Wilson, 2008).

Toward this end, San Pedro (2013) suggested the *dialogic spiral* as a tool for developing effective social relations through listening to and learning from others:

> The *dialogic spiral* is the [social] construction of a conversation between two or more people whereby the process of listening and speaking co-creates an area of trust between speakers—the space between. In this *between space,* the speaker's discourse reveals vulnerabilities and feelings [and identities].... If constructive, this dialogic spiral moves back and forth, while it also advances forward/upward by expanding prior understandings of listening and speaking. (pp. 117–118)

The spiral is, thus, grounded in relationship with participants giving back to the conversation, co-constructing social relations from shared ideas and stories. Insofar as it requires co-learning (that is, telling stories as well as hearing stories as opposed to only one person sharing stories), the dialogic spiral asks both sides to take risks, to be vulnerable, and to develop trust and understanding. It is this new level of mutuality that spirals the relationship forward and upward.

Consider, for example, the following exchange that took place among Indigenous students in an urban high school classroom:

> First, Anna asks Nisha what tribes she's from. Nisha replies saying she's full blooded Native American, but half Zuni and half Apache. Anna then lists the five tribes that she's part of. Another student Cree says, "She's a mutt!" Nisha says, "So am I!" Nisha and Anna stand up and give each other a high five. As they sit back down, Cree says, "My great Grandmother had blue eyes. I wish I had blue eyes." Eileen chimes in that she's half Navajo and half Black. Cree says she is too. Eileen tells Cree that if they cut themselves in half and then stitched the Black and Navajo halves back together, they would have two complete people— one full blood African American, the other full blooded Navajo. Anna

then says to the group, "Vince is Mexican and Pima. He looks Mexican though." She then laughs with the girls around her and Vince slumps in his desk a little more.[7] (personal communication, October 12, 2011)

This short exchange not only illustrates the ways in which Indigenous youth process, make sense of, and construct their identities in relation to one another but is also very revealing of the legacy of settler discourses: of blood; of whole, half, and mixed; and ultimately of Whiteness as desirable. While it is crucially important to listen to and validate the voices of students like Nisha, Anna, Cree, Eileen, and Vince as they are "storying" their identities (Kinloch & San Pedro, 2014), it is just as important to coax a dialogue that helps to push, guide, and educate them about the broader context in which they are situated. The hope is that the emergent dialogue would not only disrupt and complicate their perceptions of themselves as "mutts," "half," and "full blooded" Indians but also bring forth a consciousness of themselves as whole (and sovereign) peoples, deeply connected to history and defined by agency, resistance, and survivance.[8]

When work is grounded in dialogue—in the words, emotions, and understandings of those we are working with as well as our own words, emotions, and understandings—the conversation and experience can be powerful. In this sense, telling, listening to, and sharing stories can be powerful healing acts, particularly when practitioners share their own stories and speak with knowledge and understanding about the communities in which they work. In other words, the dialogic spiral grows when individuals take risks and develop trust and when participants are aware and conscious of the systemic oppression that works to invalidate, ignore, and silence stories.

This level of awareness or self-confrontation requires not only a solid foundation of historical knowledge but also a critical consciousness of how this history structures contemporary contexts. It requires an ability to see and work with Native peoples beyond the familiarized frame of "tragic victimry" and support efforts of resistance and reclamation. The following section focuses on Indigenous families and communities as principal sites where such efforts unfold.

---

[7] This story came from San Pedro's (2013) dissertation research, a three-year, longitudinal ethnography in an urban high school classroom in the Southwest United States.

[8] The term *survivance* was developed by Annishinaabe scholar Gerald Vizenor to describe an Indigenous state of being beyond mere survival. He writes, "survivance ... is more than survival, more than endurance or mere response.... [It] is an active presence ... an active repudiation of dominance, tragedy, and victimry" (Vizenor, 1999, p. 15).

Reclaiming Indigeneity through Remembrance, Regeneration, and Reclamation

For Indigenous peoples, identity is as much a matter of responsibility as it is genetics. That is, traditionally, membership in Native nations came not only through birth, marriage, and formal adoption, but also through kinship and social relations. These expanded forms of membership highlight the ways in which Indigenous identity is relational—not only influenced one's own internal understanding of who one is but also by the Indigenous community to which one belongs.

Despite the impact of the Dawes Act, extended family structures persist in most Indigenous communities, serving as just one example of how complex systems of relationality—ways of being-through-relationship—continue to be a distinctive feature of Indigenous identity formation (McGoldrick, Giordano, & Garcia-Preto, 2005; Red Horse, 1997). As Red Horse (1997) explained, "the extended kin system ... commonly referred to as the extended family ... includes vertical and horizontal dimensions. ... Some households ... may have three generations living in them [with] neighboring households of cousins, aunts, and uncles," comprising equally important family units with whom "intense daily contact occurs" (p. 244).

Gatherings to commemorate births, deaths, weddings, and holidays as well as more traditional celebrations and ceremonies such as potlatches and feast days are common places for extended families and community members to build and honor relationships. Such gatherings are so integral to sustaining identity that when tribal members live away from home, they often fear that lack of participation in gatherings will result in losing connection to community and strain membership ties. Yet it is an effect of settler colonialism that many communities remain divided by federal policies of removal and relocation, separated across (imposed) national borders between the United States, Mexico, Canada, and other parts of the world. Sustained membership in one's community thus often entails an intentional act of reunion, whereby journeys help reconnect and solidify one's belonging.

Increasingly, reunions have been eased by the development of new technologies, which in turn have given rise to wider and stronger global connections. As a result, communities are beginning to co-construct new realities of what it means to be Indigenous: adopting one another, having children together, redefining and developing Indigenous knowledge together. The increased solidarities raise new questions around what it means to be a good relative and a good envoy of one's family and community in other, particularly global Indigenous spaces. Membership in the global Indigenous community means not only connecting with other Indigenous peoples around the world but also supporting them in their struggles and celebrations and using their collective power and wisdom to sustain alternative ways of being that are not defined by capitalist visions of the good life.

Thus, to support identity development within Indigenous communities, practitioners must understand complex systems of community and relationship. This work may counter norms and practices taught in professional training and thus necessitate "confrontations with self" regarding practices that may either explicitly or inadvertently uphold the traditional nuclear family as the norm while they pathologize other family systems. As part of this process, practitioners must understand not only community stories of struggle and success but also the way individuals understand these stories. In other words, it is important for practitioners to recenter their work in the spaces, places, and people with which they work.

Toward this end, Ball and Janyst (2008) wrote about the importance of working with communities in "a good way." They called for practitioners to "demonstrate new forms of engagement that restore power to Indigenous people in their dealings with mainstream institutions and individuals of the dominant culture," recognizing their right to make decisions regarding their children and families and to "control the flow of information" (pp. 34–35). "Nothing about us without us" is a common phrase among communities working to define such an ethic of partnership, guided by the advice of elders who appeal that work be conducted "in a good way" (p. 35).

The recognition and involvement of community in co-constructing notions of health and wellness require various acts of intentionality: to remember, to reclaim, and to regenerate. In her book *Decolonizing Methodologies: Research and Indigenous Peoples,* Maori scholar Linda Smith (1999) discussed the necessity of Indigenous peoples taking back the control of the collective Indigenous future, delineating 25 indigenizing projects that are currently under way within Native communities, including claiming, storytelling, remembering, intervening, revitalizing, connecting, representing, envisioning, reframing, restoring, protecting, sharing, and naming. Although each project has a distinctive aim, as a collective they serve to challenge Western norms and center Indigenous values.

One of the main methods for recentering Indigenous values is the telling and teaching of story. Storytelling and the associated responsibility that comes with it are instrumental in navigating historically oppressive spaces. As noted by Brayboy (2005b), stories and storytelling are the mediums in which knowledge about communities and their processes are expressed, serving as "roadmaps . . . and reminders of our individual responsibilities to the survival of our communities" (p. 427). As such, we build on the work of L. T. Smith (1999) to expand on three of the "indigenizing projects" that entail story: *remembrance,* looking back into one's community history; *reclamation,* taking back spaces, places, and perspectives; and *regeneration,* moving forward as contemporary peoples while sustaining traditional values.

Remembrance

Traditional knowledge and the lessons it embodies persist, not because they are written down, but because they are held, shared, and remembered collectively by communities. Such knowledge is embedded in ways of being and passed on through story (Barnhardt, 2005). Within Indigenous communities, storytellers are carefully chosen and cultivated, explicitly taught how to share the stories that give their people direction. Stories serve to contextualize the learner or listener and are told and retold multiple times over the course of one's life at particularly relevant moments. Although this may be seen as repetitive and monotonous, in the context of Indigenous remembering, stories are shared when we need to hear them. Their lessons are intended to bring attention to one's blind spots and thus come with the expectation that they will be contemplated and applied to one's life.

When and if appropriate, practitioners can build on the power of story by working it into their own practices. In so doing, it is important to understand that stories are typically told in a way that does not judge the listener but rather are accepted with "unconditional positive regard" (Rogers, 1957) while at the same time communicating care and concern for the individual to live better, in a good way.

Regeneration

Regeneration is the act of maintaining Indigenous philosophies—ways of knowing, being, and doing through sustaining the cultural values and shared experiences that make communities unique. It is imperative, in this definition of regeneration, to maintain *cultural integrity* (Deyhle, 1995; Modiano, 2001; Tierney, 1999), understood as sustaining culturally distinct principles in the development and growth of a cohesive collection of people (Garcia & Shirley, 2012; Paris, 2012). Examples of regeneration include learning to speak one's Native language, recognizing sacred places, and understanding the Indigenous historical perspective.[9] Regeneration is the process of exercising traditional Indigenous values and applying them to contemporaneous environments; for example, bringing Indigenous languages into contemporary usage includes the development of new words that were not previously in the language, to serve the purpose of utility. Regeneration also includes recognizing new places of collective cultural importance and thinking critically about what Indigenous peoples are taught as a result of formal education. At the core, regeneration is the application of Indigenous philosophies applied to various environments and life situations.

Reclamation

Reclamation is the act of taking back not just in the literal sense but in a way that (re)connects Indigenous peoples to space, place, and philosophy. For example, Indigenous languages are place based, often explaining the significance of specific sites and locations to the community. Insofar as settler colonialism "destroys to replace" (Wolfe, 2006, p. 388), the names of many places and peoples were replaced with colonial terms. Reclamation thus can take the form of restoring original (Indigenous) names (L. T. Smith, 1999). Some examples include Native nations that have reclaimed their own names for themselves: Ho-Chunk instead of Winnebago; Diné instead of Navajo.

Reclaiming can also take the form of acknowledging places that fall outside the boundaries of current reservation lands. For instance, as a result of removal and assimilation-era policies, many peoples have had to (re)construct "home" in places that are not their traditional territories. In the period of Indian removal (approximately 1830–1880s), eastern peoples were forcibly moved westward, away from their homelands to what was designated as "Indian Territory" (the current states of Oklahoma and parts of Kansas). Over the centuries, the removed tribes have (re)cultivated and reclaimed their collective identities by (re)making homes in new territories. Similarly, as a result of termination-era (1950s–1960s) policies,[10] such as the "voluntary relocation programs," thousands of Indians migrated to designated relocation cities: Chicago, Denver, Los Angeles, San Francisco, San Jose, St. Louis, Cincinnati, Cleveland, and Dallas.

---

[9]For examples of Indigenous reclamation, see Garcia and Shirley (2012); Lomawaima and McCarty (2006); Romero-Little (2010); C. Smith (2005); Battiste (2011); Johnson and Murton (2007); A. C. Wilson (2005); and McCarty, Romero, and Zepeda (2006).

[10]By allocating tribal resources through a single per capita payment to current tribal membership, the goal of termination-era policy was to close tribal rolls and end the protected trust status of all Indian-owned lands. Congress supported the Bureau of Indian Affairs in implementing the relocation program, which assisted Indians moving away from rural communities and reservations to metropolitan areas (Fixico, 1980).

Today these urban centers have burgeoning and active Indigenous communities, remaking and regenerating new formations of Indigeneity.

Acts of remembrance, regeneration, and reclaiming take on great significance as spaces where Indigenous identity is constructed and collective histories are retained and (re)told. Ultimately, Indigenous communities are not defined by reservation borders[11] but refer to all the places where people gather to sustain cultural integrity. In working with communities, one should refrain from making assumptions and work to understand each individual's story regarding his or her relationship to place and culture. By encouraging people to examine their own connections, to revisit stories and histories, they learn to "walk with" rather than over.

Concluding Thoughts

In this chapter, we aimed to recenter Indigenous conceptualizations of self, community, and well-being in the history and contemporary experiences of Indigenous peoples. The hope is that those working and walking with Indigenous peoples develop a critical consciousness regarding their own social location and the ways in which it interfaces with community understandings. In so doing, we advocate the use of methodological tools that help to build and co-construct relationships with others, such as the dialogic spiral, which enables stories to be told, heard, and shared.

By reframing identity as something one does, rather than a set of characteristics one embodies, we also affirm an understanding of Indigenous identity as socially constructed. It is in the process of being made and remade in local and global spaces and thus not something that exists in the past or forever lost. While refocusing the shift toward the deliberate actions of survivance in Indigenous communities, we also validate Indigenous voices and ideas as legitimate sources of knowledge, shared through stories as well as acts of trust and vulnerability. As the population of Indigenous peoples continues to expand in the 21st-century United States, it will become increasingly important for educational and health practitioners to develop the necessary competencies to provide culturally appropriate services to Native American peoples and their communities (Gone, 2004). Toward this end, it is important that we learn to walk with each other "in a good way."

---

[11]"Borders" pertains to Canadian reserves, Alaska Native corporations, and U.S. reservations, pueblos, and rancherías.

References

Ball, J., & Janyst, P. (2008). Enacting research ethics in partnerships with indigenous communities in Canada: "Do it in a good way." *Journal of Empirical Research on Human Research Ethics: An International Journal, 3*(2), 33–51.

Barnes, P. M., Powell-Griner, E., & Adams, P. F. (2005). *Health characteristics of the American Indian and Alaska Native adult population, United States, 1999–2003*. Atlanta: U.S. Department of Health and Human Services, Centers for Disease Control and Prevention, National Center for Health Statistics.

Barnhardt, R. (2005). Indigenous knowledge systems and Alaska Native ways of knowing. *Anthropology & Education Quarterly, 36,* 8–32.

Battiste, M. (2011). *Reclaiming indigenous voice and vision*. Vancouver, British Columbia, Canada: UBC Press.

Bird, C. P., Lee, T. S, & Lopez, N. (2013). Leadership and accountability in American Indian education: Voices from New Mexico. *American Journal of Education, 119,* 539–564.

Brayboy, B. (2005a). Toward a tribal critical race theory in education. *Urban Review, 37,* 425–446.

Brayboy, B. (2005b). Transformational resistance and social justice: American Indians in Ivy League universities. *Anthropology & Education Quarterly, 36,* 193–211.

Bruyneel, K. (2004). Challenging American boundaries: Indigenous people and the "gift" of U.S. citizenship. *Studies in American Political Development, 18,* 30–43.

Bruyneel, K. (2007). *The third space of sovereignty: The postcolonial politics of U.S.–indigenous relations*. Minneapolis: University of Minnesota Press.

Burman, E., & Chantler, K. (2005). Domestic violence and minoritisation: Legal and policy barriers facing minoritized women leaving violent relationships. *International Journal of Law and Psychiatry, 28,* 59–74.

Chang, D. A. (2011). Enclosures of land and sovereignty: The allotment of American Indian lands. *Radical History Review, 109,* 108–119.

Deloria, V., & Lytle, C. M. (1984). *The nations within: The past and future of American Indian sovereignty*. Austin: University of Texas Press.

Deyhle, D. (1995). Navajo youth and Anglo racism: Cultural integrity and resistance. *Harvard Educational Review, 65,* 403–445.

Fixico, D. L. (1980). *Termination and relocation* (Doctoral dissertation). University of Oklahoma, Norman.

Garcia, J., & Shirley, V. (2012). Performing decolonization: Lessons learned from Indigenous youth, teachers and leaders' engagement with critical Indigenous pedagogy. *Journal of Curriculum Theorizing, 28,* 76–91.

General Allotment Act of 1887 (or Dawes Act), 24 Stat. 388, ch. 119, 25 USCA 331 (1887).

Gone, J. P. (2004). Mental health services for Native Americans in the 21st century United States. *Professional Psychology: Research and Practice, 35,* 10–18.

Gone, J. P., & Trimble, J. E. (2012). American Indian and Alaska Native mental health: Diverse perspectives on enduring disparities. *Annual Review of Clinical Psychology, 8*, 131–160.

Grande, S., & Nichols, R. (in press). Indigenous political thought. In M. Gibbons (Ed.), *The encyclopedia of political thought*. New York: John Wiley & Sons.

Indian Citizenship Act of 1924, 43 Stat. 253, (1926), 8 U.S.C. §3 (1924).

Johnson, J. T., & Murton, B. (2007). Re/placing native science: Indigenous voices in contemporary constructions of nature. *Geographical Research, 45*, 121–129.

Kinloch, V., & San Pedro, T. (2014). The space between listening and story-ing: Foundations for projects in humanization. In D. Paris & M. Winn (Eds.), *Humanizing research: Decolonizing qualitative inquiry with youth and communities* (pp. 21–42). Thousand Oaks, CA: Sage Publications.

Lomawaima, K. T., & McCarty, T. (2006). *"To remain an Indian": Lessons in democracy from a century of Native American education*. New York: Teachers College Press.

Lyons, S. R. (2010). *X-marks: Native signatures of assent*. Minneapolis: University of Minnesota Press.

McCarty, T. L., Romero, M. E., & Zepeda, O. (2006). Reclaiming the gift: Indigenous youth counter-narratives on native language loss and revitalization. *American Indian Quarterly, 30*, 28–48.

McGoldrick, M., Giordano, J., & Garcia-Preto, N. (Eds.). (2005). *Ethnicity and family therapy*. New York: Guilford Press.

Modiano, M. (2001). Linguistic imperialism, cultural integrity, and EIL. *ELT Journal, 55*, 339–347.

Paris, D. (2012). Culturally sustaining pedagogy: A needed change in stance, terminology, and practice. *Educational Researcher, 41*, 93–97.

Pratt, R. (1973). The advantages of mingling Indians with Whites. In F. P. Prucha (Comp.), *Americanizing the American Indians: Writings by the "friends of the Indian," 1880–1900* (pp. 260–271). Cambridge, MA: Harvard University Press.

Quijada Cerecer, P. (2013). The policing of native bodies and minds: Perspectives on schooling from American Indian youth. *American Journal of Education, 119*, 591–616.

Red Horse, J. (1997). Traditional American Indian family systems. *Families, Systems, & Health, 15*, 243–250.

Rifkin, M. (2011). Settler states of feeling: National belonging and the erasure of Native American presence. In C. F. Levander & R. S. Levine (Eds.), *A companion to American literary studies* (pp. 342–355). Malden, MA: Wiley-Blackwell.

Riley, L. (n.d.). *Federal recognition for Indian tribes*. University of Arizona, Native Net. Retrieved from http://www.uanativenet.com/sites/default/files/Federal%20Recognition_0.pdf

Rogers, C. R. (1957). The necessary and sufficient conditions of therapeutic personality change. *Journal of Consulting Psychology, 21*, 95–103.

Romero-Little, M. E. (2010). Best practices for Native American language learners. In G. Li & P. A. Edwards (Eds.), *Best practices in ELL instruction* (pp. 273–298). New York: Guilford Press.

Royster, J. (1995). The legacy of allotment. *Arizona State Law Journal, 27,* 1–78.

San Pedro, T. (2013). *Understanding youth cultures, stories, and resistances in the urban Southwest: Innovations and implications of a Native American literature classroom.* Available from ProQuest Dissertations and Theses database (UMI No. 3558673)

San Pedro, T. (2014). Internal and environmental safety zones: Navigating expansions and contractions of identity between indigenous and colonial paradigms, pedagogies and classrooms. *Journal of American Indian Education, 53*(3).

Smith, C. (2005). Decolonising the museum: The National Museum of the American Indian in Washington, DC. *Antiquity, 79,* 424–439.

Smith, G. (2003). *Indigenous struggles for the transformation of education and schooling.* Retrieved from http://ankn.uaf.edu/curriculum/Articles/GrahamSmith/index.html

Smith, L. T. (1999). *Decolonizing methodologies: Research and indigenous peoples.* London: Zed Books.

Strakosch, E., & Macoun, A. (2012). The vanishing endpoint of settler colonialism. *Arena Journal, 37/38,* 40–62.

Stremlau, R. (2005). "To domesticate and civilize wild Indians": Allotment and the campaign to reform Indian families, 1875–1887. *Journal of Family History, 30,* 265–286.

Tierney, W. G. (1999). Models of minority college-going and retention: Cultural integrity versus cultural suicide. *Journal of Negro Education, 68,* 80–91.

U.S. Census Bureau. (2007, May). *The American community—American Indians and Alaska Natives: 2004* (American Community Survey Reports, ACS-07). Retrieved from https://www.census.gov/prod/2007pubs/acs-07.pdf

Vizenor, G. R. (1999). *Manifest manners: Narratives on postindian survivance.* Lincoln: University of Nebraska Press.

Washburn, W. E. (1976). The historical context of American Indian legal problems. *Law and Contemporary Problems, 40,* 12–24.

Wilson, A. C. (2005). Reclaiming our humanity: Decolonization and the recovery of Indigenous knowledge. In P. French & J. Short (Eds.), *War and border crossings: Ethics when cultures clash* (pp. 255–263). Lanham, MD: Rowman & Littlefield.

Wilson, S. (2008). *Research is ceremony: Indigenous research methods.* Black Point, Nova Scotia, Canada: Fernwood.

Wolfe, P. (2006). Settler colonialism and the elimination of the Native. *Journal of Genocide Research, 8,* 387–409.

Chapter Six

White Racial Identity Development: Looking Back and Considering What Is Ahead

Lisa B. Spanierman

W hiteness often is unnamed, unmarked, and unexamined by White people (Frankenberg, 1993; Sue, 2004). Indeed, White students in my multicultural counseling courses rarely have thought about their Whiteness and its effects on their lives in general and on the therapy process in particular. Conversely, Black scholars such as W.E.B. Du Bois and James Baldwin long have been studying Whiteness to expose White hegemony, disrupt the status quo, and promote racial justice. These scholars and others underscored the importance of studying how institutional racism and White privilege shape the lives of White Americans (for example, Bowser & Hunt, 1981; Katz & Ivey, 1977; Terry, 1970). Following their directives, in this chapter, I focus on theory and research on White racial identity development—the process by which White people develop awareness of themselves as racial beings and come to acknowledge institutional racism and White privilege. Although much of the work on White racial identity development derives from the social sciences, it is important to draw from the broader interdisciplinary literature on critical Whiteness studies to understand the complexities of Whiteness.

Although a comprehensive review of critical Whiteness studies is beyond the scope of this chapter, I present key themes to help situate my discussion of White racial identity. One central theme is that race must be understood as a social construction rather than as a biological reality (Lopez, 1996). A wide range of scholarship has addressed this topic, and an educational film, *Race: The Power of an Illusion* (Adelman, 2003), is a good starting point for students. In short, there is greater genetic variation within a so-called racial group than across these groups. There is no evidence for genetic markers that are common to one racial group and not possessed by another (for a thorough discussion, see Smedley & Smedley, 2005).

In fact, Whiteness came into being in the late 1600s as a tool of White elites to exert social control over labor through both laws and cultural practices (Allen, 1994). Notably, these laws and practices considered people from certain ethnic groups, such as Irish (see Ignatiev, 1995), Italian (see Guglielmo & Salerno, 2003), and Jewish (see Brodkin, 1998), to be non-White on their arrival to the United States. Over time, however, the boundaries of Whiteness widened to include these groups to maintain elite power during times of economic stress. So we must understand that Whiteness is constructed in social, economic, and political contexts. Although Whiteness is socially constructed, it has very real consequences for people's lived experiences (Lipsitz, 1998). For example, the Pew Research Center (Taylor, Kochhar, Fry, Velasco, & Motel, 2011) found that the racial wealth gap in the United States continues to widen such that in 2009 the median wealth of White households was 19 times that of Black households and 15 times more than Hispanic households.

A related theme from critical Whiteness studies links Whiteness with privilege, resources, and dominance. Socialization processes exert strong influences on White people to understand themselves implicitly as humane, civilized, entitled, and superior to people of color (Neville, Worthington, & Spanierman, 2001). Although White individuals experience privilege and dominance differentially on the basis of other social group identities (for example, social class and gender), scholars agree that Whiteness results in material and/or psychological benefits for Whites in the United States (McIntosh, 1988). Indeed, scholars have argued that Whiteness is coveted property with a cash value obtainable only by those who could prove their Whiteness by law (Harris, 1993; Lipsitz, 1998; Moreton-Robinson, 2005). At the same time that Whiteness is property, it also acts as a means of accumulating more property, thus reproducing itself across generations (Lipsitz, 1998). To document benefits beyond the material dating back to 1935, Du Bois wrote of the "public and psychological wage" afforded to White people (Du Bois, 1935/1998). The psychological wage is linked to enhanced social status and access to various aspects of public life. Roediger (1999) explained that the psychological wages of Whiteness provided a form of compensation to working-class Whites for complying with the wishes of White elites. Thus, we cannot separate Whiteness from the many material, psychological, and social privileges that it bestows.

It is within this contextual backdrop of the social construction of a "superior" Whiteness that I review existing White racial identity development models and related empirical research. I address emerging intersectional approaches to the study of White identity, such as the influence of social class status, gender, and sexual orientation.

Models of White Racial Identity Development

In this section, I review three models of White racial identity development. Common across these models is their attention to White individuals' (1) thoughts and feelings about White people, (2) perceptions of people of color, (3) awareness of institutional racism and White privilege, and (4) White supremacist ideology. Development through the stages and statuses of these models is dependent on critical incidents that create cognitive dissonance. The ultimate goals of healthy White identity development consist of increasing one's critical consciousness of racial issues, exercising greater complexity and flexibility regarding racial issues, and abandoning race-based entitlement (Helms, 1995).

Rita Hardiman's White Identity Development Process Model

Drawing from scholarship on sexual identity development and racial identity development among people of color (for example, Cross, 1971), Hardiman (1982) analyzed autobiographies of six White antiracist authors. She examined their worldviews, dissonance events that triggered change, and the underlying motivation for such change. She was concerned with how these White individuals developed a White identity in which racial justice became a key feature. Hardiman sought "to understand whether and how Whites could escape from the effects of their racist programming ... [to] contribute to the construction of a new way to be White that was not dependent on the subjugation or denigration of people of color" (Hardiman, 1982, p. 2).

The first two stages of her five-stage developmental model involve naïveté and acceptance of the status quo. Hardiman referred to stage 1 as *lack of social consciousness* of social norms governing appropriate attitudes and behaviors surrounding race and racial interactions. Hardiman explained that White children in this stage are curious about race and learn how they are expected to act through family, the media, school, and other avenues. Subsequently, this socialization process leads to stage 2, *acceptance*. It is the period in which children are inculcated to the norms of dominant White culture, learning and internalizing beliefs and actions consistent with White supremacist ideology, such as viewing Whites as superior and normal. Whites in this stage generally ignore racial issues and do not realize that "they have been programmed to accept their worldview ... [which] seems natural" (Hardiman, 1982, p. 171). Whites can (and often do) remain in this stage throughout their lives.

Through a series of contradictions that result in dissonance, some White individuals might progress to stage 3, *resistance,* where they acknowledge the existence of racism in the United States and reject the socialized messages that they once passively accepted. Hardiman (1982) explained that resistance "represents a dramatic paradigm shift ... to an ideology that names the dominant group ... as the source of racial problems" (p. 183). Race becomes increasingly salient during resistance, and individuals become aware not only that they are racial beings but also that they have perpetrated racism and benefited unfairly from White privilege. Consequently, White individuals might experience difficult emotional reactions, such as guilt and anger regarding their participation in a racist system. As Whites abandon their racist beliefs, they might also reject their Whiteness, which could results in feelings of grief, loss, and isolation. I have observed this during my teaching. For example, numerous White students reported loss of longtime childhood friendships when they went home for the holidays espousing their new awareness of racial oppression and White privilege; they have shared similar stories of disconnection with family members in response to shifting awareness and values.

The last two stages are linked to resolution of the above-mentioned emotional conflicts. Stage 4, *redefinition,* involves an introspective time when individuals explore what it means to be White. This stage is characterized by an appreciation of differences coupled with a critical consciousness of structural and cultural racism. White individuals might experience empathy for other Whites who remain in passive acceptance of the status quo and desire to assist them toward this stage. The aim of redefinition is to develop a positive sense of White identity without feeling superior to other racial groups. Finally, *internalization* refers to stage 5, in which White individuals integrate their newly established White identity into their overall identity. Whites in this stage will engage in social justice behaviors to transform society. Although the model has not garnered much empirical support, White students resonate with Hardiman's (1982) stages. In a previous review, my coauthor and I recommended that we reinvigorate the model through qualitative research that examines the stages in the contemporary moment (Spanierman & Soble, 2010).

Janet Helms's Model of White Racial Identity Development

Helms's (1984) model has received the most empirical attention among all White racial identity development models. Helms articulated two processes of identity development: abandonment of one's racism and development of a healthy, nonracist White identity. Although, like Hardiman, her initial conceptualization reflected a linear, developmental process in which Whites increasingly acknowledge institutional racism and White privilege and enhance their sense of responsibility for dismantling racism, later iterations of the model rearticulated stages as statuses, which reflect a more fluid and dynamic approach (Helms, 1990, 1995, 2005). In the revised model, individuals can exhibit more than one status, although one usually is dominant and most often dictates a person's reactions to racial issues via particular cognitive–emotional information processing strategies.

The first phase of the model comprises three statuses that involve becoming aware of societal racism and abandoning a racist identity: *contact, disintegration,* and *reintegration. Contact* has been characterized by denial or lack of awareness of structural racism and White privilege. The information processing strategy is avoidance of racial stimuli, characterized by obliviousness of race and racism combined with a pull-yourself-up-by-your-bootstraps mentality (Helms, 1995; Pack-Brown, 1999). Most often in my teaching, I encounter White students in *contact.* They have not yet considered themselves as having a race and are quite surprised when I introduce White privilege. *Disintegration* involves the development of racial awareness, which can cause anxiety and guilt among White individuals, as they feel forced to choose between loyalty to their own group and the larger moral and humanistic issues that arise in a racist system. Information processing strategies reflect suppression and ambivalence. For example, a White individual may feel conflicted about confronting the racist behavior of a family member while simultaneously fearing rejection or humiliation (Pack-Brown, 1999). In my teaching, I have observed disintegration and subsequent transformation in responses to readings (for example, Peggy McIntosh's [1988] *Unpacking the Invisible Knapsack of Privilege*) and powerful videos, such as *The Color of Fear* (Wah, 1994). In rare cases in my courses, *reintegration* can emerge as a way to manage the emotions elicited by *disintegration* and is characterized by identification and idealization of one's own group as well as anger and intolerance toward people of color. Selective perception and negative out-group distortion reflect information processing strategies.

The second, more sophisticated phase in Helms's model (that is, *pseudoindependence, immersion/emersion*, and *autonomy*) reflects the development of a nonracist, positive White identity. In *pseudoindependence,* an intellectualized approach to racial issues, White individuals might look to people of color to explain racism or express a desire to "help" them. Helms noted that this status often is associated with paternalistic attitudes and liberal guilt. In the updated model, Helms (1990, 1995) added a status (that is, immersion/emersion). *Immersion/emersion* is defined as Whites' search for a deeper understanding of racism and how it has played a role in their lives. People in this status often will identify with other White individuals of similar status, and the goal shifts from "helping" people of color to changing White individuals. Hypervigilance is a key information processing strategy of this status. Finally, *autonomy* is characterized by an ability to let go of one's racial privilege, as well as a firm commitment to antiracism and social advocacy. Information processing strategies reflect flexibility and complexity, whereby White individuals redefine what it means to be White as well as continue to work to promote racial justice.

Helms (1984) argued that racial identity was central to human development and therefore to the therapy process. Empirical findings support this assertion and suggest that White racial identity statuses are associated with perceptions of forming a working alliance with an African American therapist (Burkard, Juarez-Huffaker, & Ajmere, 2003) and preferences for White counselors (Helms & Carter, 1991). Helms described four types of counseling relationships, grounded in racial identity statuses: progressive (counselor exhibits a higher racial identity status than the client), parallel (counselor and client exhibit same status), crossed (counselor and client's worldviews are total opposites), and regressive (client exhibits a higher status than the counselor). Progressive relationships can foster client growth, whereas the other forms of relationship potentially are problematic. For example, in a regressive relationship, a service provider might minimize the effects of racism in clients' lives, when clients themselves accurately attribute the etiology of their concerns to racial oppression. Thus, training White service providers to achieve more sophisticated racial identity statuses is vital.

Ponterotto's Model for Graduate Trainees

Derived from the racial identity theories of Cross (1971) and Helms (1984) and based on his personal experience training hundreds of White students in multicultural counseling, Ponterotto (1988) proposed a four-stage developmental model of White racial identity and consciousness among trainees. He was most concerned with White trainees' level of engagement with multicultural curricula and the impact of such curricula on their racial consciousness. Stage 1, *preexposure*, is characterized by a lack of awareness of race and racism; this is similar to Hardiman's (1982) naïveté stage. White trainees in this stage believe that racism no longer exists in the United States and are oblivious to their own Whiteness. The next stage, *exposure,* begins when White counseling trainees are made aware of societal racism as well as racial disparities within the counseling profession. During this stage, trainees typically experience guilt and anger, as well as uncertainty in conveying this newly discovered information to other White individuals for fear of being ostracized and rejected. I have seen these emotions among White students in my classes; thus, I address emotions of White racial identity in greater depth below. As students grapple with these emotions, they proceed in one of two directions that represent the third stage, *zealot–defensive*. The *zealot* represents those trainees who become passionately involved in multicultural issues and social activism, whereas the *defensive* response reflects anger, skepticism, and withdrawal from multicultural issues. In my experience teaching multicultural issues, defensive students often withdraw from the course and express hostility toward me, the instructor. Finally, stage 4 is labeled *integration* and is characterized by critical awareness of racism, along with respect and appreciation of racial and cultural differences.

Summary and Next Steps

The above-mentioned models share much in common but feature slightly different aspects of White racial identity. Collectively, they suggest that White individuals most often commence with oblivious or naive perspectives on race and racism; they passively accept the status quo. This stance could persist for a lifetime unless White individuals encounter dissonance-inducing events, such as multicultural curricula or meaningful relationships with people of color. Once dissonance ensues, White individuals can retreat further into White supremacy or break out of conditioned patterns to redefine themselves. The latter takes great commitment and appropriate support to deal with the challenges inherent in the process (Kiselica, 1998). Of particular interest are the various emotional responses that accompany development throughout the statuses and stages of White racial identity.

Dealing with Feelings: Emotions of White Racial Identity

Because emotional responses are salient among White individuals with regard to racial issues (Feagin, 2010), I highlight several emotions that are related to the above-mentioned models. Helms (1990) and Hardiman (1982), for example, underscored emotional responses such as guilt, anxiety, and anger in response to dissonance-inducing events. I have witnessed this among White students as they learn about structural racism and White privilege in my courses. Drawing from the White racial identity models as well as writings from antiracist educators (Goodman, 2011; Kivel, 2002), my colleagues and I developed a survey to measure three emotions that are related to White racial identity development: White fear, White guilt, and White empathy (Poteat & Spanierman, 2008; Spanierman & Heppner, 2004; Spanierman, Poteat, Beer, & Armstrong, 2006).

White fear focuses on anxiety and distance from people of color. Our research has linked White fear to lesser openness to diversity, racial awareness, cultural sensitivity, and ethnocultural empathy (Poteat & Spanierman, 2008; Spanierman & Heppner, 2004). White fear also has been associated with less exposure to and fewer friendships with people of color (Spanierman & Heppner, 2004). In my courses, helping White students articulate their irrational fear of people of color has been important to enhance their self-awareness as racial beings. For example, many White women have acknowledged that they clutch their purses or cross the street to avoid men of color. Raising awareness of their irrational fear helps White students to develop more flexible responses to these somewhat automatic thoughts. I suspect that White fear is prevalent among the least sophisticated racial identity statuses and stages (for example, Helms's [1990], contact status). And on the basis of my earlier research, I have found that White fear in combination with low empathy and low White guilt reflects an insensitive and frightened stance (Spanierman et al., 2006) that might be indicative of Helms's (1990) reintegration status.

When considering the dissonance-inducing events in Hardiman's (1982) resistance stage and Helms's (1990) disintegration, White guilt is implicated. It makes sense that White students might feel guilty when learning about unearned racial privilege and the myth of meritocracy. Supporting this notion, White guilt has been correlated positively with multicultural education and racial awareness in several investigations (Spanierman & Heppner, 2004; Spanierman, Poteat, Wang, & Oh, 2008). Moreover, empirical findings indicate that White guilt facilitates cultural competence (Spanierman et al., 2008) and social justice outcomes (Iyer, Leach, & Crosby, 2003).

It is interesting to note, however, that the literature regarding White guilt is mixed. Despite empirical evidence that shows the utility of White guilt in racial identity development, conceptual and anecdotal writings suggest that guilt paralyzes White students in multicultural courses. I have been asked by colleagues, "Do we want to induce guilt in our White students? Won't that be damaging?" When White guilt is coupled with White fear, it may in fact be debilitating. A White female student once approached me privately to share her distress in response to learning about her racial privilege. She thought that people of color could "see" her White privilege as she walked across campus. So, yes, learning about one's unearned privilege may be painful, although certainly not as painful as the daily injustices that people of color experience. With the proper supports, White students are able to grapple with White guilt and move toward a healthier racial identity. In my research, I have found that when White guilt is coupled with empathy for people who are oppressed by racism, guilt tends to be motivating rather than harmful. Clearly, further research is needed to tease apart the various productive and destructive dimensions of White guilt.

Racial empathy for people of color, what I termed *White empathy* in prior research, is yet another emotion relevant to the process of White racial identity development. White empathy has been linked empirically to multicultural education, racial awareness, openness to diversity, and cultural competence (Poteat & Spanierman, 2008; Spanierman & Heppner, 2004; Spanierman et al., 2008). I want to point readers to Feagin's (2010) articulation of three kinds of racial empathy: sympathy, empathy, and autopathy. Feagin suggested that sympathy is not helpful and may be harmful, whereas empathy and autopathy reflect more consistent and developed understandings of what it feels like to be oppressed. I find this work to be very useful for trainees in the helping professions and applicable to White racial identity development models. For example, in *contact* status or *pseudoindependence,* a White individual might experience sympathy for people of color, whereas the higher form of autopathy might reflect *immersion/emersion* and *autonomy*.

Intersectional Approaches to the Study of White Racial Identity

Whiteness is not monolithic, meaning that not all White individuals experience its power and privileges in the same way. Drawing from feminist scholars of color, who developed a theory of intersectionality to emphasize multiple social identities in explaining social inequality (for example, Crenshaw, 1989), I contend that contemporary approaches must incorporate intersecting social group identities to address the complexity of White racial identity. Although there are a number of social identity groups that may intersect with Whiteness, I focus on three that are prevalent in the interdisciplinary literature: gender, social class, and sexual orientation.

Whiteness and Gender

Although it has not addressed racial identity development models explicitly, sociological research has offered insight into what it means to be a White man (for example, Feagin & O'Brien, 2003) versus a White woman (for example, Frankenberg, 1993). Because of the salience of power in men's lives and taking into account masculine gender role socialization, these scholars surmised that White men's experiences of Whiteness might appear different from that of White women. See Spanierman, Beard, and Todd (2012) for a brief review of the literature on the intersection of Whiteness and gender.

Germane to the current discussion of White racial identity development models, Scott and Robinson (2001) developed the key model of White male identity development—one of the only models to my knowledge that addresses intersecting identities explicitly as they pertain to White racial identity. The initial developmental phases entail little self-exploration, whereas higher phases require self-exploration and resolution of some crisis (that is, dissonance events). The authors described their model as circular in nature, and thus movement can occur in multiple directions. Phase 1, *noncontact,* is characterized by ethnocentrism, little knowledge of race, and beliefs in White superiority. Phase 2, *claustrophobic,* is characterized by beliefs of reverse racism, victim blaming, and an overall feeling of being closed in by other groups who are vying for White male power. This phase is particularly relevant in a political context of heightened fear of Mexican immigrants and demographic changes that project that White people soon will be the numerical minority. White men who are *claustrophobic* tend to rely on stereotypes for information about people of color. Recent empirical research by Nolan Cabrera (2012) among White men at two universities revealed the prevalence of their anger when they felt threatened by race-conscious social policies in competitive environments. Moreover, in a related study, interviewees reported feeling "victimized" as a function of being White and male in contexts that valued multiculturalism (Cabrera, 2014). These findings provide keen examples of *claustrophobic* White men.

The third phase, *conscious identity,* develops in response to dissonance-creating incidents. White men who are *conscious* can venture in two possible directions: regress back to being *claustrophobic* or emerge into the *empirical type,* in which they begin to acknowledge the existence and effects of racism, as well as recognize their own White privilege. Similar to Helms's (1990) *pseudoindependence,* this type is characterized by intellectual understanding, whereby men might read about or discuss racial issues. The final phase in the model is referred to as *optimal,* which represents a worldview shift and holistic understanding of racial issues. *Optimal* men value all people, and their struggle for power over people is diminished. These White men use power and privilege in ways that foster equity and redistribution of societal resources. I hope to encourage the next generation of White racial identity scholars to theorize a model that reflects White women's unique experiences.

Whiteness and Sexual Orientation

In addition to intersections with gender, emerging empirical research has addressed the intersection of Whiteness and sexual orientation. Qualitative research, for example, highlights that White gay and lesbian individuals might be more sensitive to other forms of oppression, such as racism and White privilege. For instance, Croteau (1999) disclosed how exploration of his oppressed gay identity was crucial to understanding his White racial identity and privilege. Similarly, among a diverse sample of 18 graduate students, Croteau, Talbot, Lance, and Evans (2002) found that some White gay men highlighted how being oppressed as gay men enhanced their sensitivity toward and ability to form relationships with people of color. Similarly, in a quasi-experimental study, Kleiman, Spanierman, and Smith (in press) examined racial attitudes among gay and straight White men in Canada. Findings suggested that White gay men tended to have more positive racial attitudes, including racial empathy, than their straight counterparts. Of particular note, when White gay men were primed with a news article about a homophobic hate crime, they demonstrated the highest levels of racial empathy.

Whiteness and Social Class

Earlier in this chapter, I equated Whiteness with privilege, dominance, and supremacy. To complicate this notion, I reiterate that all White people do not benefit from white racial privilege in the same way. Working-class White men and women, for example, do not possess the same White privileges as upper-class White people. Sometimes it is difficult to ascertain how unemployed or underemployed White people benefit from any racial privilege at all. I have used Deborah Megivern's (2005) short but powerful autobiographical account as a tool to help students in these cases. Sharing her personal struggle to acknowledge racial privilege as a social work graduate student, she reflected:

Certainly, it felt to me as though my entire life had been defined by deprivation. If there were White privileges to be recognized, I could not see them. In my mind, what on earth good had it done to be White? It had not spared me hunger, frostbite, lice, poor medical care, ridicule, violence, or trauma. (Megivern, 2005, p. 19)

Educating her peers about classism took precedence over her understanding White privilege. Megivern's dissonance-inducing event was an authentic conversation with an African American peer. During this conversation, she realized that as long as she ignored her race-based privilege, she could not foster meaningful connections with peers who experienced racial oppression. I recommend that students read Megivern's narrative. Interested readers might also consult a chapter that my colleagues and I authored on the intersections of Whiteness and social class that (1) addresses how whiteness manifests across various class strata, (2) outlines implications for future research, and (3) makes links to clinical practice (Spanierman, Garriott, & Clark, 2013).

Summary, Implications, and Future Directions

The early models of White racial identity explicate a process of change toward the development of a healthy, nonracist White identity (Hardiman, 1982; Helms, 1984). Most early models suggested that White racial identity was developmental and sequential in nature, although Helms (1995) complicated this notion in several revisions of her theory. These models help explain how White people move from obliviousness to understanding and commitments to racial justice. Drawing from Helms's emphasis on the link between cognitive and affective dimensions of White racial identity, research has begun to examine the emotional responses to race and racism as important features. With notable exception (for example, Scott & Robinson, 2001), few White racial identity development models have addressed explicitly the complexities of intersecting social group identities. With its focus on White male identity development, the key model offers one innovative approach. Future scholarship should address the complexity of White identity by theorizing racial identity development for White women or working-class Whites, for example. In the meantime, White students can consider how their intersecting identities complicate their own White racial identity development. Finally, the best White racial identity development models will continue to be informed by the rich interdisciplinary Whiteness literature that includes sociological research, critical race theory, and labor history to gain the most comprehensive understanding.

References

Adelman, L. (Executive Producer). (2003). *Race: The power of an illusion.* San Francisco: California Newsreel Productions.

Allen, T. W. (1994). *The invention of the white race: Vol. 1. Racial oppression and social control.* London: Verso.

Bowser, B. P., & Hunt, R. G. (1981). *Impacts of racism on white Americans.* Thousand Oaks, CA: Sage Publications.

Brodkin, K. (1998). *How Jews became white folks and what that says about race in America.* New Brunswick, NJ: Rutgers University Press.

Burkard, A. W., Juarez-Huffaker, M., & Ajmere, K. (2003). White racial identity attitudes as a predictor of client perceptions of cross-cultural working alliances. *Journal of Multicultural Counseling and Development, 31,* 226–244.

Cabrera, N. L. (2012). Exposing whiteness in higher education: White male college students minimizing racism, claiming victimization, and recreating white supremacy. *Race Ethnicity and Education, 17,* 30–55.

Cabrera, N. L. (2014). "But I'm oppressed too": White male college students framing racial emotions as facts and recreating racism. *International Journal of Qualitative Studies in Education, 27,* 768–784.

Crenshaw, K. (1989). Demarginalizing the intersection of race and sex: A black feminist critique of antidiscrimination doctrine, feminist theory and antiracist politics. *University of Chicago Legal Forum, 140,* 139–168.

Cross, W. E. (1971, July). The Negro-to-black conversion experience. *Black World,* pp. 13–27.

Croteau, J. M. (1999). One struggle through individualism: Toward an antiracist white racial identity. *Journal of Counseling and Development, 77,* 30–32.

Croteau, J. M., Talbot, D. M., Lance, T. S., & Evans, N. J. (2002). A qualitative study of the interplay between privilege and oppression. *Journal of Multicultural Counseling and Development, 30,* 239–258.

Du Bois, W.E.B. (1998). *Black Reconstruction in the United States, 1860–1880.* New York: Free Press. (Original work published 1935)

Feagin, J. R. (2010). *The white racial frame: Centuries of framing and counter-framing.* New York: Routledge.

Feagin, J. R., & O'Brien, E. (2003). *White men on race: Power, privilege, and the shaping of cultural consciousness.* Boston: Beacon Press.

Frankenberg, R. (1993). *White women, race matters: The social construction of whiteness.* New York: Routledge.

Goodman, D. J. (2011). *Promoting diversity and social justice: Educating people from privileged groups* (2nd ed.). Thousand Oaks, CA: Sage Publications.

Guglielmo, J., & Salerno, S. (2003). *Are Italians white? How race is made in America.* New York: Routledge.

Hardiman, R. (1982). White identity development: A process oriented model for describing the racial consciousness of White Americans. *Dissertation Abstracts International, 43,* 104A.

Harris, C. I. (1993). Whiteness as property. *Harvard Law Review, 106,* 1707–1791.

Helms, J. E. (1984). Toward a theoretical explanation of the effects of race on counseling. *Counseling Psychologist, 17,* 227–252.

Helms, J. E. (Ed.). (1990). *Black and white racial identity development: Theory, research, and practice.* Westport, CT: Greenwood Press.

Helms, J. E. (1995). An update of Helms's white and people of color racial identity models. In J. G. Ponterotto, J. M. Casas, L. A. Suzuki, & C. M. Alexander (Eds.), *Handbook of multicultural counseling* (pp. 181–198). Thousand Oaks, CA: Sage Publications.

Helms, J. E. (2005). Challenging some of the misuses of reliability as reflected in the evaluations of the White Racial Identity Attitudes Scale (WRIAS). In R. T. Carter (Ed.), *Handbook of racial-cultural psychology and counseling: Theory and research* (Vol. 1, pp. 360–390). New York: John Wiley & Sons.

Helms, J. E., & Carter, R. T. (1991). Relationships of white and black racial identity attitudes and demographic similarity to counselor preferences. *Journal of Counseling Psychology, 38,* 446–457.

Ignatiev, N. (1995). *How the Irish became white.* London: Routledge.

Iyer, A., Leach, C. W., & Crosby, F. J. (2003). White guilt and racial compensation: The benefits and limits of self-focus. *Personality and Social Psychology Bulletin, 29,* 117–129.

Katz, J. H., & Ivey, A. (1977). White awareness: The frontier of racism awareness training. *Personnel and Guidance Journal, 55,* 485–489.

Kiselica, M. S. (1998). Preparing Anglos for the challenges and joys of multiculturalism. *Counseling Psychologist, 26,* 5–21.

Kivel, P. (2002). *Uprooting racism: How white people can work for racial justice* (Rev. ed.). Philadelphia: New Society Publishers.

Kleiman, S., Spanierman, L. B., & Smith, N. G. (in press). Translating oppression: The effect of sexual minority status on white men's racial attitudes. *Psychology of Men and Masculinity.*

Lipsitz, G. (1998). *The possessive investment in whiteness: How white people profit from identity politics.* Philadelphia: Temple University Press.

Lopez, I. H. (1996). *White by law: The legal construction of race.* New York: New York University Press.

McIntosh, P. (1988). *White privilege and male privilege: A personal account of coming to see correspondences through work in women's studies* (Working Paper No. 189). Wellesley, MA: Center for Research on Women.

Megivern, D. (2005). Supposed to know better: On accepting privilege. In S. K. Anderson & V. A. Middleton (Eds.), *Explorations in privilege, oppression, and diversity* (pp. 17–23). Pacific Grove, CA: Brooks Cole.

Moreton-Robinson, A. (2005). The house that Jack built: Britishness and white possession. *Australian Critical Race and Whiteness Studies Association Journal, 1*, 21–29.

Neville, H. A., Worthington, R. L., & Spanierman, L. B. (2001). Race, power, and multicultural counseling psychology: Understanding white privilege and color-blind racial attitudes. In J. G. Ponterotto, J. M. Casas, L. A. Suzuki, & C. M. Alexander (Eds.), *Handbook of multicultural counseling* (2nd ed., pp. 257–288). Thousand Oaks, CA: Sage Publications.

Pack-Brown, S. P. (1999). Racism and white counselor training: Influence of white racial identity theory and research. *Journal of Counseling and Development, 77*, 87–92.

Ponterotto, J. G. (1988). Racial consciousness development among white counselor trainees: A stage model. *Journal of Multicultural Counseling and Development, 16*, 146–156.

Poteat, V. P., & Spanierman, L. B. (2008). Further validation of the Psychosocial Costs of Racism to Whites Scale among a sample of employed adults. *Counseling Psychologist, 36*, 871–894.

Roediger, D. R. (1999). *The wages of whiteness: Race and the making of the American working class.* New York: Verso.

Scott, D. A., & Robinson, T. L. (2001). White male identity development: The key model. *Journal of Counseling and Development, 79*, 415–421.

Smedley, A., & Smedley, B. D. (2005). Race as biology is fiction, racism as a social problem is real: Anthropological and historical perspectives on the social construction of race. *American Psychologist, 60*, 16–26.

Spanierman, L. B., Beard, J. C., & Todd, N. R. (2012). White men's fears, white women's tears: Examining gender differences in racial affect types. *Sex Roles, 67*, 174–186.

Spanierman, L. B., Garriott, P. O., & Clark, D. A. (2013). Whiteness and social class: Intersections and implications. In W. M. Liu (Ed.), *The Oxford handbook of social class in counseling* (pp. 394–410). New York: Oxford University Press.

Spanierman, L. B., & Heppner, M. J. (2004). Psychosocial Costs of Racism to Whites Scale (PCRW): Construction and initial validation. *Journal of Counseling Psychology, 51*, 249–262.

Spanierman, L. B., Poteat, V. P., Beer, A. M., & Armstrong, P. I. (2006). Psychosocial costs of racism to whites: Exploring patterns through cluster analysis. *Journal of Counseling Psychology, 53*, 434–441.

Spanierman, L. B., Poteat, V. P., Wang, Y.-F., & Oh, E. (2008). Psychosocial costs of racism to white counselors: Predicting various dimensions of multicultural counseling competence. *Journal of Counseling Psychology, 55*, 75–88.

Spanierman, L. B., & Soble, J. R. (2010). Understanding whiteness: Previous approaches and possible directions in the study of white racial attitudes and identity. In J. G. Ponterotto, J. M. Casas, L. A. Suzuki, & C. M. Alexander (Eds.), *Handbook of multicultural counseling* (3rd ed., pp. 283–299). Thousand Oaks, CA: Sage Publications.

Sue, D. W. (2004). Whiteness and ethnocentric monoculturalism: Making the "invisible" visible. *American Psychologist, 59*, 761–769.

Taylor, P., Kochhar, R., Fry, R., Velasco, G., & Motel, S. (2011). *Wealth gaps rise to record highs between whites, blacks and Hispanics.* Washington, DC: Pew Research Center.

Terry, R. W. (1970). *For whites only.* Grand Rapids, MI: William B. Eerdmans Publishing.

Wah, L. M. (Director). (1994). *The color of fear.* Oakland, CA: Stir Fry Seminars & Productions.

Chapter Seven

Growing Up Multiracial in the United States

Robin Lin Miller and NiCole T. Buchanan

A child whose mother is White and whose father is Black is raised in a predominantly White, middle-class neighborhood. The child has blond, wiry hair, and blue eyes. His classmates and teachers assume he is White and treat him as such. At times, his friends make jokes and negative comments about Blacks that make him angry and unhappy, but he says nothing. One day his father arrives at the school to take him home, and the child overhears kids whispering, wondering what "that Black guy" is doing at their school. The child feels dejected and confused as he hurriedly packs his backpack and tries to leave before anyone else has the chance to make a derogatory comment about his father.

After her parent's divorce, a child whose mother is Native American and whose father is White is raised on an Indian reservation by her mother. Though she is secure in the feeling that she is loved and accepted by her family, television, magazines, and picture books reflect few images of successful, powerful people who are widely recognized as Native American. When asked whether she would prefer to be Native American or White, she says White.

A child grows up in Japan, and although he has a very light café-au-lait complexion and straight hair and strongly resembles his mother, in Japan most people consider him Black, based on the fact that his father is Black rather than Japanese and that his skin is slightly brown compared with a typical Japanese complexion. His family moves to the United States when he is 15. When among his Japanese and Japanese American friends, he is still considered Black. However, most other youths consider him Asian because of his appearance; his preference for speaking Japanese; who he has selected as his friends; and some of his cultural preferences in food, clothing, and leisure activities. His identity shifts when he goes from home to neighborhood to school; he adopts different self-perceptions, attitudes, beliefs, and behaviors in each context.

A newly married Vietnamese woman and mestizo Mexican man are expecting their first child. The couple and their parents have lived in an integrated community for most of their lives. The neighborhood has stayed stable as members of the community have worked side by side to build a good school, a community center, and a sports complex. Both families have embraced the joyful news of the new child. The couple will teach the child the customs of both cultures and the languages of both parents. They want their child to see him- or herself as both Vietnamese and Mexican.

Multiracial status affects children from many different backgrounds and families. Yet there is relatively little written on the impact of multiracial status on children and adolescents and how definitions of race and the experience of growing up in a racist society affect identity development for these youths. How will their understandings of their own and other groups change as they grow older and as society itself changes?

In this chapter, these questions will be explored, and issues related to the development of children's multiracial identity in the United States will be reviewed. The social context of racial definitions and group interactions and their impact on multiracial people will be discussed because multiracial youths achieve racial identities in the context of a complex, stratified social structure. The impact of family and neighborhood factors on the identity development of multiracial youths will also be briefly examined. Finally, we will examine the identity development process for multiracial youths in relation to traditional models of racial identity development.

Empirical and theoretical work often jointly considers features of race and ethnicity, and race is often loosely used to discuss ethnic, cultural, and physical differences among groups. However, the unequal social and economic status among racial groups in the United States can dramatically differentiate issues of ethnicity from those of race. Given that race is historically the most salient means of classifying individuals in the United States, this chapter focuses on racial background. Our discussion is primarily limited to Black, European, Asian, and Native American people. Hispanic/Latino people are not discussed as a racial group given that they may be of any race and are typically considered an ethnic group. Most non-European Hispanics represent a combination of White, Black, and indigenous Indian ancestry.

Race

What race means to multiracial children and how they select a racial reference group reflects a complex process, mirroring the complicated historical and contemporary racial dynamics of the United States. As recently as 1967, laws prohibiting interracial unions were still in force in 16 states until these were declared unconstitutional in the controversial Supreme Court decision *Loving v. Virginia*. The ultimate overturning of antimiscegenation laws at the state level took over 30 years to complete. Alabama was the last to repeal its antimiscegenation law, in 2001. Thus, for any multiracial person born in the United States in 2001 or earlier, the relationship between his or her parents was illegal in some portion of the country. Nevertheless, over the last 50 years, society's view on interracial marriage has shifted toward greater acceptance, and interracial marriages have become increasingly commonplace.

As more children are born of these unions, social scientists have taken greater interest in the identity development of multiracial children. Forming a stable identity is a key developmental task (Erikson, 1968), and forming a racial identity is among the major developmental tasks facing youths of color (Phinney & Rotheram, 1987). An individual's racial identity refers to a sense of belonging to a racial group and to the thinking, perceptions, feelings, and behavior unique to a specific racial group membership (Rotheram & Phinney, 1987). Similar to identities based on gender and sexual orientation, racial identity shapes an individual's experiences in the world. Racial identity development includes acquisition of cognitive, perceptual, attitudinal, and behavioral components and shifts at each developmental stage.

Given that race is a social construction, developing an identity based on race becomes a complicated process for the multiracial child. A child's racial identity may be determined and influenced by his or her own self-label, the family's label, or labels imposed by society and may reflect a consensus-building process across self, family, and society's labels. It is difficult to know which, if any, racial group label will exert a more powerful influence on a child, and it is possible for the child's self-label, the label chosen by the family, and the label imposed by the rest of society to be at odds. Each of the racial communities that compose a child's background may rely on superficial markers of race, such as skin color or facial features, to generate labels. The family may rely on blood ties for generating a label or may reject traditional labels. For example, a child may be considered Asian by a stranger who passes on the street, Sioux by the father's family, and Amerasian by the mother's family, while thinking of him- or herself as Vietnamese Sioux. This lack of consensus has unknown effects on a child's identity development process.

Race Is a Socially Constructed Phenomenon

We use the term *race* to mean a socially defined group for which physical features are the primary marker. To varying degrees, unique cultural and normative traditions are manifest in these socially defined groups. Our conception of race as a social rather than biological phenomenon is grounded in scientific evidence that any two people share 99.9 percent of the same DNA, demonstrating that there is considerable genetic similarity across human beings (Jorde & Wooding, 2004; Schneider et al., 2003). Genes cannot be readily used to discern one race from another (Bolnick et al., 2007; Fujimura, Duster, & Rajagopalan, 2008). Given the lack of any genetic basis for race and concern for the social consequences of racial categories, race should not be conceptualized as genetically based and should instead be understood as a social construct (Omi & Winant, 1986; Smedley & Smedley, 2005).

Government's Role in Defining Race

In the United States, definitions of race have generally functioned to promote segregation between Whites and all others as a means of enhancing the power of Whites (Smedley & Smedley, 2005). Although legal determinations of racial membership have not always used the same criteria for each racial group, in the United States, bloodlines have historically determined ascribed racial identity. The ascribed racial group of a multiracial child has typically been the least valued group according to the rule of *hypodescent*. For example, if a child had one White parent and one parent of color, the child was considered a member of the non-White group. By 1910, laws had been passed establishing the "one-drop rule" as a stringent form of hypodescent. Under these laws, a single drop of Black blood classified someone as Black, regardless of appearance or self-identification. If both parents were non-White but of different races, different rules sometimes applied (for example, if neither was Black, the father's group was ascribed to the child unless the mother was Hawaiian). This precedent was reaffirmed in a 1985 court decision (*Jane Doe v. State of Louisiana,* 1985) in which 1/32 African ancestry was deemed sufficient to keep "colored" (Black) on an individual's birth certificate (Omi & Winant, 1986). However, since 1983, racial self-identification has been legally binding in all states (Dominguez, 1986). That is, the identity a person declares will be legally accepted regardless of bloodlines, even if the particular choice an individual makes is socially contentious (for example, claiming Black identity despite "White" appearance). By contrast, Native American tribes have authority to determine whether individuals are or are not a member, and different tribes may use different minimum blood quantum criteria (Thornton, 1987) despite requirements for government entitlements being set at 8.4 percent.

A complete review of historical trends in racial classification schema is beyond the scope of this chapter; however, the legacy of how racial group memberships were officially determined still affects multiracial children today. Although as of the 2000 Census, individuals can self-identify as multiracial (N. A. Jones & Smith, 2001; Martin, Hamilton, Ventura, Menacker, & Park, 2002), research indicates that some of these legacy conventions still operate to assign children a racial group (Brunsma, 2005) and affect multiracial adults' choices for self-identification (Townsend, Fryberg, Wilkins, & Marcus, 2012).

The historical use of bloodline schema to determine racial group affiliations says as much about the historical definition of Whiteness as it does about minority racial groups. In each instance, Whiteness has been implicitly understood to mean the absence of known African, Asian, or Native American ancestry. Scholars suggest that this intentional exclusion from the majority group serves to prevent individuals with non-White ancestry from attaining the social benefits available to Whites (Fernandez, 1996; Root, 1992). Therefore, because they oppress people of color, definitions of race are a racist legacy (Root, 1992), and it is within this context of exclusion and arbitrary definitions of belonging that multiracial children seek to develop a racial identity.

Categorizing Multiracial People

The 2010 Census captured racial social identification rather than known heredity. The 2000 Census was the first to allow individuals to self-identify as belonging to more than one race, a controversial and hotly debated decision. In 2000, out of the total U.S. population of 281.4 million people, 2.4 percent, or 6.8 million people, considered themselves to be of more than one race (N. A. Jones & Smith, 2001). In the 2010 Census, over 9 million people (roughly 3 percent) identified as two or more races (Humes, Jones, & Ramirez, 2011), although the accuracy of these numbers is debated.

Conversely, some adults have refrained from selecting more than one race on the Census out of concern that doing so would have unintended negative political and financial consequences on minority communities (Elam, 2010). For example, those who select more than one race may be classified as "other" rather than as a racial minority group, thereby reducing the number of people classified as members of that particular minority group. When federal resources are allocated on the basis of proportionate representation in the population, a reduction in the population of a specific racial group because of increasing numbers of multiracially identified people could result in a loss of targeted funds. In combination, the many factors affecting personal self-identification choices suggest that the 2000 and 2010 Census data may not accurately reflect the number of U.S. citizens who could identify as multiracial.

As adults, identifying as more than one race depends on one's choice in self-identity, willingness to disclose racial information, and awareness of racial heritage (Morning, 2000). Relying on knowledge of presumed racial heritage may capture the racial ancestry of only the past one or two generations (Woo, Austin, Williams, & Bennett, 2011). Observed increases in the multiracial population may reflect more favorable attitudes toward interracial relationships, resulting in a dramatic increase in interracial marriages and the birth of multiracial children since the 1960s. In addition, the visibility of multiracial individuals, from U.S. President Barack Obama to performers such as Maya Rudolph, Alicia Keyes, and Norah Jones to athletes such as Hines Ward, Ronda Rousey, Derek Jeter, Jason Kidd, and Apolo Ohno, has created a climate in which multiracial parentage is no longer something to hide. This increasingly favorable social climate may encourage adults to claim multiracial heritage.

The Context of Multiracial Identity Formation

Ecological factors such as economics and residential segregation affect individual growth and development and how multiracial[1] children formulate their racial identity (Brunsma, 2005; Korgen, 2010; R. L. Miller, 1992; Phinney & Rotheram, 1987; Renn, 2003, 2008). For instance, Brunsma (2005) studied the identity that parents assigned to their multiracial children by using a large, nationally representative sample of kindergarteners. Brunsma observed that family socioeconomic status affected labeling of children as mono- or multiracial, such that families of lower socioeconomic status preferred a monoracial label when compared with families of higher socioeconomic status. More recently, Townsend and colleagues observed that working-class people of

---

[1]Although we use the term "multiracial" throughout this chapter, readers should note that a majority of the empirical research and theory on multiracial people focuses on those who are biracial and particularly those who have one White parent. White–other racial combinations have been of special interest to researchers because of the differences in social power and privilege associated with having one White and one non-White parent. We use the term "biracial" when we discuss research in which the sample was composed exclusively of biracial individuals or when the theoretical work was specific to biracial identification.

biracial background were more likely to use monoracial self-labels when compared with middle-class persons (Townsend et al., 2012). Fhagen-Smith (2010) argued that people of higher social class status expect greater personal freedom and choice, which in turn leads them to expect to define themselves as they choose and to have that choice respected and validated by others. Coincidentally, the activists initially advocating for recognition of biracial, as opposed to monoracial, racial identity were reared largely in middle- and upper-class families (DaCosta, 2007).

Multiracial identity formation also occurs within the context of social, cultural, and institutional racism (Root, 1992). To achieve mental health, members of disempowered racial groups must be socialized to actively cope with their racial group culture, mainstream culture, and their status as a member of a devalued group (Boykin & Toms, 1985; Cauce et al., 1992; J. M. Jones, 1988; R. L. Miller & Miller, 1990). J. M. Jones (1988) and Holliday (1985) have suggested that disempowered racial group members must be bicultural to survive. These theories imply that members of subjugated, devalued racial groups must obtain more skills in more domains to adapt to their environment (Holliday, 1985). These theories also suggest that the socialization agenda of parents of color may differ radically from that of racial-majority parents.

A multiracial child may be more vulnerable to racism than a monoracial child because the multiracial child represents an affront to racial divides. Multiracial people must often cope with reactions reflecting the internalized racism of society. For example, some people will tell multiracial children that they must identify with only one group without examining the origins of that idea in terms of racist ideologies about racial purity and the mutual exclusivity of racial groups. Others may insist that a European-looking multiracial child cannot identify with a non-European parent and that the child ought to take advantage of his or her ability to "pass," thereby denying the child's heritage and ignoring attachments to one parent, cousins, grandparents, siblings, and family history. These attitudes also reflect the tension between a strategy or a stance taken to enhance the adjustment of an individual child on mainstream terms and the socialization needs for within-group survival, group pride, and loyalty.

It remains easy to locate stories of rejection and teasing related to mixed-race parentage and of individual struggles to resolve conflicting expectations and stereotypes of racial identities. Teen Zora Howard's recorded performance of the poem "Biracial Hair" (Howard, 2006) has over 650,000 YouTube.com views, suggesting some degree of resonance with her rendering of biracial experiences. Anecdotal stories of discrimination are matched by research evidence of discrimination. A 2009 study demonstrated that mixed-race people are subject to wage discrimination similar to that experienced by Blacks (Fairlie, 2009). Comparing the rates of harassment across race, multiracial men and women reported significantly higher rates of both sexual and racial harassment compared with their White, Asian, or Black peers (Buchanan, Bergman, Bruce, Woods, & Lichty, 2009). Other studies have documented that multiracial people may be more vulnerable to negative perceptions and stereotyping than monoracial peers of color (Sanchez & Bonam, 2009) and that asserting a multiracial identity may not be met with validation by others (Lou, Lalonde, & Wilson, 2011). Exposure to prejudice and social disapproval may discourage adult self-identification as multiracial.

Family and Neighborhood Influences

Family structure and relationships form a critical part of the social environment for children. Interracial marriages may split families, limiting multiracial children's access to part of their family support network (Newsome, 2001). Some psychologists believe that White families may struggle at helping a multiracial child effectively cope with racism because White parents have not had to develop the requisite survival skills to cope with being a person of color in the United States (R. L. Miller & Miller, 1990). White family members may be less adept at detecting and helping children to cope with race-related stressors that are more subtle in nature than overt acts of racism (for example, racial microaggressions).

Neighborhood and community also influence multiracial children. In interviews with multiracial individuals, Funderburg (1994) found that those who were raised in monoracial majority and minority communities experienced pressure to identify with only one side of their racial heritage. Integrated neighborhoods may offer more opportunities for multiracial children to form positive identifications with multiple racial groups. However, an integrated neighborhood alone is not sufficient to promote a positive racial identity and cross-race interaction. Only when there are positive role models of all racial groups and cross-race tensions are low will cross-racial harmony result (N. Miller & Brewer, 1984). The child raised in such a multiracial setting may be more inclined to reject stereotypes of racial groups, perceive racial mixing as normal, and obtain language to describe groups and mixed-race people that is not based on stereotypes. Children in monoracial settings or in disharmonious integrated settings may be more likely to perceive racial segregation as rational and appropriate. For example, Hirschfeld (1995) found that children in integrated neighborhoods were less likely to adopt attitudes about the heritability of race consistent with the one-drop rule than children in predominantly White neighborhoods.

Cohort Influences

The multiracial experience today differs considerably from that of a generation ago, despite similarities across generational cohorts. Root (2004) described three contemporary adult cohorts with distinct life experiences and perceptions of their racial identity. The "exotic" generation was born in the early to mid-1960s, and the "vanguard" generation was born in the late 1960s and early 1970s, after the 1967 *Loving v. Virginia* ruling that antimiscegenation laws were unconstitutional. These generations were commonly subjected to critiques of their racial identity; demands to pick a single racial group with which to identify; invasive questions about and commentary on their distinctive physical appearance (Buchanan & Acevedo, 2004; Rockquemore & Brunsma, 2008); and rejection by members of multiple racial groups, including those to which they belong (double rejection) (Buckley & Carter, 2004; Root, 1996; Shih & Sanchez, 2005). As a result, these generations often experienced *cultural homelessness* (Vivero & Jenkins, 1999). They were seen as belonging nowhere, for example, being deemed too racial to be White among Whites, yet not racial enough among racial minority-group members. Further, the families of these first two cohorts were often rife with tension concerning race. It was not uncommon for members of these generations to grow up knowing that members of either side of their family, and sometimes the entire maternal or paternal side of their families, had disowned their parents as a result of their interracial relationship, which may have furthered their sense of isolation and negative distinctiveness.

The cohort born in the 1980s, the "biracial baby boomers," had a distinctly more positive experience (Root, 2004). Many grew up among other multiracial people who created a visible peer group in schools and neighborhoods and with positive representations of multiracial people in their communities and in the media. This group benefited from the civil rights struggles of past generations such that the various components of their racial background are acknowledged, but rules of hypodescent are no longer prominent (Root, 1998). Members of this generation perceive greater freedom to identify in multiple ways and have faced less of a backlash than did prior generations for their identity choices. For some multiracial baby boomers, race may not be highly salient. For others, their racial identity may be fluid, changing in response to situational and environmental cues. Despite greater latitude to craft a multiracial identification, this cohort has continued to face identity challenges in multiple life arenas, such as in romantic relationships.

Contemporary younger cohorts, infants through adolescents, are growing up in a racial climate unlike any other in our time. The number of multiracial people is increasing at an unprecedented rate and is concentrated among those under the age of 18 (Humes et al., 2011). Several states, such as California and Texas, have already entered a minority-majority status (Humes et al., 2011) in which the number of people of color outnumbers the White population. The entire nation is expected to share minority-majority status by 2050 (U.S. Census Bureau, 2008). The contemporary cohort is also growing up in the presence of prominent models such as President Barack Obama, the first U.S. president to acknowledge his multiracial background openly and to discuss his experiences as the child of an African father, Irish and English mother, and an Indonesian stepfather (Obama, 2004). Although the contemporary context holds promise that the racial experiences of young multiracial people will be more positive than those of previous generations, it would be a mistake to assume that they no longer have unique challenges in identity formation that warrant attention.

Racial Awareness

The recognition and understanding of one's own and other racial groups is called *racial awareness*. This term typically refers to the use of racial labels in assigning others to groups on the basis of physical characteristics, an ability generally acquired by first grade. With increasing age, however, racial awareness comes to include awareness of customs, values, beliefs, and behavior patterns of other groups. Racial awareness becomes more differentiated and integrated with age and experience (Aboud, 1980; Katz, 1973). For example, Kerwin, Ponterotto, Jackson, and Harris (1993) found that younger children described themselves in terms of physical characteristics (for example, skin color), whereas older children and adolescents preferred to describe themselves in terms of racial labels. The degree of differentiation in racial concepts is based on the child's cognitive–developmental level, as well as on the degree of exposure to other racial groups (Ramsey, 1987).

Awareness varies substantially depending on the social situation and whether the child is a member of a racial group that is of lower status in the culture or of the dominant group (Aries et al., 1998; Goodman, 1964). *Minority status* refers both to having an unequal share of the political, economic, and social power of the culture and to being a minority in numbers (Rotheram & Phinney, 1987). Children of the dominant racial group may not need to attend to the norms, values, and customs of minority groups unless they have direct exposure to minority groups in their neighborhoods and schools. However, children of minority races are exposed to the norms, values, and customs of the dominant group through interaction with most institutions, as well as through television, books, and other media. Success and sometimes survival of minority children depend on their awareness of the norms of the majority group.

Racial Attitudes

Attitudes about one's own racial group, as well as other racial groups, are formed initially by about age four or five. Racial attitudes appear to be formed by about age eight to 10 and stay relatively stable from that point. In particular, prejudice and stereotypes are often resistant to change (Brand, Ruiz, & Padilla, 1974). Although there appear to be more positive cross-race attitudes within the United States with cohorts succeeding the civil rights era (Doyle & Aboud, 1995; Jenkins, 1982), contemporary research suggests that cross-race attitudes have not dramatically evolved (Hutchings, 2009).

Racial Preference

Racial preference refers to the recognition that one race is preferred or dominant in a culture; it has been a very controversial construct. When young children are shown pictures or dolls of various racial groups and are asked to choose a picture that looks like them, Black children in the United States are likely to choose a picture of a White face (Bogan & Slaughter-Defoe, 2012; Clark & Clark, 1947; Gopaul-McNicol, 1992). It is not clear whether the Black children think they really belong to this group, would like to belong, or recognize that the group has higher status in the culture. Little research exists to describe mediating and moderating factors on racial preference. However, contemporary research suggests that awareness of racial preferences may influence how multiracial adults identify and constrain the identity options for people who derive part of their racial heritage from a group that is not socially preferred (Townsend et al., 2012).

Reference Group

Reference group refers to a child's selection of a group to emulate. It is not surprising that there are sometimes strong sanctions among group members to discourage too close an alignment with the White group, which is perceived as the oppressor. For example, the ethnic slur *apple* refers to those who are seen as Native American or aboriginal on the outside and White on the inside—that is, people who are perceived to think and behave more like Whites than like Native Americans or Indigenous persons ("Red Apple," n.d.). Other minority groups have similar terms for group members who are too closely aligned with or who demonstrate behavior patterns of the dominant White racial group, such as "oreos" among Blacks and "bananas" among Asians. For the majority group, such terms serve as mechanisms to maintain distance and power; among members of minority races, these terms of disparagement serve to question a member's loyalty and pride toward the minority group and to point out that these individuals have lost touch with their cultural origins. Given the sanctions associated with identification with White culture, multiracial children with White parentage who select White culture as a reference group may experience more adjustment difficulties than those who choose a minority or multiracial reference group.

Self-Identification

Self-identification refers to the process of acquiring one's own racial label. Self-identification is based on how others see the child (ascribed criteria), the extent to which the child acts like a group member (performance criteria), and the degree to which the child believes and feels himself or herself to be a member of a particular group (personal criteria) (Newsome, 2001). Ascribed criteria are likely to become important when a child has physical characteristics, such as skin color and facial features, that signal his or her membership in particular racial group as opposed to others. Thus, a dark-skinned multiracial child with one Black parent is likely to be considered Black by most people, regardless of how the child feels and behaves. Ambiguity in appearance may provide greater opportunity for personal criteria to influence self-identification. Conversely, identity development can be more complicated when one's racial identification is ambiguous and not clearly definable to others (Buchanan & Acevedo, 2004). Nevertheless, research shows that multiracial children are more likely to self-identify at an earlier age and with greater accuracy than their monoracial peers (Green, 1980). This may indicate that race is made salient for multiracial children, potentially as a consequence of frequent questions about their race and differences in phenotypic markers, behavioral routines, and racial attitudes and preferences among family members. Increases in the number of multiracial people in U.S. society over the past two decades has provided multiracial children with an alternative reference group on which to model themselves and with whom to affiliate. Research on reference group orientation among biracial Black–White youths suggests that adolescents who identify with a Black or biracial reference group have more positive self-concepts than those who identify with a White reference group (Field, 1996). Recent research indicates that for multiracial people who choose multiracial labels, validation from others who share those labels promotes identity integration and a healthy self-concept (Lou et al., 2011).

Developmental Stages of Identity Development

Each of the following developmental stages has been investigated with monoracial children in the United States (see Aboud, 1987, or Phinney, 1990, for a review of the literature), but there are fewer data on these processes among multiracial children. Our discussion is approached from the standpoint that multiracial status dramatically shapes the development of racial identity and children's adjustment. Whether the impact is positive or negative will vary on the basis of environmental setting, age, personality, and family background and resources of a child or adolescent. The issue of the multiracial child's potential for choosing an identity of one racial group reemerges at each developmental period. Multiracial identity development is not a static process (Root, 1990) but an evolving social process across the life span.

Early Childhood (Ages Four through Six)

Children initially learn from others (particularly their parents) how to label their race. Thus, multiracial children first acquire their racial self-identification on the basis of their family's assignment, typically by age four or five. Because U.S. society is socially stratified by race (Root, 1990), parents may perceive that they are constrained in their choice of labels for their children. A child with one White parent and one Black parent typically does not choose the label White in a social environment that labels people with any African heritage Black. Some data suggest that parents of Black–White biracial children consciously elect to raise their child as Black, hoping to minimize any problems the child might later face and to prepare the child for life in a racist society (Spencer, 1987).

A multiracial child's skin color and physical features may affect whether others accept a nontraditional label. The desire to ensure that their multiracial children will value their racial heritage leads some parents to teach their children to label themselves *multiracial* (Brunsma, 2005), a label that is at odds with ascribed racial labels (Morrison, 1995). Brunsma provides the only contemporary research on this topic, so it is difficult to assess the impact of a family's choice of racial labels for their children.

Children under age five may learn to articulate that they are multiracial, but the concept will have little meaning to them. Although it is uncertain whether children this young understand the term "multiracial" to mean "several and neither," their cognitive skills may be too limited to accommodate the concept. Labels become increasingly differentiated and elaborated with age.

In each family, whether multiracial or monoracial, issues of dominance hierarchies and bonding patterns will be initiated while the children are quite young. These issues will be magnified and acquire different meanings when members of the family have radically different social status ascribed to them by the dominant culture.

When communities and families do not force multiracial children to adopt a single racial label, children need substantial exposure to models of each race and of other multiracial people to acquire an understanding of the meaning of "multiracial" and to acquire cultural coping skills. The results of a series of cross-racial adoption studies confirmed the importance of neighborhood factors for healthy racial identification among children of color. These same studies confirmed that extrafamilial factors may affect a multiracial child's adjustment. Positive adjustment of transracially adopted children appears to depend on the social integration of racial groups in the community (Halahan, Betak, Spearly, & Chance, 1983). In communities with positive intergroup relations, transracially adopted children have high self-esteem; cross-racial tension appears to affect children's adjustment negatively (McRoy, Zurcher, Lauderdale, & Anderson, 1982). The United States remains a country in which there are few integrated, stable, tension-free multiracial communities. Thus, most multiracial children are raised in racially unbalanced settings and in settings where cross-racial tension may be evident.

Middle Childhood (Ages Seven through 11)

Middle childhood is also characterized by understanding race in terms of concrete and specific markers associated with each group. Categorizations are expanded and become more elaborate; however, cognitive conceptualizations of racial groups are intertwined with affective associations. Concepts are emotional to children of this age, and transmission of prejudice and stereotypes often occurs during the process of teaching children about racial differences.

The development of cross-racial attitudes and prejudice has consequences for multiracial children in terms of their relationships with their parents, teachers, and peers, as well as their own self-concept.

Multiracial children may have their self-labels, attitudes, and conceptualizations of themselves challenged by a majority group that has stereotypic notions of race. This is particularly likely when children are raised to adopt patterns of each racial group within their family. Children can respond to the stereotypes of others in a variety of ways: by challenging the stereotypes, internalizing the norms of the dominant group and feeling negatively toward the racial groups that have lower status within society, or choosing to ignore the issue and the reactions of others.

The social ecology of the child's environment is likely to influence the reaction pattern. Children in environments that are unsupportive of their multiracial identity are less likely to emerge with positive feelings about their multiracial identity and about each of the racial groups in their heritage. Children who respond by internalizing society's negative stereotypes of their racial heritage may increasingly face interpersonal challenges, such as embarrassment at being seen with one or the other parent. A multiracial heritage may be ignored during this developmental period, but the challenges presented by maintaining identification and loyalty to groups that are differentially valued by society must be resolved by each multiracial individual at some point.

Race is typically not the primary determinant of cross-race interactions during middle childhood. Children are likely to maintain cross-racial acquaintances and friendships. Friendships and play groups are more likely to be segregated by gender, rather than race, at this age. Although cross-race contact is maintained, middle childhood often marks the onset of cliques and ingroup/outgroup teasing. If there are strong community sanctions against cross-racial contact, racial insults and derogatory prejudicial comments can characterize peer networks (Schofield, 1981).

There is substantial evidence that racial attitudes become crystallized during middle childhood. Children who are fortunate enough to have been exposed to and to have acquired the norms, values, and beliefs of all their heritage races may have multicultural identities as well as multiracial status. Evidence suggests that exposure to different cultural patterns increases both behavioral and cognitive flexibility (Ramirez & Castenada, 1974). For example, in interviews with biracial children of Black–White heritage, Kerwin et al. (1993) found that the majority of the respondents identified as biracial but did not express feelings of marginality as suggested by older theories of bicultural identity. Instead, these youths exhibited a clear understanding and affiliation with both groups' cultures and values. These and other findings suggest that there are positive aspects associated with multicultural and multiracial identification.

Adolescence and Early Adulthood

The primary developmental task of adolescents in Western culture is to establish their personal identity (Erikson, 1968). Adolescents' social identities of gender, race, and socioeconomic status are central determinants of their search for personal identity. Two general dimensions characterize adolescents' search for identity: (1) exploration of optional life paths in the domains of occupation, political and religious beliefs, sex roles, and racial and ethnic groups; and (2) commitment to a reference group within each domain (Phinney, 1990) and to a set of goals, beliefs, values, and attitudes.

Although community sanctions and norms shape the possible choices of reference groups for younger multiracial children, these issues become more intense and complex in adolescence. The strong racial tension in the United States (Root, 1990) is associated with same-race cleavage in adolescence (Kerwin et al., 1993). Friendships that flourished in middle childhood often end abruptly (Kochman, 1976; Schofield, 1982). This pattern is associated with limited cross-racial dating. Indeed, research on adolescents and young adults indicate that a majority of sexual and romantic partnerships formed during these periods are racially homogeneous (for example, Ford, Sohn, & Lepkowski, 2002). Racial divisiveness in the United States may force multiracial adolescents to choose one group with which to align. Because racial groups are not of equal power and status (Root, 1990), choosing one group means either abandoning a group that is struggling to maintain its identity in the face of economic and social inequities or aligning with a group in which the adolescent anticipates and experiences racism and prejudice. Multiracial adolescents who moved freely across groups and were comfortable in multicultural settings at earlier ages often confront a need to choose a single racial group as their reference at this developmental period (Poston, 1990; Townsend et al., 2012).

Multiracial Identity Development

Racial identity derives from a person's self-identification and the racial assignment of others in the community. Poston (1990) suggested that societal pressure initially influences multiracial children to identify with a single racial group. As multiracial children mature, they begin to exhibit feelings of guilt for selecting a monoracial identity that does not completely reflect their racial background. This guilt prompts multiracial individuals to explore their parental cultures. They obtain a multiracial identity when they fully recognize and incorporate their parental cultures as part of their identity. Whereas the final identity for monoracial children is unambiguous, and the developmental process follows a linear course (R. L. Miller, 1992), for the multiracial adolescent, the end state of such developmental processes is not static, singular, or unambiguous. Although Poston (1990) posited a linear course toward the development of a biracial identity, Root (1990) suggested that biracial adolescents may resolve their identity status in several ways. Biracial adolescents may identity with one group, both groups, or a new group (for example, biracial) or accept community labels (Newsome, 2001; Root, 1990; Xie & Goyette, 1997). This diversity in identification possibilities and the dynamic shifting over time that may occur are captured in Rockquemore and Laszloffy's (2005) continuum of biracial identity model and Renn's discussion of situational identity (Renn, 2000).

Reference group orientation may continually shift across social contexts for multiracial adolescents (Renn, 2000, 2008). Shih, Sanchez, Bonam, and Peck (2007) found that multiracial people are more likely to view race as socially constructed when compared with monoracial peers. They also observed that viewing race as a social construction rather than as heritable was protective against racial stereotypes that could undermine multiracial children's personal well-being. For example, Root (1998) found that experiences external to the identity development process, such as hazing at school and family dysfunction, affected identity development among biracial siblings, who often claimed different racial identities. Brown (1995) found that biracial young adults coped with societal resistance to a biracial identity by compartmentalizing their public and private racial identities. In public, they identified as African American, whereas in private they identified as biracial. Acquiring an understanding of the social norms of the dominant racial group prohibits participating in the rituals and activities of another group without an awareness of the prejudices or attitudes of the dominant group. Even if the views of the dominant group are rejected, awareness of the prejudices exists as a norm being violated.

Renn (2000, 2003) observed five distinct identity patterns among biracial college students. The first type was characterized by having a foot in both worlds, holding multiple monoracial perspectives simultaneously and in parallel. The second type followed a pattern of situation-determined identification in which the individual made conscious shifts in identification to suit the immediate context. The third type was a multiracial identification that

Renn described as "sitting on the border." Her fourth type was a monoracial identification. Type 5 individuals declined to label themselves with a racial social identity. Lou et al. (2011) observed similar diversity in identification in a sample of Black–White and Asian–White biracial people.

In regard to biracial identity development, there is evidence that both gender and social class have significant influences on the life experiences and identification of biracial people. Intersectionality theory (Crenshaw, 1989) encourages the integrated examination of multiple systems of oppression to understand individual lived experiences. Incorporating an intersectional analysis requires simultaneous consideration of multiple social identities (for example, race, gender, social class) and how the unique intersections of these identities create and define experiences and interpretations of events for a given individual (Cole, 2009). As such, interesectionality theory highlights the fact that people understand who they are not in a compartmentalized manner but through their social position at the intersection of multiple social categories. Identity will reflect where an individual is positioned relative to these multiple categories, each of which may have distinct implications for daily social experience separately and when taken together. Intersectionality suggests that the development of a racial identity is a fluid process of complex transactions between the individual and his or her broader social environment and is informed by other social identities, such as gender and sexual orientation.

Psychological Well-Being

Emerging empirical evidence casts doubt on the utility of monoracial identity development theories for understanding multiracial people's long-term psychological adjustment. In a comprehensive review of all the available evidence on multiracial children's adjustment, Shih and Sanchez (2005) observed that a multiracial identification may better serve a child's mental health and social adjustment than a monoracial identity. Problems and stressors associated with being multiracial have declined over time, such that studies conducted earlier contain more reports of negative experiences than do studies conducted more recently. Yet Shih and Sanchez also found that the outcomes being studied, the comparisons being made among racial identity groups, and the nature of the multiracial population being examined (for example, clinical versus nonclinical; composition of racial component identities) all had an impact on whether the multiracially identified children did better or worse than their monoracial peers. For instance, in the studies they reviewed, multiracial children were more often depressed than monoracial White youths but less often depressed than monoracial youths of color; multiracial children often had higher school performance than monoracial youths of color; and multiracial children often perceived lower regard for their racial background than their monoracial peers perceived. Lou and colleagues observed that validation of identity choices for multiracial persons was an important predictor of the quality of their self-concept (Lou et al., 2011). Current theories regarding identity development fail to capture these person–environment complexities adequately.

Despite a more complicated racial identity process, most multiracial people are as psychologically healthy as members of other racial groups. However, some studies have found that multiracial children have higher rates of victimization compared with monoracial peers (Gibbs & Moskowitz-Sweet, 1991). Research with biracial women reveals that they have higher lifetime rates of sexual victimization than monoracial women (Nakashima, 1992). For example, biracial women are often deemed "exotic" and are more likely to be sexualized than biracial men (Root, 1994, 2004). Narratives surrounding appearance and beauty are infused throughout biracial women's stories of identity formation (Bowles, 1993) and differ considerably from those of biracial men (Gillem, Cohn, & Throne, 2001; Hall, 2004; Rockquemore & Brunsma, 2004). Although there are certain to be challenges in identity formation that are concentrated among biracial men, they are rarely the focus of research, and little is known about their unique experiences.

By college, multiracial students report higher rates of sexual and racial harassment than do monoracial peers (Buchanan et al., 2009), which may reflect higher rates of rejection and further a sense of cultural homelessness (Vivero & Jenkins, 1999). These increased rates of victimization and rejection may make multiracial children, adolescents, and adults more vulnerable to psychological distress in the form of depression, anxiety, and posttraumatic stress. It is essential that these symptoms are not defined as deficits inherent to being multiracial and are instead recognized as common reactions to victimization.

Implications

Counselors, teachers, therapists, and members of other helping professions serving multiracial populations face many challenges. They might presume to know an individual's race on the basis of his or her physical characteristics. Typically, little background information is gathered on racial self-identification, cultural routines, same or cross-ethnic norms, and attitudes of the individual and his or her family. Without inquiring about these aspects of developmental history, it is difficult to understand a child's world. This background is particularly important when children are being evaluated for problem behaviors, programs for the gifted, or remediation. Therefore, racial, cultural, and socioeconomic background should always be reviewed when conducting an evaluation.

Service providers' and educators' intervention strategies will vary on the basis of their training and their own racial background, personal values, the societal values prevalent during their childhood (for example, the 1960s versus the 1990s), and the geographic environment as characterized by varying levels of cross-racial tension and balance. Interventionists must consider how their professional and personal worldviews and experiences shape their perceptions of multiracial children and families (Nishimura, 1995; Winn & Priest, 1993).

Despite its intuitive appeal, a color-blind racial ideology is not recommended when working with multiracial children and families. In the context of therapy, color-blind racial ideology has been associated with lower levels of multicultural counseling competence, difficulty understanding the true origins of clients' problems, and lower levels of empathy for client concerns (Neville, Spanierman, & Doan, 2006). Color-blindness is often an attempt to focus on the individual value of each person and minimize the focus on race; however, color-blind ideology often has the unintended consequence of silencing discussion and acknowledgment of differences related to race and culture (Markus, Steele, & Steele, 2002) and race-based injustices (Bonilla-Silva, 2010). Teaching children to be color-blind when they may face experiences directly due to race negates their reality and may result in a child internalizing negative experiences as inherent to his or her value and worth, rather than understanding bias and structural inequities that may motivate others' behaviors.

A counselor typically addresses problems of individuals and promotes choices that are likely to reduce the individual's stress and enhance individual coping skills. Multiracial children are often challenged by situations that pit reducing the individual's external stress (for example, passing as monoracial) against maintaining group pride and promoting change in cross-race relations over the long term. Sensitization and education to the norms of many cultures are critical when conducting cross-racial counseling. With multiracial children, this means an analysis of the conflicting cultural routines, the meaning attributed to the routines, and potential ways of resolving conflicting cultural norms.

Yet not all of the issues a multiracial youth might present are necessarily related to racial identity. Counselors and others working with multiracial children must be careful to assess when issues are a function of racial identity versus other factors. As stated previously, the identity formation process will evolve, often in a complex manner. Choices made by multiracial children at one stage of development are likely to be rethought and reevaluated at later developmental stages (Xie & Goyette, 1997). This results not only from the developmental processes at the individual level, but also because group cultural norms evolve. For example, a multiracial child who was raised in the 1990s, when multiracial pride and heritage were commonly endorsed and societal supports of interracial relationships were more evident, may have been more likely to assert multiracial pride than a multiracial child who was raised in the 1970s. Similarly, children raised in 2010 may be perplexed by a focus on their racial identity if they have grown up with a large cohort of multiracial peers.

Parents of multiracial children often need help with the special problems they confront as their families face prejudice from others. Hud-Aleem and Countryman (2008) highlighted environmental factors that can facilitate the positive identity development of multiracial children. They suggested that therapists help parents and their children to (a) encourage the child's discussion of his or her racial background, (b) acknowledge that the child's racial heritage differs from that of the parents, (c) facilitate opportunities for the child to develop relationships with other children and role models from a variety of racial backgrounds by living in integrated neighborhoods with integrated schools, and (d) form an identity as a multiracial family. To address these factors, parents must make decisions about how to enhance their child's developing racial identity, whether to live in an integrated or segregated neighborhood, how to help their child negotiate challenges presented by harassing peers, and how to obtain social support for themselves (Hershel, 1995). Most of these decisions require the parents to clarify their own values and goals; when parents come from different racial backgrounds, this clarification often involves recognition and resolution of conflicting values and goals around racial identity. Counselors may be able to help parents negotiate these decisions, but they must recognize their own heritage and values before they can help others resolve their differences in background.

Single parents may benefit from additional assistance in finding ways to reinforce their child's positive racial identity. Clinicians may be able to help single parents find ways to connect their children to all of their racial cultures. It will be especially important that the parent be cognizant of the ways in which racial issues may affect the child. Parents can help their children by teaching them to recognize and value their racial identity and acknowledge the ways race affects their lives, positively and negatively.

The San Francisco–based organization iPride (Interracial Intercultural Pride) is one of the oldest multiracial groups in the United States and the founder of the Association of MultiEthnic Americans (AMA). The Biracial Family Network started in Chicago and grew out of the AMA. These organizations have spread to many areas of the United States, especially in major urban areas, and are committed to enhancing the development and well-being of multiracial children and adults. They specifically seek to enhance multiracial families by offering parents a means of social support, advocating for the elimination of monoracial biases (such as "check one only" forms), and helping parents transmit to their children the values, attitudes, and behavior patterns consistent with their heritage. Counselors and other helping professionals can help families connect with such organizations as an ongoing venue of support.

Conclusion

Multiracial children in the United States grow up in a society stratified by race. This stratification influences a child's identity at each developmental period. Typically it puts external pressure on children to identify with whichever racial heritage group has a lower status. Thus, children must often resolve a tension between adopting survival strategies for individual success and adjustment within the majority culture while demonstrating pride in and loyalty to a racial group that may be of lower status.

Parents and family can substantially influence this process when children are young; multiracial children can be exposed to positive models from each racial group and acquire a self-concept, attitudes, and behaviors that reflect all groups (Hershel, 1995) and an alternative multiracial perspective. However, as children grow up, society's sanctions are likely to have an increasing influence. Among children in middle childhood, the establishment of entrenched cross-ethnic attitudes and their increased awareness of differences highlight any discrepancies among the values of the family, school, peers, and the child. This conflict is typically an internal one during middle childhood. However, the increasing racial cleavage of adolescence often forces multiracial youths to reconsider their multiracial identity. Whether the transaction between developmental challenges and social forces has a positive or negative influence is not clear, but support of these youths regarding the range of self-identifications from which they may select may have a substantial influence on their adoption of a consolidated and positive racial identity.

References

Aboud, F. E. (1980). A test of ethnocentricism with young children. *Canadian Journal of Behavioral Science, 12*, 195–209.

Aboud, F. E. (1987). The development of ethnic self-identification and attitudes. In J. S. Phinney & M. J. Rotheram (Eds.), *Children's ethnic socialization: Pluralism and development* (pp. 32–50). Beverly Hills, CA: Sage Publications.

Aries, E., Olver, R. R., Blount, K., Christaldi, K., Fredman, S., & Lee, T. (1998). Race and gender as components of the working self-concept. *Journal of Social Psychology, 138*, 277–290.

Bogan, E. D., & Slaughter-Defoe, D. T. (2012). Through the eyes of a child: The development and consequences of racial stereotypes in Black and White children. In D. T. Slaughter-Defoe (Ed.), *Racial stereotyping and child development* (pp. 1–19), Farmington, CT: Karger.

Bolnick, D. A., Fullwiley, D., Duster, T., Cooper, R. S., Fujimura, J. H., Kahn, J. S., et al. (2007, October 19). The science and business of genetic ancestry testing. *Science, 318*, 399–400.

Bonilla-Silva, E. (2010). *Racism without racists: Color-blind racism and racial inequality in contemporary America* (3rd ed.). Lanham, MD: Rowman & Littlefield.

Bowles, D. D. (1993). Bi-racial identity: Children born to African-American and White couples. *Clinical Social Work Journal, 21*, 417–428.

Boykin, A. W., & Toms, F. (1985). Black child socialization: A conceptual framework. In H. P. McAdoo & J. L. McAdoo (Eds.), *Black children: Social, educational, and parental environments* (pp. 33–52). Newbury Park, CA: Sage Publications.

Brand, E. S., Ruiz, R. A., & Padilla, A. M. (1974). Ethnic identification and preference: A review. *Psychological Bulletin, 81*, 860–890.

Brown, U. M. (1995). Black/White interracial young adults: Quest for a racial identity. *American Journal of Orthopsychiatry, 65*, 125–130.

Brunsma, D. L. (2005). Interracial families and the racial identification of mixed-race children: Evidence from the early childhood longitudinal study. *Social Forces, 84*, 1131–1157.

Buchanan, N. T., & Acevedo, C. (2004). When face and soul collide: Therapeutic concerns with racially ambiguous and non-visible minority women. *Women & Therapy, 27*, 119–131.

Buchanan, N. T., Bergman, M. E., Bruce, T. A., Woods, K. C., & Lichty, L. F. (2009). Unique and joint effects of sexual and racial harassment on college students' well-being. *Basic and Applied Social Psychology, 31*, 267–285.

Buckley, T. R., & Carter, R. T. (2004). Biracial (Black–White) women: A qualitative study of racial attitudes and beliefs and their implications for therapy. *Women & Therapy, 27*, 45–64.

Cauce, A. M., Hiraga, Y., Mason, C., Aguilar, T., Ordonez, N., & Gonzales, N. (1992). Between a rock and a hard place: Social adjustment of biracial youth. In M.P.P.

Root (Ed.), *Racially mixed people in America* (pp. 207–222). Newbury Park, CA: Sage Publications.

Clark, K., & Clark, M. (1947). Racial identification and racial preference in Negro children. In J. M. Newcomb & E. L. Hartley (Eds.), *Readings in social psychology.* New York: Holt, Rinehart & Winston.

Cole, E. R. (2009). Intersectionality and research in psychology. *American Psychologist, 64*, 170–180.

Crenshaw, K. (1989). Demarginalizing the intersection of race and sex: A Black feminist critique of antidiscrimination doctrine, feminist theory and antiracist politics. *University of Chicago Legal Forum, 140*, 139–167.

DaCosta, K. M. (2007). *Making multiracials: State, family, and market in the redrawing of the color line.* Stanford, CA: Stanford University Press.

Dominguez, V. R. (1986). *White by definition: Social classification in Creole Louisiana.* New Brunswick, NJ: Rutgers University Press.

Doyle, A., & Aboud, F. E. (1995). A longitudinal study of White children's racial prejudice as a social cognitive development. *Merrill-Palmer Quarterly, 41*, 210–229.

Elam, M. (2010, March 3). 2010 Census: Think twice, check once. *Huffington Post.* Retrieved from http://www.huffingtonpost.com/michele-elam/2010-census-think-twice-c_b_490164.html

Erikson, E. H. (1968). *Identity: Youth and crisis.* New York: W. W. Norton.

Fairlie, R. W. (2009). Can the "one-drop rule" tell us anything about racial discrimination? New evidence from the multiple race question on the 2000 Census. *Labour Economics, 16*, 451–460.

Fernandez, C. A. (1996). Government classification of multiracial/multiethnic people. In M.P.P. Root (Ed.), *The multiracial experience: Racial borders as the new frontier* (pp. 15–36). Thousand Oaks, CA: Sage Publications.

Fhagen-Smith, P. E. (2010). Social class, racial/ethnic identity, and the psychology of "choice." In K. Korgen (Ed.), *Multiracial Americans and social class: The influence of social class on racial identity* (pp. 59–70). New York: Routledge.

Field, L. D. (1996). Piecing together the puzzle: Self-concept and group identity in biracial Black/White youth. In M.P.P. Root (Ed.), *The multiracial experience: Racial borders as the new frontier* (pp. 211–226). Thousand Oaks, CA: Sage Publications.

Ford, K., Sohn, W., & Lepkowski, J. (2002). American adolescents: Sexual mixing patterns, bridge partners, and concurrency. *Sexually Transmitted Diseases, 29*, 13–19.

Fujimura, J. H., Duster, T., & Rajagopalan, R. (2008). Introduction: Race, genetics, and disease: Questions of evidence, matters of consequence. *Social Studies of Science, 38*, 643–656.

Funderburg, L. (1994). *Black, White, other: Biracial Americans talk about race and identity.* New York: William Morrow.

Gibbs, J. T., & Moskowitz-Sweet, G. (1991). Clinical and cultural issues in the treatment of biracial and bicultural adolescents. *Families in Society, 72*, 579–592.

Gillem, A. R., Cohn, L. R., & Throne, C. (2001). Black identity in biracial Black/ White people: A comparison of Jacqueline who refuses to be exclusively Black and Adolphus who wishes he were. *Cultural Diversity and Ethnic Minority Psychology, 7*, 182–196.

Goodman, M. E. (1964). *Race awareness in young children* (Rev. ed.). New York: Collier.

Gopaul-McNicol, S. A. (1992). Racial identification and racial preference of Black preschool children in New York and Trinidad. In A.K.H. Burlew, W. C. Banks, H. P. McAdoo, & D.A.Y. Azibo (Eds.), *African American psychology: Theory, research, and practice.* Thousand Oaks, CA: Sage Publications.

Green, P. (1980). The doll technique and racial attitudes. *Pacific Sociological Review, 23*, 474–490.

Halahan, C., Betak, J., Spearly, J., & Chance, B. (1983). Social integration and mental health in a biracial community. *American Journal of Community Psychology, 11*, 301–311.

Hall, C.C.I. (2004). Mixed race women: One more mountain to climb. *Women & Therapy, 27*, 237–246.

Hershel, H. J. (1995). Therapeutic perspectives on biracial identity formation and internalized oppression. In N. Zack (Ed.), *American mixed race: The culture of microdiversity.* Lanham, MD: Rowman & Littlefield.

Hirschfeld, L. A. (1995). The inheritability of identity: Children's understanding of the cultural biology of race. *Child Development, 66*, 1418–1437.

Holliday, B. G. (1985). Developmental imperatives of social ecologies: Lessons learned from Black children. In H. P. McAdoo & J. L. McAdoo (Eds.), *Black children: Social, educational, and parental environments* (pp. 53–71). Newbury Park, CA: Sage Publications.

Howard, Z. (2006, September 18). Biracial hair [Video file]. Retrieved from http:// www.youtube.com/watch?v=RTnxJdxhU7o

Hud-Aleem, R., & Countryman, J. (2008). Biracial identity development and recommendations in therapy. *Psychiatry, 5*, 37–44.

Humes, K. R., Jones, N. A., & Ramirez, R. R. (2011). *Overview of race and Hispanic origin: Census 2010 brief.* Retrieved from http://www.census.gov/prod/cen2010/briefs/c2010br-02.pdf

Hutchings, V. L. (2009). Change or more of the same? Evaluation racial attitudes in the Obama era. *Public Opinion Quarterly, 73*, 917–942

Jane Doe v. State of Louisiana, 479 So. 2d 369 (La. Ct. App. 1985).

Jenkins, A. (1982). *The psychology of the AfroAmerican: A humanistic approach.* New York: Pergamon.

Jones, J. M. (1988). Racism in Black and White: A bicultural model of reaction and evolution. In P. A. Katz & D. A. Taylor (Eds.), *Eliminating racism: Profiles in controversy* (pp. 117–135). New York: Plenum Press.

Jones, N. A., & Smith, A. S. (2001). *The two or more races population: Census 2000 brief.* Retrieved from http://www.census.gov/prod/2001pubs/c2kbr01-6.pdf

Jorde, L. B., & Wooding, S. P. (2004). Genetic variation, classification and "race." *Nature Genetics, 36,* S28–S33.

Katz, P. A. (1973). Perception of racial cues in preschool children: A new look. *Developmental Psychology, 8,* 295–299.

Kerwin, C., Ponterotto, J. G., Jackson, B. L., & Harris, A. (1993). Racial identity in biracial children: A qualitative investigation. *Journal of Counseling Psychology, 40,* 221–231.

Kochman, T. (1976). Perception along the power axis: A cognitive residue of interracial encounters. *Anthropological Linguistics, 18,* 271–274.

Korgen, K. O. (2010). *Multiracial Americans and social class: The influence of social class on racial identity.* New York: Routledge.

Lou, E., Lalonde, R. N., & Wilson, C. (2011). Examining a multidimensional framework of racial identity across different biracial groups. *Asian American Journal of Psychology, 2,* 79–90.

Loving v. Virginia, 388 U.S. 1 (1967).

Markus, H. R., Steele, C. M., & Steele, D. M. (2002). Color blindness as a barrier to inclusion: Assimilation and nonimmigrant minorities. In R. A. Shweder, M. Minow, & H. R. Markus (Eds.), *Engaging cultural differences: The multicultural challenge in liberal democracies* (pp. 453–472). New York: Russell Sage Foundation.

Martin, J. A., Hamilton, B. E., Ventura, S. J., Menacker, F., & Park, M. M. (2002). Births: Final data for 2000. *National Vital Statistics Reports, 50*(5), 1–101.

McRoy, R., Zurcher, L., Lauderdale, M., & Anderson, R. (1982). Self-esteem and racial identity in transracial and inracial adoptees. *Social Work, 27,* 522–526.

Miller, N., & Brewer, M. (1984). *Group in conflict: The psychology of desegregation.* New York: Academic Press.

Miller, R. L. (1992). The human ecology of multiracial identity. In M.P.P. Root (Ed.), *Racially mixed people in America* (pp. 24–36). Newbury Park, CA: Sage Publications.

Miller, R. L., & Miller, B. (1990). Mothering the biracial child: Bridging the gaps between African-American and White parenting style. *Women & Therapy, 10,* 169–180.

Morning, A. (2000). Who is multiracial? Definitions and decisions. *Sociological Imagination, 37,* 209–229.

Morrison, J. W. (1995). Developing identity formation and self-concept in preschool-aged biracial children. *Early Child Development and Care, 111,* 141–152.

Nakashima, C. L. (1992). An invisible monster: The creation and denial of mixed-race people in America. In M.P.P. Root (Ed.), *Diversity and complexity in feminist therapy* (pp. 185–206). New York: Harrington Park Press.

Neville, H., Spanierman, L., & Doan, B. (2006). Exploring the association between color-blind racial ideology and multicultural counseling competencies. *Cultural Diversity and Ethnic Minority Psychology, 12,* 275–290.

Newsome, C. (2001). Multiple identities: The case of biracial children. In V. H. Milhouse, M. K. Asante, & P. Nwosu (Eds.), *Transcultural realities: Interdisciplinary perspectives on cross-cultural relations* (pp. 145–161). Thousand Oaks, CA: Sage Publications.

Nishimura, N. J. (1995). Addressing the needs of biracial children: An issue for counselors in a multicultural school environment. *The School Counselor, 43*, 52–57.

Obama, B. H. (2004). *Dreams from my father: A story of race and inheritance.* New York: Random House.

Omi, M., & Winant, H. (1986). *Racial formation in the United States: From the 1960s to the 1980s.* New York: Routledge and Kegan Paul.

Phinney, J. S. (1990). Patterns of social expectations between Black and Mexican American children. *Child Development, 61*, 542–556.

Phinney, J. S., & Rotheram, M. J. (1987). Children's ethnic socialization: Themes and implications. In J. S. Phinney & M. J. Rotheram (Eds.), *Children's ethnic socialization: Pluralism and development* (pp. 274–292). Newbury Park, CA: Sage Publications.

Poston, W.S.C. (1990). The biracial identity development model: A needed addition. *Journal of Counseling and Development, 69*, 152–155.

Ramirez, M., III, & Castenada, A. (1974). *Cultural democracy, bicognitive development and education.* New York: Academic Press.

Ramsey, P. G. (1987). *Teaching and learning in a diverse world: Multicultural education for young children.* New York: Teachers College Press.

Red apple. (n.d.). In *Urban dictionary.* Retrieved from http://www.urbandictionary.com/define.php?term=red+apple

Renn, K. A. (2000). Patterns of situational identity among biracial and multiracial college students. *Review of Higher Education, 23*, 399–420.

Renn, K. A. (2003). Understanding the identities of mixed-race college students through a developmental ecology lens. *Journal of College Student Development, 44*, 383–403.

Renn, K. A. (2008). Research on biracial and multiracial identity development: Overview and synthesis. *New Directions for Student Services, 123*, 13–21.

Rockquemore, K., & Brunsma, D. L. (2004). Negotiating racial identity: Biracial women and interactional validation. *Women & Therapy, 27*, 85–102.

Rockquemore, K. A., & Brunsma, D. L. (2008). *Beyond Black: Biracial identity in America* (2nd ed.). Thousand Oaks, CA: Sage Publications.

Rockquemore, K., & Laszloffy, T. A. (2005). *Raising biracial children.* Lanham, MD: AltaMira Press.

Root, M.P.P. (1990). Resolving "other" status: Identity development of biracial individuals. In L. Brown & M.P.P. Root (Eds.), *Diversity and complexity in feminist therapy* (pp. 185–205). New York: Haworth Press.

Root, M.P.P. (1992). Within, between, and beyond race. In M.P.P. Root (Ed.), *Racially mixed people in America* (pp. 3–11). Newbury Park, CA: Sage Publications.

Root, M.P.P. (1994). Mixed race women. In L. Comas-Diaz & B. Greene (Eds.), *Women of color: Integrating ethnic and gender identities in psychotherapy.* New York: Guilford Press.

Root, M.P.P. (1996). The multiracial experience: Racial borders as a significant frontier in race relations. In M. P. P. Root (Ed.), *The multiracial experience: Racial borders as the new frontier* (pp. xiii–xxviii). Thousand Oaks, CA: Sage Publications.

Root, M.P.P. (1998). Experiences and processes affecting racial identity development: Preliminary results from the Biracial Sibling Project. *Cultural Diversity and Mental Health, 4,* 237–247.

Root, M.P.P. (2004). From exotic to a dime a dozen. *Women & Therapy, 27,* 19–31.

Rotheram, M. J., & Phinney, J. S. (1987). Introduction: Definitions and perspectives in the study of children's ethnic socialization. In J. S. Phinney & M. J. Rotheram (Eds.), *Children's ethnic socialization: Pluralism and development* (pp. 10–28). Beverly Hills, CA: Sage Publications.

Sanchez, D. T., & Bonam, C. M. (2009). To disclose or not to disclose biracial identity: The effect of biracial disclosure on perceiver evaluations and target responses. *Journal of Social Issues, 65,* 129–149.

Schneider, J. A., Pungliya, M. S., Choi, J. Y., Jiang, R., Sun, X. J., Salisbury, B. A., et al. (2003). DNA variability of human genes. *Mechanisms of Ageing and Development, 124,* 17–25.

Schofield, J. (1981). Complementary and conflicting identities: Images and interactions in an interracial school. In S. R. Asher & J. M. Gottman (Eds.), *The development of children's friendships.* New York: Cambridge University Press.

Schofield, J. (1982). *Black and White in school: Trust, tension or tolerance?* New York: Praeger.

Shih, M., & Sanchez, D. T. (2005). Perspectives and research on the positive and negative implications of having multiple racial identities. *Psychological Bulletin, 131,* 569–591.

Shih, M., Sanchez, D. T., Bonam, C., & Peck, C. (2007). The social construction of race: Biracial identity and vulnerability to stereotypes. *Cultural Diversity and Ethnic Minority Psychology, 13,* 125–133.

Smedley, A., & Smedley, B. (2005). Race as biology is fiction, race as a social problem is real: Anthropological and historical perspectives on the social construction of race. *American Psychologist, 60,* 16–26.

Spencer, M. B. (1987). Black children's ethnic identity formation: Risk and resilience of castelike minorities. In J. S. Phinney & M. J. Rotheram (Eds.), *Children's ethnic socialization: Pluralism and development* (pp. 103–116). Beverly Hills, CA: Sage Publications.

Thornton, R. (1987). *American Indian holocaust and survival: A population history since 1492.* Norman: University of Oklahoma Press.

Townsend, S.S.M., Fryberg, S. A., Wilkins, C. L., & Markus, H. R. (2012). Being mixed: Who claims a biracial identity? *Cultural Diversity and Ethnic Minority Psychology, 18,* 91–96.

U.S. Census Bureau. (2008). *An older and more diverse nation by midcentury*. Retrieved from http://www.census.gov/newsroom/releases/archives/population/cb08-123.html

Vivero, V. N., & Jenkins, S.R.C.A. (1999). Existential hazards of the multicultural individual: Defining and understanding "cultural homelessness." *Cultural Diversity and Ethnic Minority Psychology, 5*, 6–26.

Winn, N. N., & Priest, R. (1993). Counseling biracial children: A forgotten component of multicultural counseling. *Family Therapy, 20*, 29–36.

Woo, M., Austin, S. B., Williams, D. R., & Bennett, G. G. (2011). Reconceptualizing the measurement of multiracial status for health research in the United States. *Du Bois Review, 8*, 25–36.

Xie, Y., & Goyette, K. (1997). The racial identification of biracial children with one Asian parent: Evidence from the 1990 Census. *Social Forces, 76*, 547–570.

Chapter Eight

What It Means to Be American

Jennie Park-Taylor, Joshua Henderson,
and Michael Stoyer

Examining the many facets of what it means to be American is more than a mere scholarly endeavor. Given recent evidence suggesting that the way individuals describe American identity is related to their opinions on important legal and social issues, such as racial profiling (Schildkraut, 2009) and official English-language policies (Schildkraut, 2003), studying American identity is critical because of the high stakes involved. Moreover, considering the increasing diversity in the United States and the globalization of the world, the nation's war on terror and the rise in discrimination and hate crimes against Muslim Americans post-9/11 (Ali, 2011; Disha, Cavendish, & King, 2011; Mir, 2001), and the difference between explicit and implicit views of who is American (Devos, Huynh, & Banaji, 2012; Devos & Ma, 2013; Park-Taylor et al., 2008), American identity is both complex and multilayered.

An individual's ethnic, racial, or national identity development has been studied primarily as an individual experience, and it is generally accepted that this process is influenced largely by a person's social environment. In examining the notion of an American identity, where, heretofore, the terms "America" or "American" refer to the United States or a person of the United States, we have chosen to use Uri Bronfenbrenner's (1979, 1986) ecological systems model of human development as a framework for this investigation. This perspective posits that development involves a dynamic relationship between a teleological individual and the changing variables of the immediate contexts in which the person lives, as well as the interactions between these settings and the larger system in which the settings are held (Bronfenbrenner, 1979). This model has been depicted as a set of concentric circles and has also been visualized as a collection of Russian *matryoshka* nesting dolls, with each circle or doll representing another layer of contextual influence.

Considering the ecology of human development, we argue that an individual's American identity is one that develops through his or her direct contact and interaction with various microsystems (for example, family, peers, work, school), as well as the influence of the exosystem, which refers to the circle where all the microsystems are embedded (for example, neighborhood, city, or state) and the larger macrosystem (for example, sociocultural–political context of the United States). Moreover, it is through this dynamic process that individuals develop their social identities (for example, American identity), which are understood as part of individuals' self-concept that emerges from their understanding of their membership in a social group (or groups) together with their emotional attachment to those groups (Tajfel, 1978; Tajfel & Turner, 1979).

In line with an ecological perspective, to be the individual is both changed by and is the change agent of his or her environment, we believe that the American identity that is embraced by the nation at any given time is also influenced by this dynamic process. That is, an examination of the self and identity must be understood within a social context in which thoughts and feelings about oneself are influenced by membership in a larger unit and in which these feelings and thoughts transcend the self to shape a view of the collective (Banaji & Prentice, 1994). Finally, Bronfenbrenner's (1979, 1986) emphasis on chronological time, which he calls a *chronosystem*, is certainly germane in a discussion of the development of an American identity, as it is clear both at the individual and larger systemic level that what it means to be American has evolved over time and differs on the basis of the generation and developmental stage of the individual.

Although there are many microsystems that may affect an individual's American identity development, for the present chapter we have chosen to limit our focus to a brief discussion of the influences of an individual's family and school or workplace. At the exosystem level, our chapter will highlight regional influences that may be involved in American identity development both at the individual and at the larger societal level. Specifically, we will outline the potential significance of one's region and state of residence in the development of an American identity. We then follow with a description of the influence of the larger macrosystem on how an individual understands, endorses, embodies, and embraces his or her American identity. In this discussion, we describe how a predominant American identity ideal influences the extent to which an individual feels a sense of belonging to or inclusion within the American identity and a sense of power and influence to change how the American identity is defined. Finally, we point to the role that chronological time plays in the development of an American identity.

Microsystems

Family and American Identity

From our very first days, perhaps our most influential microsystem is our family. Our identity, at least on some level, emerges from our being members of a family unit, and given that family is unlike any other relationship context, it affects both the contents and processes of identity development (Scabini & Manzi, 2011). The significance of family in identity processes can clearly be seen when examining parent and child relationships and the important role parents play in their children's identity development. Schacter and Ventura (2008) introduced the concept of *identity agents,* which they described as individuals who actively interact with children with the intention of participating in their identity development and who moderate influences from the larger social systems that interact with the developing child. From this definition, the authors argued that parents clearly fit the description of identity agents as they are active and intentional coparticipants in their children's identity formation and later identity development. The influence of parents as identity agents does not just apply for young children, but also extends to adolescents, for whom parents continue to play a significant role in attitudes about identity and self in relation to others. For instance, a study by Edmonds and Killen (2009) investigated how adolescents' perceptions of their parents' messages about cross-race relationships were related to their self-reported levels of intergroup contact and found that the degree of intimacy in cross-race relationships was related to perceptions of parents' racial attitudes.

When considering the case of ethnic and racial minority families, parents' role as identity agents may include an emphasis on preparing their children to live in a country where being American is associated with a racial hierarchy (Devos et al., 2012). Furthermore, Portes and Rivas (2011) argued that racialized stereotypes that are pervasive in society provide particularly negative self-identity messages for Black and Latino youths that tend to last over generations. In their study, they found that racialized self-perceptions among Mexican American students persisted into the third and fourth generations. Considering the ubiquity of racialized stereotypes, research that demonstrates the impact of parental racial socialization provides strong evidence for the notion that parents serve as much-needed cultural identity agents for their children. Racial socialization has been understood as the process that ethnic and racial minority parents engage in to instill in their children a strong sense of ethnic or racial pride as well as prepare their children for bias and discrimination (Hughes, 2003). For instance, Neblett, Smalls, Ford, Nguyen, and Sellers (2009) found that racial socialization practices affected adolescents' racial centrality, assimilationist ideology, and nationalist ideology. In this study, researchers determined that various patterns of racial socialization experiences played an important role in how adolescents made meaning of their race as African Americans.

In terms of instilling ethnic pride and preserving culture of origin within a cultural context that often leans toward assimilation, ethnic and racial minority parents may do this through an intergenerational transmission of cultural values (Koh, Shao, & Wang, 2009) as well as efforts to teach or maintain the family's language of origin (Kang, 2012). Thus, it would seem that parents' engagement in the racial socialization of their children is a mechanism through which they can provide their children with an understanding of what it means to be a person of color in America and how to negotiate their multiple identities within a racialized social context.

Schools and the American Identity

Historically and currently, one of the major goals of public education is to help students learn about the responsibilities of American citizenship (Benninga & Quinn, 2011). Indeed, one of public education's primary functions is to prepare young people to become responsible citizens (Feinberg, 1998). School is an excellent vehicle for instilling a strong sense of civic duty as well as a strong American identity, as they are places where young persons learn and practice democracy (Quinn, 2011). Given the significant amount of time that youths spend in school and the fact that the school is an essential vehicle for the transmission of the cultural norms, values, and ideals of a society, it becomes a critical context for children to develop a sense of belongingness to the larger macrosystem (that is, the United States) and the identity of that macrosystem (that is, American identity). Taken together, the role of the school context in the social identity development of its students as well as the professed goals of public education provide a strong rationale for the examination of the impact of the school microsystem on American identity.

The messages that young people may receive regarding what it means to be American are powerful because although attitudes about America, citizenship, and so forth are abstract, they are formed via concrete experiences youths have in their microsystems (for example, family, peer group, and schools; Parissa, 2011). In a recent study of youth perspectives on American identity, it was found that some specific experiences that affected American identity development among youths included an attachment to American ideals, a mismatch between ideals and reality, experiences with diversity, opportunities for civic and political participation, and ideas about the American dream (Parissa, 2011). This study's results point to the significance of microsystems, such as the school and peer group, in American identity development for young people, and thus, it can be expected that as youths negotiate their multiple identities to form an affiliation and identification with the nation, they will seek information from their microsystem for validation and support for their identity formation.

Unfortunately, both at the institutional level and at the individual level, nonmajority students are challenged to develop a sense of belongingness to the school unit, the larger national unit, and American identity. For instance, a recent study of five- to 11-year-old European American children's attitudes regarding immigrants, immigration policy, and what it means to be an American found that the majority had strong American identities and also held specific ideas about what it means to be an American. Participants believed that one must love America, live by its rules, and be White. Furthermore, the study found that although participants were in favor of legal immigration as a policy, they believed that only illegal immigrants who were employed should be allowed to stay in the country. Younger participants thought that illegal immigrants should go to jail. Many of the children surveyed also held negative attitudes about Mexican immigrants, and these attitudes were found among those with prototypical national in-group identity (Brown, 2011). The impact of racialized messages from both their peer and school contexts may be significant for older ethnic minority youths as these messages likely add complexity to their identity negotiations. For example, in a recent qualitative investigation of the life stories of a group of middle-class African American students attending affluent and predominantly White suburban middle schools, the researcher found that participants discussed their identity development within their peer groups and academic environments in terms of their sense of "otherness" (Gordon, 2012).

In addition to the potential negative impact of peers who may hold negative views of immigrants and strong exclusionary American identities, the classroom environment may be an activating context for students to feel either included or excluded from the fabric of the nation and American identity. Anti-immigration sentiment, which is associated with an exclusionary definition of what it means to be American, was identified by education scholars to be such a pervasive problem within school contexts that recently a team of education scientists from the United States and Europe engaged in collaborative efforts to examine how educators can challenge anti-immigration discourses in school and community contexts (Allexsaht-Snider, Buxton, & Harmon, 2012). When a school context is characterized as endorsing or even not actively fighting against anti-immigrant attitudes, it can be argued that it is supporting what Bond (2006) referred to as an *internal exclusion* orientation, which he defined as one in which minority citizens do not feel included within their own country

Workplace and American Identity

Although the school context is arguably the second most important microsystem for school-age youths in terms of identity development, the first being the family microsystem, the workplace occupies a parallel level of significance for many adults. Indeed, full-time employed adults spend approximately 1,750 hours per year at work (U.S. Department of Labor, Bureau of Labor Statistics, 2012). What we do in terms of our career or occupation is personal and has a strong influence on our identity. Given the significant amount of time that employed adults spend at work, the workplace microsystem context may be particularly influential in individuals' national identity negotiations and affiliations. Furthermore, the ways in which individuals are perceived in terms of their national identity may influence their overall work experience.

Although the notion of a glass ceiling in the world of work has been a thoroughly investigated phenomenon that has affected many different subgroups of individuals (for example, women, ethnic minority individuals), this and other kinds of work-related barriers may also be significant for individuals who are not perceived to fit in the national identity. People of color and individuals who speak English as a second language may be particularly at risk for being perceived as not fitting into the societally accepted definition of what it means to be American, and these perceptions may influence their work experiences. For instance, Chen, Rao, and Ren (2013) found that research and development scientists who were foreign-born Americans of Asian descent experienced a glass ceiling that they attributed, in part, to prevailing stereotypes of Asians, ethnocentrism of the workplace, and workplace prejudice and discrimination. Another study that examined Asian American social workers found that participants' perceptions of a glass ceiling were influenced by ethnic discrimination as well as the number of Asian American managers within the participant's organization (Hwang, 2007).

Although there may be personal aspects of individual identity development, others' perceptions of one's social identities have public consequences.

That is, there may be negative work-related repercussions when individuals are perceived as not belonging to the national identity. For example, a recent study found that supervisors' perceptions of their employees' national identity and English-language fluency influenced their quality ratings of their employees' science contributions. The researcher concluded that despite popular belief that science does not discriminate, the concept of *good science* was based, on some level, on the identity and English-language proficiency of the subject (Wells, 2013). Similarly, in an experimental study of business students' perceptions of a labor pools' ethnic and gender identity, it was found that these perceptions were related to compensable factor weightings. Findings from the researcher's two-study investigation demonstrated significant discriminatory weighting of compensable factors on the basis of both the ethnic and gender identity of the labor pool (D. E. Martin, 2011). Furthermore, in a survey based on hypothetical cases of college students' employment-related decisions, Hosoda and Stone-Romero (2010) found that compared with French-accented applicants, Japanese-accented applicants fared worse on employment-related decisions even after controlling for applicant understandability and location. Collectively, these data suggest that the extent to which an individual is perceived as fitting into the American national identity in terms of racial and ethnic identity and English-language ability may have serious consequences in terms of their work experiences and potential for upward mobility. Although the influence of microsystems, such as family, school, and work, is certainly significant, these influences must be understood within an outer systemic layer that is dynamically related to the microsystems (that is, the exosystem). Below, we briefly highlight how the exosystem may shape and influence the American identity.

Exosystem

As Campbell, Converse, Miller, and Stokes (1960) argued, "In most groups formed along occupational, ethnic, or religious lines, membership is more likely to determine attitudes than are attitudes to determine membership" (p. 323). We extend this line of thinking to explain the effect of the exosystem on American identity development with a specific focus on regional differences. We assert that geographically bound individuals will have aspects of their identity influenced by the other individuals within that regional context. One particularly fruitful geographic comparison is the examination of differences in how urban and rural communities endorse, express, and feel a sense of belongingness to the American identity. For example, Doran and

Littrell (2013) analyzed individuals' responses on a measure of personal values that relate to American identity and found significant differences between urban and rural populations. Their findings may be interpreted to suggest that whereas the American identity endorsed in a rural setting is more individualistic, conservative, conforming, and traditional, urban populations seem to endorse an American identity that places significantly greater emphasis on cultural factors and universalism and less weight on conformity and security.

In addition to urban–rural comparisons, on a state-to-state scale, one might expect variations in cultural values that in turn may influence an individual's identity as an American. Macnab, Worthley, and Jenner (2010) examined specific cultural variations between individuals in Florida and Hawaii. Within the dimensions tested, Hawaiian respondents tested higher than their Floridian counterparts on collectivism and uncertainty avoidance. Given that Hawaii's Asian population is the majority racial group in the state (U.S. Census Bureau, 2014), these results can be interpreted to support Hofstede's (1980) observation that Asian cultures have a greater inclination to be represented by higher levels of collectivism and uncertainty avoidance. This finding further suggests that factors such as the Harper racial–ethnic composition of a state can greatly influence specific values that would further distinguish regional differences within the greater American identity. Furthermore, states that are geographically close to other countries (for example, California and Arizona) may differ in their expression or endorsement of American identity values because of their proximity to the nation's border. According to Smith and Tarallo (1995), the passing of Proposition 187, which effectively denied basic social services to undocumented immigrants, represents an anti-immigrant sentiment that is rooted in California's own history and political conditions (for example, economic ties with Mexico, political–economic integration of the Latino population in California). Furthermore, the political framing of ethnic and racial minority groups and of individuals who support less strict immigration policies as being somehow less American or anti-American has proven to be powerful (Orozco, 2012). In his analysis of the process in which a kindergarten to 12th-grade Mexican studies program was dismantled in Arizona through the political agenda of certain state officials, Orozco demonstrated the potential utility of anti-immigrant sentiment in swaying voters to support a rigid and limited notion of what it means to be American.

Beyond state boundaries, regions defined by geographic barriers have molded unique American identities. Roggenkamp (2008) described one of these identities as a *hillbilly* and further elaborated its association to individuals from the Appalachian Mountains area of the United States. Two studies showed that the amount of time individuals had lived in western North Carolina was positively related to their development of a regional, Appalachian identity, which was characterized by an increased opposition to regional growth, a greater likelihood to support green space preserves, and greater likelihood to support ordinances to restrict steep slope development (Cooper & Knotts, 2012; Cooper, Knotts, & Livingston, 2010). Furthermore, both studies found that despite some regional-specific values, participants were more prone to identify with a national identity, which portrayed a greater attachment to America. These results suggest that Appalachian identity does not inhibit the greater national identity but alternatively creates another layer to an individual's American identity. These findings about Appalachian identity provide a clear example of how an exosystem can add another layer of complexity to how an individual defines his or her American identity. The microsystems and exosystem relevant to an individual's identity development are all influenced and informed by a larger societal context or macrosystem.

Macrosystem

The extent to which an individual feels a sense of membership in an American identity is significantly influenced by the values, norms, and structure of the larger macrosystem (for example, the United States). In line with the premise set forth by Sidanius and Pratto (1999) asserting that relations with groups are usually organized in a hierarchy, we believe that individuals will have differential levels of American identity status and power and belongingness on the basis of demographic differences. While the growing body of evidence suggesting a racial hierarchy of Americanness points to the significance of race as an identity belongingness and power anchor, we believe that the same might be true for other social identities, such as religion, socioeconomic status, and language.

Belongingness is an essential human need to form stable attachments and relational bonds with others (Baumeister & Leary, 1995). It is the feeling of personal investment in a social system, the self-perception of being an essential part of that system (Anant, 1966). Individual and social identities are developed to fulfill this need for belongingness (Simon & Hamilton, 1994). It follows, then, that immigrant groups would be motivated to establish new identities to feel like they belong in the collective. However, for people to belong, they must be recognized by the majority and they must feel a part of that group. In the social construction of American identity, we propose *domains of belonging,* defined here as implicit social structures, rooted in American historical narratives that serve to define the meaning of being an American. Whether these narratives are factual does not matter as much as how people remember them and how they are socially transmitted in American culture. A brief look at the holidays celebrated in the United States provides an example of how the American narrative is widely understood.

Perhaps no two holidays are more emblematic of the narrative of American founding history than Thanksgiving and Independence Day. The modern celebration of Thanksgiving commemorates the preservation of Puritan settlers during their first winter in the New World. We often see the image of the White Europeans' gratitude to the native peoples who taught them how to survive during harsh conditions. According to the narrative, were it not for the benevolence of the native peoples, the European settlers would have perished. We celebrate the preservation of the Europeans, yet there is no national day of remembrance for the plight of the native peoples. When U.S. citizens celebrate Independence Day, an event that took place more than 150 years after the first Thanksgiving in the country's history, the founding fathers are remembered for crafting the document that substantiated the creation of a new nation. English-born White men are commemorated for the fortitude, wisdom, and foresight to plan for the country's future greatness with the framework of "life, liberty, and justice for all."

Consider, for a moment, some of the characteristics of the people being commemorated in the narrative underlying these American holidays: Whites, English speakers, Protestants, and mostly men. These characteristics represent categories—or domains—that serve as the basis of the American identity as it was first established. Over the course of American history, certain subgroups within each domain have embodied the American identity to a greater degree than others. Within several major domains (that is, race, religion, social class, and language), we suggest there are hierarchies along which some characteristics are more likely to engender belongingness into the American identity. To understand the American identity is impossible without considering the hierarchical structure of the society that creates and perpetuates it (Correa de Oliveira, 2012).

Hierarchical Domain of Race

The hierarchy within the domain of race can be viewed historically from a review of the U.S. Census. In 1790, the Census asked four questions specifically regarding race: the number of free White males, the number of free White females, the number of other free persons, and the number of slaves in a household (U.S. Census Bureau, 2012a). American identity, as assessed by the Census from the outset, concerned only Whites and "others." No other racial group was considered important to include for description. Thirty years later, the 1820 Census made its first distinction for a racial category other than White, in this case "free colored males and females" (U.S. Census Bureau, 2013). Though it is likely this term was meant to be applied to liberated African slaves, the implicit message continued to be "Whites and others." Not until 1850 did the U.S. Census give differentiation within the racial domain to non-Whites, with the addition of the categories of "Black" and "mulatto" (U.S. Census Bureau, 2012b). In 1870, Census respondents were given additional racial options for Chinese or Indian (U.S. Census Bureau, 2012c). Over the next 12 decades, the U.S. Census continued to add differentiation to the racial category, but the foundation was set from the beginning: Whites are at the top of the hierarchy, and all "others" follow.

In recent studies, it has been found that most individuals implicitly (and sometimes explicitly) attribute American identity more readily to White people than to Black, Asian, or Latino people (Dasgupta & Yogeeswaran, 2011). Devos and Banaji (2005) explored the association between people's explicit and implicit judgments of African Americans, Asian Americans, and White Americans and their relationship to the category "American." They found that although people tend to endorse an explicitly strong commitment to racially equal views for what it means to be "American," they have implicit attitudes that White Americans are most strongly related to the American national identity. Experimental studies by Devos and Banaji (2005) found that people are more likely to implicitly associate a known foreign-born White person with Americanness than a known American-born ethnic minority individual. Despite these strong findings, which have now been referred to as the "American = White effect" (Devos & Banaji, 2005), recent researchers have found that participants were more likely to include an African American individual in the American identity when the individual was presented positively (Rydell, Hamilton, & Devos, 2010).

In terms of how individuals see themselves in relation to American identity, Devos and Banaji (2003) found that people may strive to maintain egalitarian beliefs in society but cannot consciously control prejudicial attitudes toward members of groups, even those to which they themselves belong. These implicit beliefs may constitute some of the influence on how ethnic minority individuals perceive themselves in relation to American identity. Through a mixed-methods investigation of people's feelings about and meanings related to American identity, Rodriguez, Schwartz, and Whitbourne (2010) found that ethnic minority (but U.S.-born) individuals felt less American and were perceived as less American than their White counterparts. Finally, researchers found some differentiation among racial minority subgroups with regards to the extent to which they associated their group with American identity. They discovered that whereas Asian American participants implicitly associated their group to be less American than the "White" group, for African American participants, the association of Americanness just as strongly defined their own group as it did the "White" group (Devos & Banaji, 2005).

Numerous other studies have demonstrated that people unconsciously associate Americanness with race, specifically that White or European Americans are implicitly seen as more American than Asian Americans, African Americans, and Latino Americans (Devos, Gavin, & Quintana, 2010; Devos & Heng, 2009; Devos & Ma, 2008). Park-Taylor et al. (2008) deconstructed the hierarchy from a qualitative perspective: 10 second-generation American graduate students, from multiple ethnic and racial backgrounds, were interviewed. It was found that the majority of participants described a prototypical American as being White or having characteristics of a White individual.

The racial hierarchy of American identity was established from the outset on an institutional level. We propose the domain of American identity, derived from the historical narrative in the country's collective consciousness, to be arranged in the following order, with those at the top having the greater likelihood of feeling belongingness: Whites, Blacks, Latinos, and Asians. We posit that it would be more challenging for racial minority Americans to feel a sense of belongingness to the American identity.

Hierarchical Domain of Religion

Our second hierarchical domain of belongingness centers on religion. Although America has never officially been a Christian nation, biblical imagery has been a part of American civil life since its inception. As the narrative goes, the Puritans fled persecutory conditions in Europe and settled in America to practice their religion. Early founder John Winthrop envisioned Boston as the "city upon a hill," a reference to the New Testament book of Matthew (Bremer, 2003). Roger Williams founded the town that would become the capital of Rhode Island as the "land of God's merciful providence" (Gaustad, 2005). One hundred fifty years later, the founding fathers inked the Constitution.

Though considered by scholars to be a secular document affirming America as a nation of religious liberty rather than a Christian state (Lambert, 2003), the "overwhelmingly Protestant" makeup of the 1787 Constitutional Convention holds weight in the American narrative. Of the 55 delegates present, only two were Roman Catholics ("America's Founding Fathers," n.d.). Being Protestant Christian seems to represent the greatest degree of Americanness in politics as well. John Fitzgerald Kennedy was the first non-Protestant president, and he was highly scrutinized for being a Catholic. The country has not elected another non-Protestant since Kennedy. Most recently, similar religious skepticism was cast on Republican presidential candidate W. Mitt Romney in 2008 and 2012 for being a member of the Mormon faith. Some have suggested that these criticisms evidence a "politico-religious mold" by which American voters judge their candidates (Sheets, Domke, & Greenwald, 2011, p. 460). These authors further proposed that people's implicit validations of political candidates' Americanness is largely dependent on their being White and Christian (though these views seem to vary in degree according to one's political party, which is beyond the scope of our discussion; Sheets et al., 2011).

In the United States, "civil-religious references to God have evolved and broadened since the founding from generic Protestant to Protestant-Catholic to Judeo-Christian" (Morley & Halliwell, 2008, p. 135). Given this historical precedent, it is much easier for a Christian-identifying person to feel included in the American identity than for a non-Christian. Although national sentiment toward Jewish Americans shifted swiftly after World War II (Sacks, 1994) and granted them greater entry into the American polity, Jewish Americans still face anti-Semitism, which may challenge their feeling of inclusion into the American identity. Among all religious groups, being accepted into the American identity may be presently most difficult for Muslim Americans. As they strive to assert their place in the patchwork of American identity, Muslims in America have faced a dramatic increase in hate crimes since 9/11 (Disha et al., 2011). Furthermore, some Muslims in the United States fear that their loyalty to America is under suspicion (Ali, 2011). The proportion of hate crimes against Muslims was found to be greater in American counties where Muslims are represented in the smallest numbers, reflecting the influence of power differential on incidents of discrimination (Disha et al., 2011). Of the demographically largest religions in the United States (Newport, 2012), we theorize the hierarchy within this domain of American identity to follow this order: Protestant, Catholic, Jewish, nonmainstream Christian religions (for example, Mormon and Jehovah's Witness), and Islam.

Hierarchical Domain of Social Class

Social class is a critical component of the American identity, and it represents the third domain of our model. Here we propose that the middle class embodies the greatest degree of Americanness, given the middle class's sociological foundations of democratization, industrialization, and urbanization (Kroos, 2012). These three components were deeply woven into the American historical narrative, especially after World War II, in the advent and affordability of the automobile, prosperous postwar economic conditions, increased access to higher education, and abundant industrialization that helped lead to the explosive growth of the middle class (Sacks, 1994).

Although social class is an often unmentioned and even taboo subject in American discourse, research has found that most Americans not only believe that they are middle class but strive to be perceived as middle class, even when their subjective class identity differs from objective measures of social class. A recent nationwide poll probed Americans' perceptions of what it takes to make it in the middle class ("Heartland Monitor Poll," 2013). A majority of respondents selected a description of the middle class as "having the ability to keep up with expenses and hold a steady job while not falling behind or taking on too much debt" (Brownstein, 2013). Among poll respondents, 46 percent identified themselves as middle class, with only 17 percent identifying themselves as upper or upper-middle class (Brownstein, 2013). In one study, participants' objective class status was compared with their self-reported class position, and several key findings indicated that most people perceived themselves as middle class despite true class status (Sosnaud, Brady, & Frank, 2013). More than two-thirds of those in the upper-middle class showed a deflated view of their class status, and greater than a third of the working class exhibited an inflated class status. Only half of the objectively measured middle class showed concordant subjective perceptions of their class status. What these results show is that people in the United States want to be perceived as belonging to the middle class. Consider the contrivance of American presidential candidates who roll up their shirtsleeves in appeal to middle-class values: This is a political message of humility, sincerity, and truth, meant to target the middle-class sensibility of the candidates' voter bases (Givhan, 2003). Though most candidates come from the upper class, they bare their forearms in attempts to express their ability to relate to the middle class.

On the basis of public perception, people from the lower and upper classes are more likely to feel marginalized in the American identity, for different reasons relating to American beliefs in hard work and earning one's wealth. People of lower-class status are less comfortable with and less expressive toward members of the upper class (Garcia, Hallahan, & Rosenthal, 2007). Lesser financial means can restrict access to housing, transportation, and employment, which in turn limits social mobility. Certain discriminatory practices are seen by some to keep the poor from elevating beyond the lower social class (Parker, 2014). Upper-class people may be perceived negatively by individuals from other social classes (Piff, Stancato, Mendoza-Denton, Keltner, & Coteb', 2012). A qualitative study found that upper-class students fought to dispel stereotypes against them that they are out of touch with American values of hard work and earning one's place in society (Sanders & Mahalingam, 2012). Compared with upper-class individuals, who tend to place greater importance on wealth, lower-class Americans tend to prioritize their sense of community and belongingness within society (Piff, Stancato, Martinez, Kraus, & Keltner, 2012).

Hierarchical Domain of Language

Although the United States has never adopted an official language, English may be considered the de facto language. The founders of the country spoke English as their native tongue. The Constitution was written in English. Laws and legislation all are written in English. Twenty-two states have enacted laws to observe an English-only governance, thereby restricting legal protection for minority-language speakers. In contrast, only Hawaii officially recognizes a language other than English (Hawaiian), and Louisiana recognizes the right for preserving the linguistic origins of its primarily French Caribbean Creole subpopulations (Faingold, 2012). Yet as many as 57 million Americans speak a language other than English at home (U.S. Census Bureau, 2012d).

There is mixed sentiment in American civic discussion about making English the official language. On the one hand, support for pro-official-English policies is thought to derive in part from the notion that these laws will preserve what it means to be American: that a unifying language will protect the American way of life. On the other hand, some people think that such monolingual laws violate certain freedoms that support the definition of Americanness (Schildkraut, 2005). Observing English-only legislation is a practice that some see as discriminatory (Southern Poverty Law Center, 2009). Others have proposed that official-English policies serve only to make immigrants—particularly Latinos and Asians—feel unwelcome (Schildkraut, 2005).

However, there appears to be further distinction within the language domain of American identity: accented use of the English language. The ability to speak American English without an accent is the greatest distinguishing factor for "bona fide" Americans (Akomolafe, 2013, p. 9). Equal opportunity cannot be denied a person who speaks English with an accent, and discrimination against English-as-second-language individuals is illegal in many cases under protection of national origin (U.S. Department of Justice, 2000; U.S. Equal Employment Opportunity Commission, 2014). Yet, even for U.S.-born individuals, speaking with an accent is related to the experience of feeling unaccepted by American society. A significant relationship has been found between Chinese American high school students who spoke English with an accent and their perception of being stereotyped as "perpetual foreigners," a finding that was also related to perceptions of discrimination (Kim, Wang, Deng, Alvarez, & Li, 2011, p. 289). Furthermore, Mexican Spanish–accented individuals are disadvantaged in job applications compared with American English–accented applicants (Hosoda, Nguyen, & Stone-Romero, 2012). People who speak English fluently and without a foreign accent are more likely to feel belongingness in the American identity redundant with "without a foreign accent."

In addition to the influences of the outer system layer, which is depicted in Bronfenbrenner's (1979, 1986) model as the microsystem, that are highlighted above and framed as American identity anchors, there is also the significant influence of chronological time or the chronosystem to consider. In the following section, which rests on historical milestones, we briefly review the major reasons why people have immigrated to the United States as well as some examples of national attempts to restrict immigration over the course of the country's history and how these factors influence society's definition of what it means to be American as well as individual Americans' national identity negotiations.

Chronosystem

Reasons for Immigration

"Once I thought to write a history of the immigrants in America. Then I discovered that the immigrants were American history" (Handlin, 1951, p. 3). In line with this observation, we also believe that the history of our country is inextricably linked to our immigration history. Immigration characterized our country at the outset and continues to be a defining force today. In 2013, there were approximately 46 million immigrants in the United States, more than any other country and more than quadruple the number reported in the second country on this list, Russia, with approximately 11 million immigrants (Connor,

Cohn, Gonzalez-Barrerra, & Oates, 2013). For the purposes of our argument, immigrants to the United States can be categorized according to two distinct groups: those who were forced to migrate (for example, Africans during the slave trade) and those who chose to immigrate to this country. In the following, we review forced migration and its potential influence on American identity.

Although there are several groups of people that were forced to migrate to this country for labor (for example, convict labor; Menard, 2001) and population growth (for example, women; S. Martin, 2011), the forced migration of Africans via the slave trade has left perhaps the most significant mark on the nation's history and the development of its collective national identity (Eyerman, 2001; Pinderhughes, 1990). Indeed, Eyerman (2001) purported that the symbolic construction of the American identity is intertwined with a crisis in the African American identity that he refers to as the *cultural trauma* of slavery. In trying to understand the profound and comprehensive effects of slavery, Pinderhughes (2011) used the term "internal colonialism" not only to describe the plight of African Americans and their devalued position in the nation, but also to describe the functioning of the country as a system of inequality and oppression. Drawing on nationwide statistics that demonstrate significant health disparities, continued residential segregation, and extreme educational inequality, he argued that African Americans represent colonized groups or "a nation within a nation" within their own country. Collins (2001) described several important ways in which the cultural trauma of slavery has affected the development of a national identity. First, she noted the discrepancy between supposed American values, such as equality, and the reality of racial discrimination as the paradox of American identity. She further stated that the racial and ethnic hierarchy that characterizes the nation engenders a racialized understanding of U.S. national identity. Beyond the collective national identity that, on some level, includes a legacy of and continued effects of slavery, there is also the question of how individual African Americans negotiate their American identity.

In addition to forced migration, a majority of Americans have immigrant ancestors or are immigrants themselves who chose to migrate to the United States. Many individuals who immigrated voluntarily to the United States were motivated by reasons that influence their identity negotiations. Lazarus's (1883) invitation to "Give me your tired, your poor, your huddled masses yearning to breathe free" is emblematic of an essential piece of what has become known as the *American dream*. Adams (1931) first coined this term to refer to how individuals in America have freedom and are able to pursue happiness regardless of birth or position. With the American dream in mind, immigrants have made the journey to establish a new life in this country in search of better opportunities; to escape persecution, violence, and economic and political hardships; and chase the promise of riches. The American dream has continued to be such a provocative image that many immigrants were willing to risk personal safety and sacrifice everything they left behind for a chance to chase what has now become an essential part of the identity of America (Harper, 2006). As the narrative of the American dream spread across the world and as the passage to America became more affordable and less dangerous, the diversity of the U.S. immigrant population increased, resulting in an overall shift in the country's demographic makeup (Harper, 2006). That is, individuals from around the world sought the United States as their new home and continue to do so today.

Lazarus's exhortation and the American dream characterize the United States as the land of the free and the protector of the vulnerable. Thus, with an outward message that identifies the nation as a strong country that is responsible for protecting individuals around the world, the country's narrative and identity have evolved to include acting as a safe haven for refugees. The United States has a long history of accepting refugees from other nations. In fact, the country has accepted approximately 2 million refugees for resettlement over the last 60 or so years (Haines & Rosenblum, 2010). Some specific examples include a wave of refugees from Cuba following Castro's 1959 revolution (S. Martin, 2011) and the conflict in Vietnam, which brought another significant wave of refugees. Between 1975 and 1979, 10 separate authorizations granted Vietnamese individuals parole status (Kelly, 1986). Although there are unique aspects of the refugee acculturation experience that are distinct from the acculturation processes of an immigrant who chooses to come to this country on his or her own terms and within his or her own chosen time frame, there is literature to suggest that, similar to immigrants, refugees long to be included in the fabric of the nation's identity and want to belong (Haines & Rosenblum, 2010).

Lazarus's message and the compelling draw of the American dream are indeed critical components of the American identity and enduring American narrative. However, the country's history of resistance to immigrant groups and shifting attitudes toward immigrants across time provide another essential piece of the American identity and narrative.

Barriers to Entry

One needs to only briefly examine the history of immigration laws to know that what it means to be American is influenced by sociopolitical factors that have changed over time. For instance, from the time of the first European colonizers, lines between "us" and "them" were created when colonizers called themselves "Americans," yet referred to Native Americans as "Indians." Even some Western European descendants were once considered a threat to American culture, as, for example, during the massive immigration waves of 18th-century German and Scotch Irish groups (Dinnerstein & Reimers, 1999).

Over the last 130 years, various ethnic groups have been targeted by law and policy makers because, given the sociopolitical context of the time period, they were considered threats to national security ("History of U.S. Immigration Law and Policy," n.d.). The immigration laws that either restricted or prohibited entry of certain groups at different points in time reflect national attitudes toward immigrants from those countries or regions of the world.

In 1882, the Chinese Exclusion Act was passed, an aptly titled policy that denied citizenship to Chinese immigrants and prohibited individuals from China from entering the country ("History of U.S. Immigration Law and Policy," n.d.). Less than 40 years later, in 1924, President Coolidge signed the Johnson-Reed Act into law, creating a quota-based system that relied on immigration figures from the 1890 Census. This act effectively restricted Southern and Eastern Europeans and Japanese from entering the country for the purpose of becoming U.S. citizens. These immigration laws placed a legal restriction around American identity by singling out those individuals who were "not American" and could not be included in the American identity. Furthermore, although not an immigration law, when President Roosevelt authorized the internment of Japanese and Japanese Americans during World War II by signing Executive Order 9066, he authorized the relocation of all persons deemed a threat to national security, which cleared the way for Americans of Japanese descent to be deported to internment camps. With a stroke of a pen, he effectively redefined American identity to exclude Japanese Americans.

Although there have been times when the national boundaries are loosened because of economic needs, entry into the country does not always mean that individuals are welcomed to adopt the American national identity. During the period between 1942 and 1964, as the United States emerged from World War II and the country began to prosper economically, the bracero program brought nearly a million agricultural guest workers to the United States ("History of U.S. Immigration Law and Policy," n.d.). These workers were predominantly of Mexican descent, and the Latino population drastically increased in the American Southwest as a result. In stark contrast to the bracero program, Operation Wetback, implemented under President Eisenhower, deported nearly a million Mexican immigrants in response to the swelling numbers of illegal Mexican immigrants in 1954. These two events in American history help to capture the attitudinal ambivalence toward immigrants at the middle of the 20th century.

Our nation's ethnic and racial diversity dramatically increased, in large part, as a result of immigration policies that were developed during the civil rights era. During this time, the nation appeared to be straddling between a national identity rooted in an exclusive past and one that was more reflective of openness and diversity. At the height of the American civil rights movement, the Immigrant and Nationality Act of 1965 was passed in Congress, abolishing race-based immigration quota policies. President Johnson signed this act, which, instead of using quotas still in effect from the 1920s, based eligibility on prospective immigrants' specialized work abilities and ties to family within the United States ("History of U.S. Immigration Law and Policy," n.d.). As a result, African, Latino, and Asian immigrant groups extended into the American landscape and the dialogue of American identity. Shortly thereafter, in response to the sociopolitical fallout from the Vietnam War, legislation was passed in 1975 to facilitate the resettlement of Southeast Asian refugees in the United States.

Just as historical immigration laws provide information about the national zeitgeist regarding American identity and who should be included in that identification at various points in time, today's tough policies against undocumented immigration may reflect anti-immigrant sentiment and a stricter and closed sense of who may be included in the American identity (Mukherjee, Molina, & Adams, 2013). As an example, more than 40 years after the American government introduced Operation Wetback, California passed Proposition 187, which prohibited illegal immigrants from receiving access to health services, public education, and welfare. Although the Immigration and Nationality Act of 1995 was supported by some groups for its financially conservative policies, it was also widely criticized for its discriminatory effect on Americans' attitudes toward Mexicans (Lee, Ottati, & Hussain, 2001).

At times, stricter immigration regulations have been supported by scholars. For example, recently, Huntington (2004) warned about the possibility that the increase of Mexican immigrants would forever change American culture, leading it away from the Anglo-Protestant culture that has been at its core for centuries. Perlman (2005) stated that Hispanic immigrants are the new depiction of a perceived threat that can harm American culture. This echoes previous discrimination against immigrant groups that includes signs that read "No Irish need apply" following the potato famine (Kennedy, 1964). History is repeating itself currently, and it is important to understand the sociopolitical climate that sparked these immigrant policy debates and that can be seen as precautionary measures that protect against Huntington's (2004) argument.

Conclusion

Indeed, in today's modern pluralistic society, it is safe to assume that people belong to a variety of groups, both given and chosen, and as the world becomes more diverse, opportunities to compare and contrast oneself with others will only increase (Devos et al., 2012). In this chapter, we reviewed some of the major systems that dynamically relate to influence an individual's American identity development as well as the American identity that is embraced by the country at any given time. Throughout U.S. history, the definition of American has shifted considerably and the answer to the question "What does it mean to be an American?" has also changed from generation to generation.

Although an individual's self-attribution of American identity is important, the multitude of barriers that have been imposed on immigrant and ethnic and racial minority groups suggests that American identity also depends on the society's acceptance of the individual. Indeed, for immigrants engaged in the acculturation process, their cultural adjustment and ethnic and national identity development largely depend on the characteristics of the receiving country. Given the U.S. historical and current endorsement of a melting pot metaphor to describe the goal of acculturation (Elmes & Connelley, 1997), it is evident that an assimilation strategy of acculturation is the preferred strategy, and thus immigrants are expected, to a large extent, to let go of their culture of origin and assimilate and eventually fully adopt American culture and values.

According to our review, American identity can be understood as one that evolves across time, is significantly influenced by history (for example, legacy of slavery), and is highly dependent on multiple spheres of influence (for example, microsystems, exosystem, macrosystem). Whereas the American identity that is endorsed explicitly and publicly highlights such things as democratic ideals, civic participation, freedom, and independence, the American identity that is supported implicitly reveals a hierarchy of Americanness across multiple identity domains (for example, race, class, religion, and language). Implicit beliefs as well as hidden biases result in real and felt exclusionary experiences (for example, racism, religious, and language-based discrimination) for individuals who are not perceived as fitting within the predominant characteristics of a "typical" or "true" American. Thus, we propose that *belongingness* is a key factor that contributes to the continual development of American identity: An individual can feel belongingness to the group, yet the group must express attitudes that allow the individual to feel belongingness. Finally, if we are to truly become a pluralistic society, the country must come to terms and honestly deal with the paradoxical American identity that values equality and democracy but still endorses assimilationist views and a hierarchy of Americanness (Collins, 2001; Elmes, & Connelly, 1997).

References

Adams, J. (1931). *The epic of America.* Boston: Little, Brown.

Akomolafe, S. (2013). The invisible minority: Revisiting the debate on foreign-accented speakers and upward mobility in the workplace. *Journal of Cultural Diversity, 20,* 7–14.

Ali, M. (2011). Muslim American/American Muslim identity: Authoring self in post-9/11 America. *Journal of Muslim Minority Affairs, 31,* 355–381.

Allexsaht-Snider, M., Buxton, C. O., & Harmon, R. (2012). Challenging anti-immigration discourse in school and community contexts. *International Journal of Multicultural Education, 14*(2), 1–9.

America's founding fathers: Delegates to the constitutional convention. (n.d.). Retrieved from http://www.archives.gov/exhibits/charters/constitution_founding_fathers_overview.html

Anant, S. S. (1966). The need to belong. *Canada's Mental Health, 14,* 21–27.

Banaji, M. R., & Prentice, D. A. (1994). The self in social contexts. *Annual Review of Psychology, 45,* 297–332. doi:10.1146/annurev.ps.45.020194.001501

Baumeister, R., & Leary, M. (1995). The need to belong: Desire for interpersonal attachments as a fundamental human motivation. *Psychological Bulletin, 117,* 497–529.

Benninga, J., & Quinn, B. (2011). Enhancing American identity and citizenship in schools. *Applied Developmental Science, 15,* 104–110.

Bond, R. (2006). Belonging and becoming: National identity and exclusion. *Sociology, 40,* 609–626.

Bremer, J. (2003). *John Winthrop: American's forgotten founding father.* New York: Oxford University Press.

Bronfenbrenner, U. (1979). *The ecology of human development: Experiments by nature and design.* Cambridge, MA: Harvard University Press.

Bronfenbrenner, U. (1986). Ecology of the family as a context for human development: Research perspectives. *Developmental Psychology, 22,* 723–742.

Brown, C. S. (2011). American elementary school children's attitudes about immigrants, immigration and being an American. *Journal of Applied Developmental Psychology, 32,* 109–117.

Brownstein, R. (2013). *Meet the new middle class: Who they are, what they want, and what they fear.* Retrieved from http://www.theatlantic.com/business/archive/2013/04/meet-the-new-middle-class-who-they-are-what-they-want-and-what-they-fear/275307/

Campbell, A., Converse, P. E., Miller, W. E., & Stokes, D. E. (1960). *The American voter.* New York: John Wiley & Sons.

Chen, C. C., Rao, A., & Ren, I. Y. (2013). Glass ceiling for the foreign-born: Perspectives from Asian-born American R&D scientists. *Asian American Journal of Psychology, 4*, 249–257.

Collins, P. H. (2001). Like one of the family: Race, ethnicity and the paradox of the U.S. national identity. *Ethnic and Racial Studies, 24*, 3–28.

Connor, P., Cohn, D., Gonzalez-Barrerra, A., & Oates, R. (2013). *Changing patterns of global migration and remittances.* Retrieved from http://www.pewsocialtrends.org/files/2013/12/global-migration-final_12-2013.pdf

Cooper, C. A., & Knotts, H. G. (2012). Overlapping identities in the American South. *Social Science Journal, 50*, 6–12. doi:10.1016/j.soscij.2012.04.001

Cooper, C. A., Knotts, G., & Livingston, D. (2010) Appalachian identity and policy opinions. *Journal of Appalachian Studies, 16*, 26–41.

Correa de Oliveira, P. (2012). *American society is hierarchical.* Retrieved from http://nobility.org/2012/02/09/america-hierarchy/

Dasgupta, N., & Yogeeswaran, K. (2011). Obama-nation? Implicit beliefs about American nationality and the possibility of redefining who counts as "truly" American. In G. S. Parks & M. W. Hughey (Eds.), *The Obamas and a (post)-racial America?* (pp. 72–90). New York: Oxford University Press.

Devos, T., & Banaji, M. (2003). Implicit self and identity. In M. R. Leary & J. P. Tangney (Eds.), *Handbook of self and identity* (pp. 153–175). New York: Guilford Press.

Devos, T., & Banaji, M. (2005). American = White? *Journal of Personality and Social Psychology, 88*, 447–466.

Devos, T., Gavin, K., & Quintana, F. (2010). Say "adios" to the American dream: The interplay between ethnic and national identity among Latino and Caucasian Americans. *Cultural Diversity and Ethnic Minority Psychology, 16*, 37–49.

Devos, T., & Heng, L. (2009). Whites are granted the American identity more swiftly than Asians: Disentangling the role of automatic and controlled processes. *Social Psychology, 40*, 192–201.

Devos, T., Huynh, Q., & Banaji, M. R. (2012). Implicit self and identity. In M. R. Leary & J. P. Tagney (Eds.), *Handbook of self and identity* (2nd ed., pp. 155–179). New York: Guilford Press.

Devos, T., & Ma, D. (2008). Is Kate Winslet more American than Lucy Liu? The impact of construal processes on the implicit ascription of a national identity. *British Journal of Social Psychology, 47*, 191–215.

Devos, T., & Ma, D. S. (2013). How "American" is Barack Obama? The role of national identity in a historic bid for the White House. *Journal of Applied Psychology, 43*, 214–226.

Dinnerstein, L., & Reimers, D. M. (1999). *Ethnic Americans: A history of immigration*. New York: Columbia University Press.

Disha, I., Cavendish, J. C., & King, R. D. (2011). Historical events and spaces of hate: Hate crimes against Arabs and Muslims in post-9/11 America. *Social Problems, 58*, 21–46. doi:10.1525/sp.2011.58.1.21

Doran, C., & Littrell, R. (2013). Measuring mainstream U.S. cultural values. *Journal of Business Ethics, 117*, 261–280. doi:10.1007/s10551-012-1515-z

Edmonds, C., & Killen, M. (2009). Do adolescents' perceptions of parental racial attitudes relate to their intergroup contact and cross-race relationships? *Group Processes and Intergroup Relations, 12*, 5–21.

Elmes, M., & Connelley, D. L. (1997). Dreams of diversity and the realities of intergroup relations in organizations. In P. Prasad, A. J. Mills, M. Elmes, & A. Prasad (Eds.), *Managing the organizational melting pot: Dilemmas of workplace diversity* (pp. 148–167). Thousand Oaks, CA: Sage Publications.

Eyerman, R. (2001). *Cultural trauma: Slavery and the formation of African American identity*. New York: Cambridge University Press.

Faingold, E. D. (2012). Official English in the constitutions and statutes of the fifty states in the United States. *Language Problems & Language Planning, 36*, 136–148.

Feinberg, W. (1998). *Common schools/uncommon identities: National unity and cultural diversity*. New Haven, CT: Yale University Press.

Garcia, S. M., Hallahan, M., & Rosenthal, R. (2007). Poor expression: Concealing social class stigma. *Basic & Applied Social Psychology, 29*, 99–107. doi:10.1080/01973530701330835

Gaustad, E. S. (2005). *Roger Williams: Lives and legacies*. New York: Oxford University Press.

Givhan, R. (2003). *Shirtsleeves as a political message*. Retrieved from http://articles.chicagotribune.com/2003-12-14/features/0312140502_1_sleeves-candidates-presidential

Gordon, B. M. (2012). "Give a brother a break": The experiences and dilemmas of middle class African American male students in White suburban schools. *Teachers College Record, 114*, 1–26.

Haines, D. W., & Rosenblum, K. E. (2010). Perfectly American: Constructing the refugee experience. *Journal of Ethnic Migration Studies, 36*, 309–406.

Handlin, O. (1951). *The uprooted: The epic story of the great migrations that made the American people*. Boston: Little, Brown.

Harper, M. (2006). Journeys and migrations: North Irish roots, Ireland to America. *North Irish Roots, 17*, 16–24.

Heartland Monitor Poll. (2013). Retrieved from http://www.theheartlandvoice.com/wp-content/uploads/2013/04/Heartland-Monitor-Poll-Final.pdf

History of U.S. Immigration Law and Policy. (n.d.). Retrieved from http://www.gcir.org/system/files/219-222_history_of_US.pdf

Hofstede, G. (1980). *Culture's consequences: International differences in work-related values.* Beverly Hills, CA: Sage Publications.

Hosoda, M., Nguyen, L. T., & Stone-Romero, E. F. (2012). The effect of Hispanic accents on employment decisions. *Journal of Managerial Psychology, 27*, 347–364. doi:10.1108/02683941211220162

Hosoda, M., & Stone-Romero, E. (2010). The effects of foreign accents on employ-ment-related decisions. *Journal of Managerial Psychology, 25*, 113–132.

Hughes, D. (2003). Correlates of African American and Latino parents' messages to children about ethnicity and race: A comparative study of racial socialization. *American Journal of Community Psychology, 31*, 15–32.

Huntington, S. P. (2004). *Who are we? The challenges to America's identity.* New York: Simon & Schuster.

Hwang, M. J. (2007). Asian social workers' perceptions of glass ceiling, organizational fairness and career prospects. *Journal of Social Service Research, 33*, 213–224.

Kang, H. (2012). Korean-immigrant parents' support of their American-born chil-dren's development and maintenance of their home language. *Early Childhood Education Journal, 41*, 431–438.

Kelly, G. P. (1986). Coping with America: Refugees from Vietnam, Cambodia, and Laos in the 1970s and 1980s. *Annals of the American Academy of Political and Social Science, 487*(1), 138–149. doi:10.1177/0002716286487001009

Kennedy, J. F. (1964). *A nation of immigrants.* New York: Harper & Row.

Kim, S., Wang, Y., Deng, S., Alvarez, R., & Li, J. (2011). Accent, perpetual foreigner stereotype, and perceived discrimination as indirect links between English profi-ciency and depressive symptoms in Chinese American adolescents. *Developmental Psychology, 47*, 289–301. doi:10.1037/a0020712

Koh, J.B.K., Shao, Y., & Wang, Q. (2009). Father, mother, and me: Parental value orientations and child self-identity in Asian American immigrants. *Sex Roles, 60*, 600–610.

Kroos, K. (2012). Becoming conscious of the American middle class (un)conscious-ness. *Integrative Psychological & Behavioral Science, 46*, 312–334. doi:10.1007/s12124-012-9206-y

Lambert, F. (2003). *The founding fathers and the place of religion in America.* Prince-ton, NJ: Princeton University Press.

Lazarus, E. (1883). *The new colossus.* Retrieved from http://xroads.virginia.edu/~cap/liberty/lazaruspoem.html

Lee, Y., Ottati, V., & Hussain, I. (2001). Attitudes toward "illegal" immigration into the United States: California Proposition 187. *Hispanic Journal of Behavioral Sci-ences, 23*, 430–443.

Macnab, B., Worthley, R., & Jenner, S. (2010). Regional cultural differences and eth-ical perspectives within the United States: Avoiding pseudo-emic ethics research. *Business & Society Review, 115*, 27–55. doi:10.1111/j.1467-8594.2009.00356.x

Martin, D. E. (2011). Internal compensation structuring and social bias: Experimental examinations of point. *Personnel Review, 40*, 785–804.

Martin, S. (2011). *A nation of immigrants.* New York: Cambridge University Press.

Menard, R. R. (2001). *Migrants, servants, and slaves: Unfree labor in colonial British America.* Surrey, United Kingdom: Ashgate.

Mir, S. (2001). "Just to make sure people know I was born here": Muslim women constructing American selves. *Discourse: Studies in the Cultural Politics of Education, 4*, 547–563.

Morley, C., & Halliwell, M. (2008). *American thought and culture in the 21st century.* Edinburgh , Scotland: Edinburgh University Press.

Mukherjee, S., Molina, L., & Adams, G. (2013). "Reasonable suspicion" about tough immigration legislation: Enforcing laws or ethnocentric exclusion? *Cultural Diversity and Ethnic Minority Psychology, 19*, 320–331. doi:10.1037/a0032944

Neblett, E. W., Smalls, C. P., Ford, K. R., Nguyen, H. X., & Sellers, R. M. (2009). Racial socialization and racial identity: African American parents' messages about race as precursors to identity. *Journal of Youth and Adolescence, 38*, 189–203.

Newport, F. (2012). *In U.S., 77% identify as Christian.* Retrieved from http://www.gallup.com/poll/159548/identify-christian.aspx

Orozco, R. A. (2012). Racism and power: Arizona politicians' use of the discourse of anti-Americanism against Mexican American studies. *Hispanic Journal of Behavioral Sciences, 34*, 43–60.

Parissa, J. (2011). American identity in the USA: Youth perspectives. *Applied Developmental Science, 15*, 79–93.

Parker, A. (2014). *Dispatches: Obama ignores anti-poor discrimination in U.S.* Retrieved from http://www.hrw.org/news/2014/01/29/dispatches-obama-speech-ignores-anti-poor-discrimination-us

Park-Taylor, J. J., Ng, V. V., Ventura, A. B., Kang, A. E., Morris, C. R., Gilbert, T. T., et al. (2008). What it means to be and feel like a "true" American: Perceptions and experiences of second-generation Americans. *Cultural Diversity and Ethnic Minority Psychology, 14*, 128–137. doi:10.1037/1099-9809.14.2.128

Perlman, J. (2005). *Italians then, Mexicans now.* New York: Russell Sage Foundation.

Piff, P. K., Stancato, D. M., Martinez, A. G., Kraus, M. W., & Keltner, D. (2012). Class, chaos, and the construction of community. *Journal of Personality and Social Psychology, 103*, 949–962. doi:10.1037/a0029673

Piff, P., Stancato, D., Mendoza-Denton, R., Keltner, D., & Coteb´, S. (2012). Higher social class predicts increased unethical behavior. *Proceedings of the National Academy of Sciences of the United States of America, 109*, 4086–4091. doi:10.1073/pnas.1118373109

Pinderhughes, C. (1990). The legacy of slavery. In M. Mirkin (Ed.), *The social and political contexts of family therapy* (pp. 289–305). New York: Gardner Press.

Pinderhughes, C. (2011). Toward a new theory of internal colonialism. *Socialism and Democracy, 25*, 235–256.

Portes, A., & Rivas, A. (2011). The adaptation of migrant children. *Future of Children, 21*, 219–246.

Quinn, B. (2011). The school as a democratic community. *Applied Developmental Science, 15*, 94–97.

Rodriguez, L., Schwartz, S. J., & Whitbourne, S. K. (2010). American identity revisited: The relation between national, ethnic and personal identity in a multiethnic sample of emerging adults. *Journal of Adolescent Research, 25*, 324–349.

Roggenkamp, K. (2008). Seeing inside the mountains: Cynthia Rylant's Appalachian literature and the "hillbilly" stereotype. *The Lion and the Unicorn, 32*, 192–215.

Rydell, R. J., Hamilton, D. L., & Devos, T. (2010). Now they are American, now they are not: Valence as a determinant of inclusion of African Americans in the American identity. *Social Cognition, 28*, 161–179.

Sacks, K. (1994). How Jews became White. In S. Gregory & R. Sanjek (Eds.), *Race* (pp. 78–102). New Brunswick, NJ: Rutgers University Press.

Sanders, M. R., & Mahalingam, R. (2012). Under the radar: The role of invisible discourse in understanding class-based privilege. *Journal of Social Issues, 68*, 112–127. doi:10.1111/j.1540-4560.2011.01739.x

Scabini, E., & Manzi, C. (2011). Family processes and identity. In S. J. Shwartz, L. Koen, & V. L. Vignoles (Eds.), *Handbook of identity theory and research* (pp. 565–584). New York: Springer.

Schachter, E. P., & Ventura, J. J. (2008). Identity agents: Parents as active and reflective participants in their children's identity formation. *Journal of Research on Adolescence, 18*, 449–476.

Schildkraut, D. J. (2003). American identity and attitudes toward official-English policies. *Political Psychology, 24*, 469–499. doi:10.1111/0162-895X.00337

Schildkraut, D. J. (2005). *Press one for English: Language policy, public opinion, and American identity.* Princeton, NJ: Princeton University Press.

Schildkraut, D. J. (2009). The dynamics of public opinion on ethnic profiling after 9/11: Results from a survey experiment. *American Behavioral Scientist, 53*, 61–79. doi:10.1177/0002764209338786

Sheets, P., Domke, D. S., & Greenwald, A. G. (2011). God and country: The partisan psychology of the presidency, religion, and nation. *Political Psychology, 32*, 459–484. doi:10.1111/j.1467-9221.2010.00820.x

Sidanius, J., & Pratto, F. (1999). *Social dominance: An intergroup theory of social hierarchy and oppression.* New York: Cambridge University Press.

Simon, B., & Hamilton, D. L. (1994). Self-stereotyping and social context: The effects of relative in-group size and in-group status. *Journal of Personality and Social Psychology, 66*, 699–711. doi:10.1037/0022-3514.66.4.699

Smith, M., & Tarallo, B. (1995). Proposition 187: Global trend or local narrative? Explaining anti-immigrant politics in California, Arizona and Texas. *International Journal of Urban and Regional Research, 19*, 664–676.

Sosnaud, B., Brady, D., & Frenk, S. M. (2013). Class in name only: Subjective class identity, objective class position, and vote choice in American presidential elections. *Social Problems, 60*, 81–99. doi:10.1525/sp.2013.60.1.81

Southern Poverty Law Center. (2009). *Language barrier*. Retrieved from http://www.splcenter.org/publications/under-siege-life-low-income-latinos-south/6-language-barrier

Tajfel, H. (Ed.). (1978). *Differentiation between social groups: Studies in the social psychology of intergroup relations.* London: Academic Press.

Tajfel, H., & Turner, J. C. (1979). An integrative theory of intergroup conflict. In W. G. Austin & S. Worchel (Eds.), *The social psychology of intergroup relations* (pp. 33–47). Monterey, CA: Brooks/Cole.

U.S. Census Bureau. (2012a). *1790*. Retrieved from http://www.census.gov/history/www/through_the_decades/index_of_questions/1790_1.html

U.S. Census Bureau. (2012b). *1850*. Retrieved from http://www.census.gov/history/www/through_the_decades/index_of_questions/1850_1.html

U.S. Census Bureau. (2012c). *1870*. Retrieved from http://www.census.gov/history/www/through_the_decades/index_of_questions/1870_1.html

U.S. Census Bureau. (2012d). *American community survey*. Retrieved from http://www.census.gov/compendia/statab/2012/tables/12s0053.pdf

U.S. Census Bureau. (2013). *1820*. Retrieved from http://www.census.gov/history/www/through_the_decades/index_of_questions/1820_1.html

U.S. Census Bureau. (2014). *State & county quickfacts*. Retrieved from http://quickfacts.census.gov/qfd/states/15000.html

U.S. Department of Justice. (2000). *Federal protections against national origin discrimination.* Retrieved from http://www.justice.gov/crt/legalinfo/natorigin.php

U.S. Department of Labor, Bureau of Labor Statistics. (2012). *Average annual hours worked per employed person in the United States, 2011 report.* Retrieved from https://research.stlouisfed.org/fred2/series/USAAHWEP

U.S. Equal Employment Commission. (2014). *Employees and applicants*. Retrieved from http://www.eeoc.gov/employees/index.cfm

Wells, C. (2013). Controlling "good science": Language, national identity and occupational control in scientific work. *Management Communication Quarterly, 27*, 319–345.

About the Editors

Elizabeth Pathy Salett, **MSW**, was the founder and former president of the National MultiCultural Institute, whose mission was to create a society that is strengthened and empowered by its diversity. In 2013, she was named a pioneer by NASW. She is president of the OLP Foundation that focuses on diversity, education, human trafficking and modern-day slavery (http://www.humantraffickingsearch.net). She is a graduate of Wellesley College; she earned an MA from Columbia University, Teachers College, and an MSW from the University of Maryland, School of Social Work.

Diane R. Koslow, PhD, is a licensed psychologist in private practice in Rockville, Maryland. She was director of training for the National Multi-Cultural Institute, where she contributed to publications, presentations, marketing, and proposal development. Dr. Koslow is listed in Who's Who Among Human Service Professionals, and Who's Who in the East.

About the Contributors

Elsie Achugbue is a writer with 15 years' experience in the nonprofit sector and a focus on social equity and inclusion. Currently programs manager for Success Measures at NeighborWorks America, she is also the author of *A Diversity Glossary,* the National MultiCultural Institute's best-selling publication, and articles such as "Nontraditional Market Analyses: Dismantling Barriers to Retail Development in Underserved Neighborhoods." She holds an MA in city planning from MIT and a BA from Macalester College.

Phillip Akutsu, **PhD,** is an associate professor in the Psychology Department at California State University, Sacramento. He has published over 30 journal articles and book chapters on ethnic minority mental health and Asian American psychology. He was a faculty member at Pacific Graduate School of Psychology and the University of Michigan and is a fellow of the Asian American Psychological Association.

Mollie Bradlee is a master's candidate at the Lyndon B. Johnson School of Public Affairs. She received her bachelor's degree in Spanish and Latin American Studies from Washington University in St. Louis and subsequently worked in immigration law before pursuing her master's degree. At graduate school, Mollie specializes in social policy with a focus on health care and immigration.

NiCole T. Buchanan, PhD, is an associate professor of clinical psychology at Michigan State University. She has published papers on racially ambiguous and nonvisible minority women, racialized sexual harassment, and harassment in schools and the workplace. Dr. Buchanan identifies as a biracial Black woman of Black, Irish, Swedish, Danish, German, Scottish, and English descent.

Sandy Grande, PhD, is an associate professor and chair of the Education Department at Connecticut College. Her research interfaces critical Indigenous theories with the concerns of education. Her book, *Red Pedagogy: Native American Social and Political Thought,* is being published in a 10th anniversary edition. Other publications include "Accumulation of the Primitive: The Limits of Liberalism and the Politics of Occupy Wall Street," *The Journal of Settler Colonial Studies;* and "American Indian Geographies of Identity and Power," *Harvard Educational Review.*

Joshua Henderson is a doctoral candidate in counseling psychology at Fordham University–Lincoln Center. His research focuses on interventions for at-risk urban adolescents in New York City, specifically targeting complex trauma, vocational hope, and school engagement. He practices relational psychotherapy with English- and Spanish-speaking patients. Before beginning doctoral training, Joshua was a social services worker with homeless and low-income populations in the urban center of Salt Lake City, Utah.

Lee Jenkins, PhD, LP, a psychoanalyst in private practice and published poet, is professor emeritus of English at John Jay College of Criminal Justice, City University of New York, and faculty member at the National Psychological Association for Psychoanalysis, Blanton-Peale Institute, and the Harlem Family Institute. Among his works in literature, psychology, and race relations are "Black–Jewish Relations: A Social and Mythic Alliance," and *Faulkner and Black–White Relations: A Psychoanalytic Approach* (Columbia University Press).

Greg Kim-Ju, PhD, is currently a professor in the Department of Psychology and the director of the Asian Studies Program at California State University, Sacramento. He conducts research on ethnic identity and psychological correlates and prevention and intervention programs that address academic performance and at-risk behavior. He received his degree in cultural psychology from Boston College.

Robin Lin Miller, PhD, is professor of ecological-community psychology at Michigan State University. She studies HIV prevention and care initiatives among people affected by HIV, with a special focus on programs targeting Black sexual-minority adolescents and young adults. She also conducts research on how theories of program evaluation are used in evaluation practice. Dr. Miller identifies as Black biracial. Her European ancestors hail from Scotland, Sweden, England, and France.

Jennie Park-Taylor, PhD, is an associate professor of counseling psychology in the Division of Psychological and Educational Services at Fordham University. She is the coordinator for the School Counseling MA Program. Her research focuses on exploring the intersections of individuals' ethnic, racial, national, career, gender, and religious identities.

Alan Roland, PhD, is a training analyst and faculty member of the National Psychological Association for Psychoanalysis. He authored three relevant books: *In Search of Self in India and Japan: Toward a Cross-Cultural Psychology,* Princeton University Press; *Cultural Pluralism and Psychoanalysis: The Asian and North American Experience,* Routledge; *Journeys to Foreign*

Selves: Asians and Asian Americans in a Global Era, Oxford University Press. He is an exhibiting artist and a produced playwright.

Timothy San Pedro, PhD, is an assistant professor of multicultural and equity studies in education at Ohio State University. His scholarship focuses on intricate links between motivation, engagement, and identity construction to curriculums and pedagogical practices that recenter content and conversations on Indigenous histories, perspectives, and literacies. He has worked with the Navajo nation, leading professional development workshops that co-envisioned lessons and pedagogical decisions working to sustain the cultures and languages of students.

Lisa B. Spanierman, PhD, is an associate professor in the Faculty of Counseling and Counseling Psychology at Arizona State University and faculty research affiliate at the Southwest Interdisciplinary Research Center. She serves as vice president for scientific affairs in the American Psychological Association's Society of Counseling Psychology and as editorial board member for the *Journal of Counseling Psychology* and the *Journal of Diversity in Higher Education.* Her research examines racial attitudes among White individuals and their applications for educators and mental health providers.

Michael Stoyer is a military veteran and a doctoral student in counseling psychology at Fordham University–Lincoln Center. His research explores the intersection of multiple identities and multicultural instruction. Recent topics have focused on military veteran identity development, specifically exploring the reintegration process of veterans postseparation.

Sweeney Windchief, EdD, is a member of the Fort Peck Assiniboine Tribe in Northeastern Montana and is an assistant professor in Adult & Higher Education at Montana State University in Bozeman. His research agenda includes Indigenous intellectualism, American Indian experiences in higher education, tribal college leadership development, and Indigenous values-based leadership. He received his doctorate in educational leadership and policy with a focus in higher education at the University of Utah in 2011.

Luis H. Zayas, PhD, is dean of the School of Social Work and the Robert Lee Sutherland chair in mental health and social policy at the University of Texas at Austin. He is the author of *Latinas Attempting Suicide: When Cultures, Families, and Daughters Collide* (Oxford, 2011) and *Forgotten Citizens: Deportation, Children, and the Making of American Exiles and Orphans* (Oxford, 2015). He earned his MSW and PhD in developmental psychology from Columbia University.

Index